THE BIG CON

THE BIG CON

*How the Consulting Industry Weakens our
Businesses, Infantilizes our Governments
and Warps our Economies*

Mariana Mazzucato
and Rosie Collington

ALLEN LANE
an imprint of
PENGUIN BOOKS

ALLEN LANE

UK | USA | Canada | Ireland | Australia
India | New Zealand | South Africa

Allen Lane is part of the Penguin Random House group of companies
whose addresses can be found at global.penguinrandomhouse.com.

First published by Allen Lane 2023
001

Copyright © Mariana Mazzucato and Rosie Collington, 2023

The moral rights of the authors have been asserted

Set in 12.6/15.4 pt Fournier MT Std
Typeset by Jouve (UK), Milton Keynes
Printed and bound in Great Britain by Clays Ltd, Elcograf S.p.A.

The authorized representative in the EEA is Penguin Random House Ireland,
Morrison Chambers, 32 Nassau Street, Dublin D02 YH68

A CIP catalogue record for this book is available from the British Library

ISBN: 978–0–241–57308–2
TPB ISBN: 978–0–241–57309–9

www.greenpenguin.co.uk

To all who challenge the hollowing out of their organizations, and to our friends and colleagues at the UCL Institute for Innovation and Public Purpose.

Contents

Acknowledgements   xi

1   Introduction: The Big Con –
A Confidence Trick   1

    In every room   2

    Surfing capitalism's trends   4

    Unlearning by not doing   7

2   What is the Consulting Industry?   11

    A taxonomy   17

    Meet the consultants   21

    The scale of consulting   23

    Getting in the room   26

    Interrogating the omnipresence   29

3   Where Consulting Came From: A Brief
History   31

    When consultants counselled   34

    From engineering to the matrix   38

    Consulting by numbers   40

    Shaping post-war capitalism   43

    Neoliberalism's opportunities   47

    Privatization and the growth of
consulting giants   50

Consultants without borders   55

Lucrative transitions   58

Taming a Goliath?   62

4   The Outsourcing Turn: Government by Consultancy and the Third Way   68

Contracts at scale and scope   71

'Reinventing' government   74

Who contracts the contractors?   78

Digital era outsourcing   83

Consulting the financial crisis   88

Contracting for austerity   92

Auditing the outsourcers   97

5   The Big Confidence Trick: Consultology and Economic Rents   104

Why bring in the consultants?   106

Extracting rents   111

The best and brightest   113

Talent drain   117

Case-savvy and PowerPoint-ready   121

Quasi-academia and fast fashions   127

Rubber stamping   131

6   Evading the Risks, Reaping the Rewards: The Business Model   133

Consulting risk   136

The art of limited liability   139

Shareholder value in public firms   141

Risk shifts after acquisitions   145

7   Infantilizing Organizations: When Learning Is Undermined Across Government and Business   149

Extortionate costs for likely failures   153

How do organizations learn?   157

Learning from consultants?   159

Beyond budgets: The consequences for future learning   161

Capture by brochuremanship   164

'Cronyism' and incapacity   167

Skeletonizing business   171

Apotheosis: Betting on management, stripping out science   175

8   Colliding Interests: Consultancies and Democracy   180

Privatizing bankruptcy, avoiding blame   183

Both sides of the street?   187

Poachers and gamekeepers   191

Hidden capital, minimized taxes   195

Arresting development   198

Bargaining against labour   201

Democracy dies in the shadow government   205

CONTENTS

9 Climate Consulting: An Existential
Threat? 208

The turning point 211

The dawn of climate consulting 213

A brief history of (market-driven)
climate governance 217

Manipulating models 222

Conflicting interests: Running
democracy on fumes 226

Resisting accountability: The case
of ESG 228

Future-proofing: Commitment
with action 233

10 Conclusion: A Government That
Rows So It Can Steer 235

Innovating from within 236

A government that rows so it
can steer 252

Bibliography 255
Notes 281
Index 333

Acknowledgements

The book you hold in your hands began as a series of questions: Why do so many governments outsource critical activities to consulting companies? Why has the market for consulting services grown so much in recent decades – and globally? What do consultants do, and what role does the consulting industry play in the economy overall? Why do so many well-meaning and smart graduates choose to work for these companies? And what might this tell us about contemporary capitalism?

We wanted to unpack what happens to the brain of an organisation when it is not learning by doing because someone else is doing the doing. To explore these questions, we had conversations with government leaders, civil servants, business executives, employees on both sides of consulting contracts, and colleagues and friends who shared their stories with us. From them, we learned not only about current challenges, but what alternatives might look like. Above all, they showed us that even within the most hollowed out of government departments and the most denigrated of workforces, visions of a better future endure – of more capable organisations, more responsive governance and more inclusive, sustainable and innovative economies. We hope this book not only starts a conversation about the problems with how our governments and businesses are run today, but provides some tools and inspiration for creating public purpose within them in the future.

Mariana founded the Institute for Innovation and Public Purpose (IIPP) at University College London five years ago with an ambition to strengthen the public sector's remit and capacity. Rosie joined

IIPP as Mariana's PhD student in 2020. It has been a delight partnering on the book. This process brought together Mariana's experiences writing about the theory and practice of a more ambitious, entrepreneurial and mission-oriented public sector, driven by public value and purpose, with Rosie's earlier research on what happens when critical infrastructures and skills are outsourced to others.

We couldn't have imagined a better intellectual home to carry out the research and make sense of the consulting industry. Our colleagues working across economics and public policy and IIPP's partners in governments, businesses and communities have been a constant source of inspiration, reflection and challenge. We are immensely grateful for the research seminars, public lectures, workshops and conversations with students and staff – whether over Zoom or in the kitchen at the Institute – that have helped to shape this book in its development. Everyone at IIPP, from our wonderful students and academics to facilities staff and teams working across policy, partnerships and communications, helps to make the Institute a place for confronting the biggest challenges our societies face today.

Indeed, like all books, this one has benefitted from the collective knowledge and support of many people.

The current and former consultants and people who contract them that we have interviewed and spoken to while researching for the book have been tremendous guides as we've sought to navigate the complicated world of consulting. We are grateful for their openness, insights and honesty. Special thanks go to the young consultants who have shared their experiences of recruitment, training and the early years of a consultancy career. We have agreed not to name them here.

Others have answered specific questions we had about consulting and its role in the parts of the global economy where they have expertise. They include Damon Silvers, a trade union specialist and Visiting Professor at IIPP; Professor Léonce Ndikumana; health policy specialist Els Toreele; David White from the International Association of Machinists and Aerospace Workers; historian and public sector consultant Dr Antonio Weiss; Simon Gallow, Andreas Smith Jørgensen and Nora Lambrecht. We are also grateful to those who alerted us to particular cases in their home countries. These include IIPP MPA students Hafiz Noer, Dan Yore and Abhilaasha Kaul, and Hanna Söderling.

A number of people have read chapters and early drafts of the book. We thank Zia Khan from the Rockefeller Foundation, Sonny Bardhan from the Omidyar Foundation, industrial relations scholar Dr Matt Cole, Professor Rainer Kattel, Michael Amery, Adrienne Buller, Dr Rasmus Corlin Christensen, Toke Dahler, Fausto Gernone, Simon Gallow, and Katie Kedward. Any errors are, of course, ours.

We are grateful to our agent, Sarah Chalfant, as well as Jessica Bullock and Rebecca Nagel from The Wylie Agency for believing in this project from the outset. Stuart Proffitt and Will Heyward from Penguin's publishing houses on both sides of the Atlantic have been the best editors that writers can hope for: creative and critical, astute and apt to transform our occasionally academic jargon into something people might enjoy reading. Working with them and others at Penguin – Alice Skinner, Rebecca Lee, Natalie Coleman, Tamsin Shelton, Sarah Hutson and Juli Kiyan – has been a pleasure. Dominique Garcia, Alex Homans, Adam Albrecht, Luca Kuehn von Burgsdorff and Sarah Doyle provided critical support from the IIPP Directors Office, making sure our work flow continued to progress on earth, water and air! Thank you for your diligence and patience.

Finally, to our family and friends: thank you. Research and writing are often solitary and slow endeavours. For both of us, moments of joy with the ones we love have been the lifeblood that pulses through the fingertips at the laptop keys, especially when we've been writing late at night and far away from home. Mariana would like to thank her children, Leon, Micol, Luce and Sofia – and their friends – who never stop pushing on the need for all of us to do better in fighting against inequities so visible across the entire globe, and on our doorstep. Rosie would like to thank her parents for their unflagging support, particularly during the weeks they shared their house with her and a legion of notebooks. She would also like to thank Toke Dahler, whose love and crosswords on the sofa have made the experience of writing a book for the first time all the more glorious and far less daunting than it otherwise might have felt.

While the list of individuals we want to thank is long, it could be much longer. We have had the privilege of working with leaders in the business sector and civil society who recognise the necessity of genuine partnerships between organizations that requires not only capacity and ambition, but also a different type of social contract that has mutualism at its core. This book has also benefitted enormously from our interactions with civil servants globally through our research and work at IIPP, who notwithstanding what seems like a constant attack on their competences, continue to dedicate their lives to the common good. It is to them we dedicate this book.

1. Introduction: The Big Con – A Confidence Trick

To overcome the great challenges of our time – from pandemics to the climate crisis – requires ambition and prowess. All types of organizations in our economies must be guided by experience and technical knowledge, and people with project management skills. Businesses, governments and organizations from civil society with these capabilities can then work together to meet our collective social, economic and environmental needs.

And yet this does not describe the world we live in. Many governments have stopped investing in their own capacity and capabilities, and because they fear failure they do not take risks. Many businesses have shirked responsibility for change, and are focused on earning short-term profits through easy, unproductive strategies, such as buying back their own shares to boost stock prices, or not paying workers their fair share. Bad governance in both business and the state has over the last half century caused short-termism to overshadow investments needed for progress. These trends have depleted organizations of knowledge, skills and vision.

And one group of actors has ridden the wave of this form of capitalism, and the underlying depletion of capabilities, earning huge sums of money in the process: the consulting industry.

Consulting companies, such as McKinsey, Boston Consulting Group (BCG) and Bain & Company (often referred to as the 'Big Three' strategy firms) and PwC, Deloitte, KPMG and EY (the 'Big Four' accountancies), are hired by governments, businesses and other organizations to perform different types of tasks on their behalf. When consultancies are hired by businesses, the tasks they are given sometimes relate to corporate strategy, sometimes to the management and execution of a specific project, and sometimes to a particular capacity such as IT or financial planning. Governments often contract consultancies to help deliver critical functions, from the development of climate adaptation strategies to the rollout of vaccination programmes and the commissioning of welfare services.

Today, the size of the consulting industry, and the contracts it receives, have become eye-wateringly large. Their growth shows no sign of slowing down. In 2021, estimates of the global consulting services market ranged from between almost $700 billion to over $900 billion[1] (£525 billion to £674 billion) – though these figures do not give the full picture of consultancies' activity.

In every room

The omnipresence of consultants across the economy is striking. Indeed, during the first two years of the COVID-19 pandemic (2020–21), governments spent unprecedented figures on contracts with the big consultancies. By July 2020, McKinsey had already secured over $100 million (£75 million) from the federal government in the United States for pandemic-related tasks.[2] In the United Kingdom, Deloitte received at least £279.5 million ($372.9 million) from central government in 2021.[3] One estimate suggests that in the UK over £2.5 billion ($3.34 billion) worth of consultancy contracts were awarded by public bodies in 2021.[4] In Italy, McKinsey was contracted to help organize the country's €191.5 billion share of the EU pandemic recovery fund.[5] Consultants have also been at the highest tables of decision-making during many of the past decade's global economic upheavals, from the eurozone debt crisis, to the recovery of Puerto Rico in the wake of Hurricane Maria. During that time, the

Big Three and the Big Four have also been hired to help design smart cities, develop national net zero carbon strategies, propose education reforms, counsel armies, manage the construction of hospitals, draft medical ethics codes, write tax legislation, oversee the privatization of state-owned enterprises, manage mergers between pharmaceutical companies and govern the digital infrastructure of countless organizations. Consulting contracts span value chains and sectors, across countries and continents, affecting all levels of society.

Does any of this matter? Should we be worried about it? After all, aren't they just helping to make their clients more efficient, to do things the clients can't? This book shows why the growth in consulting contracts, the business model of big consultancies, the underlying conflicts of interest and the lack of transparency matter hugely. The consulting industry today is not merely a helping hand; its advice and actions are not purely technical and neutral, facilitating a more effective functioning of society and reducing the 'transaction costs' of clients. It enables the actualization of a particular view of the economy that has created dysfunctions in government and business around the world.

The confidence tricks – or 'cons' – of late-nineteenth-century America's Gilded Age used offers of proprietary information, awe-inspiring technology and linguistic tricks as a means for criminal acts of theft and illegal forms of wealth extraction. What we call the Big Con is not about criminal activity. It describes the confidence trick the consulting industry performs in contracts with hollowed-out and timid governments and shareholder value-maximizing firms. These contracts enable the consulting industry to earn incomes that far exceed the actual value it provides – a form of 'economic rents', or 'income earned in excess of the reward corresponding to the contribution of a factor of production to value creation'.[6] These rents are not necessarily derived from the ownership of scarce valuable knowledge assets, but from the ability to create an impression of value. Consulting practices and the immense resources and networks of big consultancies help to instil confidence in the value of a consultancy and the consulting profession.

While consulting is an old profession, the Big Con grew from the 1980s and 1990s in the wake of reforms by both the 'neoliberal' right and 'Third Way' progressives – on both sides of the political spectrum. Companies were increasingly run in the short-term interests of their shareholders. Public sectors were transformed under the credo of New Public Management – a policy agenda that sought to make governments function more like businesses and diminished faith in the abilities of civil servants. These trends also meant that those working within companies and government organizations became insecure, constantly needing to justify their decisions to others – business executives to their shareholders, and civil servants to an ever sceptical populace and media, which would blame them for any failure or mistake.

Surfing capitalism's trends

The Big Con is of course not responsible for all the ills of modern capitalism, but it thrives on its dysfunctionalities – from speculative finance, to the short-termist business sector and the risk-averse public sector. It has capitalized on genuine ambition among some publics, politicians and business leaders to take on challenges including the climate crisis, the pandemic and growing inequality, which are viewed as opportunities to advise organizations that must adapt. There is an entrenched and mutually reinforcing relationship between the consulting industry and today's inherited governance forms in business and government. It is successful because of the unique structural power that the big consultancies wield through extensive contracts and networks across the economy, and their historic reputation as objective brokers of expertise.

Indeed, there is a place for consultants in our economy. Consulting advice and capacity is productive when it comes from the sidelines, from capable actors with genuine knowledge that creates value. The problem is not the act of consulting or the intentions of consultants, who often hope to effect change through their roles, but the ever expanding consulting industry which moves from the sidelines to the centre. It feeds off the weaknesses in our economies, hollowing out clients in the process, rather than helping them, which later only creates more opportunities for the rents accrued. It would be like a psychotherapist having no interest in her clients becoming independent with strong mental health, but rather using that ill health to create a dependency and an ever greater flow of fees.

Since we began research for this book in 2019, scandals involving consultancies have been brought to light by investigative journalists and government inquiries with increasing frequency. Barely a week goes by without news of yet another case of corruption, conflict of interest or avoidable accident involving a global consultancy. But the consulting fiascos that make the headlines are only the tip of the iceberg. Instances of clear failure or abuse by a big consulting company are often manifestations of broader, systemic problems – though they are rarely understood as such. Consultancies' numerous contracts, their claims to expertise, their financial incentives and the influence that large firms are granted over important areas of government and business are not scrutinized as symptoms of wider and deeper structural problems in the ways we have organized our capitalist system.

And the reality is that most of the time, most voters and employees do not know when consultants are at the table, how much they are being paid, who their other clients are, the extent of their often conflicting interests and what roles they have been contracted to perform. They do not know if the contracted consultancy has performed the task well or badly – and when it goes wrong, who is responsible. The nature of consulting contracts, limited liability and the business models of big consultancies mean that it is their clients' employees and citizens that most often end up taking the risks of consultancy failure. This difference between the rewards reaped (large) and the actual risks taken (little) makes the rents earned even greater.

The history of modern consulting is, in the end, the history of modern capitalism: every trend has been surfed by the Big Con. In government, big consultancies have promoted and profited from trends in privatization, management reform, private financing, public services outsourcing, digitalization and austerity. In business, they have helped to entrench new models and forms of corporate management – from the spread of cost accounting to the proliferation of multidivisional corporations in the decades after the Second World War across Europe, and the rise of shareholder value maximization around the world from the 1980s. These policies were not the brainchild of consultancies, but consultancies have helped to spread and shaped them, and ultimately used them to extract value. As the world is waking up to the ills of modern capitalism, and the need for more 'purpose' behind corporate governance, the consulting industry is promising to reverse the problems it helped create: the current boom in contracts for 'environmental, social and governance' (ESG) advice is the latest example.

In no area might the Big Con have greater consequences than in the fight against climatic breakdown. The consulting industry helped to embed forms of production driven by short-term profit maximization that have intensified carbon emissions. Now, in the face of growing concern about the climate crisis, it is riding a new wave, obstructing the large-scale transformations that are needed across our carbon-intensive economies. It is providing governments and businesses with frameworks that offer a veil of commitment without a requirement for action, including through the creation and promotion of ESG tools that former BlackRock executive-turned-whistleblower Tariq Fancy has called a 'dangerous distraction'. The consulting industry is one group of many actors that have shaped and profited from a market-driven response to the climate crisis, but it is future generations and those living today in the regions most exposed to the climate crisis who will bear the risks of that response failing.

In other words, the consequences of the Big Con for our collective ability to meet the immense challenges of today are stark and more urgent than ever.

Unlearning by not doing

To respond to changes in political, social and – increasingly – environmental demands, both government and business sector organizations must be able to adapt in order to govern complicated systems and provide goods and services that people want and need. The existing activities within an organization are the building blocks for the capabilities it will need to develop in the future. Organizations in the economy are not static entities but are constantly developing. The capabilities of organizations don't simply exist but evolve over time. They are dynamic.[7]

The more governments and businesses outsource, the less they know how to do, causing organizations to become hollowed out, stuck in time and unable to evolve. With consultants involved at every turn, there is often very little 'learning-by-doing'. Consultancies' clients become 'infantilised' – as the British Conservative minister Lord Agnew described the effects of outsourcing on UK civil servants in 2020.[8] A government department that contracts out all the services it is responsible for providing may be able to reduce costs in the short term, but it will eventually cost it more due to the loss in knowledge about how to deliver those services, and thus how to adapt the collection of capabilities within its department to meet citizens' changing needs. Learning, of course, also relies on interaction and engagement with other organizations. 'Closed' systems of central state planning are not amenable to this kind of learning.[9] But neither are organizations that rely on contracting out to deliver their goals.

While consultants can help clients to achieve their objectives, the claims that the consulting industry adds value to the economy and society by brokering knowledge and reducing costs is exaggerated. In the public sector, the costs incurred are often much higher than if government had invested in the capacity to do the job and learned how to improve processes along the way. Internal expertise all too often gets shunned in favour of contracting a global consultancy. Sometimes this is because the consulting firm offers to do the work pro bono or at a fee far below market rates. This is tempting for civil servants in risk-averse departments that lack resources after years of budget cuts. By charging nothing or very little in the initial contract – lowballing – the consultancy can not only shape important decisions, but also gather important knowledge about the client and gain a first mover advantage for future contracts.

It is especially striking that even in cases where the government clearly has a capability advantage, the consultancies often still win out. In Australia, for example, CSIRO (the Commonwealth Scientific and Industrial Research Organisation) holds extensive climate expertise. But in 2021, those in-house scientists were denied the funding to develop the country's net zero strategy, when the government chose to work with McKinsey instead.[10]

The consulting industry often provides legitimacy for controversial decisions. When a corporate senior manager wishes to convince their board of something, or when a government minister wants to win over others to their vision or stall meaningful action, a supportive report from a Big Three or Big Four firm can go a long way at the expense of other objectives — or even of labour agreements.

And the big consultancies that are intimately involved in important political and corporate decision-making often have egregious conflicts of interest themselves. Clients rarely have access to information about a consultancy's other clients, even when they are serving 'both sides of the street'. In climate consulting, for example, big consulting firms work simultaneously for governments whose populations would like to see lower emissions *and* for the fossil fuel companies that contribute most to the climate crisis.

For too long, the consulting industry has evaded scrutiny, undermining progress and democracy. This book not only offers a critique, but also provides concrete solutions to the current impasse. We examine the consulting industry's history, contextualize its growth within broader transformations of capitalism, and scrutinize the justifications for its widespread use among government managers, business leaders and academics. We show that even headline-grabbing cases are not anomalies but symptoms of broader dysfunctions in our economies. We draw on research that we and others have previously published in policy reports and academic journals, reports produced by consultancies, historical policy reports and contracting documents, and investigations by journalists who have closely followed consulting activities over many decades. We also use first-hand accounts from consultants and those who have worked with them in business and government. We have agreed to anonymize all potentially identifying information about the people we interviewed who are cited in the book, such as their name, job title and function. Our own experiences working with governments that have relied extensively on consultancies large and small have also been important sources of reflection.

Our analysis of the consulting industry paints a dark picture of the current situation. The scale of contracts with the consulting industry – via roles as advisors, legitimators of controversial decisions and outsourcers – weakens our businesses, infantilizes our governments and warps our economies. The cumulative use of big consultancies that operate with extractive business models stunts innovation and capacity development, undermines democratic accountability and obfuscates the consequences of political and corporate actions. In the end, we all pay the price through the lack of in-house investment and learning: public funds and other resources are wasted, decisions in government and business are made with impunity and little transparency, and our democratic societies are deprived of their dynamism. The Big Con imperils us all.

Examining the consulting industry in this way also offers a lens for rethinking how to build economies that are fit for purpose. The global missions of the future that are needed to meet great challenges, such as the climate crisis, require collective intelligence across the organizations and communities that make up our economies.[11]

It is possible to build a stronger economy, but only by investing in much-needed knowledge and capacity in business and government, bringing public purpose back into the public sector, and ridding the system of the consulting industry's obfuscation and costly intermediation. In this relationship, organizations and individuals with genuine knowledge and capacity can be a valuable source of advice; but they should advise and 'consult' from the sidelines in a transparent way that brings real knowledge and expertise – rather than be allowed to run the show from the centre. Ultimately this expertise must render those being advised stronger, not weaker.

Battling any addiction begins with admitting the gravity of the problem. Only then can we reduce the dependency, and steer a way forward.

2. What is the Consulting Industry?

At the beginning of February 2021, French lawmaker Véronique Louwagie obtained documents that would spark uproar nationwide. It had been almost a year since COVID-19 reached France, and the country was struggling to contain the latest wave of cases. The launch of its vaccine programme had been a disaster: just 5,000 people had been vaccinated by the beginning of January, compared to 316,000 in Germany and 139,000 in Spain, which had started their programmes at around the same time.[1] News of the sluggish rollout made headlines around the world. For a country that had long prided itself on its public health system and civil service bureaucracy, the numbers were galling. It didn't take long for media outlets to uncover that McKinsey had been at the helm of the vaccine rollout.

Louwagie was a member of the conservative Republican party and admitted to being generally unfazed about using management consultancies in government. But in her role as budget rapporteur, responsible for holding the Health Ministry budget to account, the news that McKinsey had been involved in what many considered a huge failure of government raised red flags. She wanted to know: how many contracts did the French government have with management consultancies for its COVID-19 response? What exactly had they been doing? What she discovered through her questioning of the Health Ministry was, for many French officials and citizens, alarming – though worse was yet to come.

Between March 2020 and February 2021, the Health Ministry had signed twenty-eight contracts with six consulting firms for tasks related to the COVID-19 crisis. The contracts totalled €11 million, with €4 million going to McKinsey alone.[2] Consultants were not merely being used as a source of expert external knowledge. Rather, they had become central to decision-making processes and the management of the vaccine rollout. McKinsey was responsible for defining distribution routes for the Pfizer and Moderna vaccines, and coordinating 'a vaccination task force of officials from numerous agencies, with some decision chains involving up to 50 authorities'.[3] One of the daily Zoom meetings attended by senior officials from the Health Ministry was chaired by a consultant from McKinsey. French consulting firm Citwell had been contracted to support the logistics of vaccines and personal protective equipment. Accenture had been recruited to deliver IT services related to the vaccination campaign.[4]

Given the extent of consultancies' involvement in the rollout and logistics of the vaccination programme, perhaps it is not surprising that the country was lagging when it came to getting the vaccine into the arms of citizens. These companies do not have decades of experience in population-level vaccination programme delivery. As one researcher at the French National Centre for Scientific Research put it to the *New York Times*, the consultancies tended to import operating models used in other industries that didn't necessarily work effectively in public health. 'Afterwards,' he said, 'the government doesn't go back to evaluate whether what the consultancies did worked well or not. It's too early to tell if McKinsey and others are adding value in this campaign, but I think we'll never know.'[5]

The French government's use of consultants would only grow as the pandemic wore on. In March 2022, a report published by the conservative-dominated Senate revealed that central government ministries alone had spent almost €900 million (£760 million; $950 million) on management consulting fees in 2021 – a figure more than double what had been spent in 2018.[6] The news came just weeks ahead of the Presidential election, with rivals to the incumbent President branding the revelations the '*Scandale McKinsey*'.[7] McKinsey was certainly not the only firm under interrogation – and the probe also extended beyond the pandemic. Among cases highlighted in the report was a contract with Boston Consulting Group and EY worth €558,900 to organize a convention for public sector officials that never actually took place.[8]

When asked about the government's extensive use of consultancies during the pandemic by journalists from the online magazine *POLITICO*, one senior civil servant claimed it had been necessary because the public sector lacked capacity – internal staff were struggling with burnout and fatigue.[9] During a crisis, it is almost inevitable that governments will need to recruit additional capacity to deliver the response that the public expects of them. Some countries, such as Germany, were nonetheless able to redeploy staff from parts of the public sector where normal activity had ceased. But in France, as with other nations, the outsourcing of important management and operational functions in the French state and elsewhere was not merely a crisis-induced anomaly. The pandemic may have been unprecedented, but the French government's reliance on the consulting industry was not. Consultants 'began to play a role in administrative reform, first in local governments following the 1982 decentralization, and then in the central state in 1987 at the same time that the consulting industry became stronger because of state initiatives designed to stimulate its development'.[10] And much as Emmanuel Macron's political opponents sought to weaponize the issue against him during the Presidential election, the use of consultants had long transcended party lines. During his term in office from 2007 to 2012, the centre-right government of President Nicolas Sarkozy had spent hundreds of millions of euros on contracts with consulting firms ostensibly to improve efficiency in the state. His

Socialist Party successor, François Hollande, did little to reverse the trend. The revelations about the Macron government's reliance on consulting firms in the pandemic were, for many, simply confirmation that the role of consultants had stretched far beyond providing expertise to the government, with one politician even arguing that the recent employment of American consulting firms had undermined French sovereignty.[11]

The tendency to outsource operational and management capacity during the pandemic was also not unique to France. Contracts in the United States were just as wide-ranging. In March 2020, leaders at the Department of Veterans Affairs, which usually spends months developing tenders, signed a $12 million (£9 million) no-bid contract with McKinsey to spend up to a year consulting on 'all aspects' of its healthcare system's operations during the pandemic in a tendering process that took less than twenty-four hours. Within weeks, the firm had been contracted to 'help obtain medical supplies' for the Department of Health and Human Services, 'serve on a task force developing a strategy to get defense contractors, many of them McKinsey clients, to produce medical supplies during the pandemic', and a host of contracts with individual states including Illinois, Tennessee, California and Virginia. In New York, Governor 'Andrew Cuomo's team hired McKinsey to draw on existing epidemiological models to project hospital capacity and medical supply needs'.[12]

Back across the Atlantic, in the United Kingdom, tens of millions of pounds were also being spent on consulting firms.[13] Where the wider economy shrunk, and millions of people lost work, the UK consulting industry actually grew by 2.5 per cent in 2020, in no small part due to government contracts.[14] In its January 2022 update, the sector's industrial body, the Management Consultancies Association (MCA), suggested growth had reached 16 per cent over the course of 2021, with its members anticipating even further growth in 2022.[15]

The contracts that Deloitte received from the public sector in the United Kingdom during the first year of the pandemic ranged from the more traditional advisory services to core operational and management tasks. It was not only contracted for 'urgent Covid-19 consultancy', but also 'the provision of digital solution design, build and live service of a digital platform'.[16] It secured contracts for the 'identification and procurement of personal protective equipment'[17] – a task that the National Health Service (NHS) has fulfilled since its inception. The company was also contracted by the Health Research Authority – a public body responsible for ensuring that health research in the NHS is ethically reviewed and approved – to 'revise its research ethics review model, building on the lessons learned from reviewing COVID-19 research'.[18]

Deloitte's role as part of the UK government's 'Test and Trace' system came under public and political scrutiny as it emerged that the consultancy was earning £1 million ($1.3 million) per day from the contracts. According to the parliamentary Public Accounts Committee, a cross-party group of MPs responsible for examining government spending, Test and Trace had 'not achieved its main objective to help break chains of Covid-19 transmission and enable people to return to a more normal way of life'.[19] An inquiry by the Committee concluded that the programme had been 'overly reliant on expensive contractors and temporary staff': 'as of April 2021, consultants accounted for nearly half of all NHS Test and Trace's central staff'. It found that Test and Trace did 'not have a firm grip on its overall spending on consultants', suggesting nonetheless that it 'is likely to cost taxpayers hundreds of millions of pounds'.[20] When questioned about why the programme's use of consultants continued to be so high more than a year after the pandemic reached the UK, a former head of Test and Trace informed the Committee that 'the skills [the NHS] was trying to recruit for, in data, digital, and operational and project delivery roles', were in short supply in the civil service', suggesting the government's relationship with the consulting industry and the scale and scope of its outsourcing contracts were systemic issues.

One person who worked in projects related to the pandemic response during the first year shared insights on what the day-to-day operations entailed. It became clear in the beginning that the government had contracted an unprecedented number of consultants, some of whom had been brought in via subcontracts with other consultancies. This scale – 'the huge amounts of people hired because of the fog of war stuff, the roving consultants' – became an operational hindrance:

> The impression I had was that the organization stood up so many new teams all at once, so there was always someone new wanting to talk to you about some new thing that was upcoming. But they often didn't even know what they were asking for . . . It just seemed like every project had loads of wandering Deloitte people. And it strikes me that the sheer volume of them that were around created the situation of these zombie emails just arriving all the time asking really basic questions that we had to respond to, taking our attention away from actual work.[21]

The junior consultants that were brought in rarely had specialist expertise in the relevant area. Their job titles for the contracts they worked on tended to be 'Product Owner' or 'Product Manager', but 'unlike in a well-functioning digital team' – where such positions are usually found – 'the consultants with these titles did not have really specific duties'. When asked whether they felt value had been added by the consultants, the interviewee noted that 'not everyone I dealt with was incompetent – I remember a Deloitte person in charge of a project who was competent and good'.

This scale and scope of the consulting industry's contracts during the pandemic is emblematic of many organizations' reliance on consultants. Already, by the time COVID-19 arrived, contracting out had become the convention across many governments – and the consulting industry was enmeshed in all aspects of it.

A taxonomy

Globally, the consulting industry is dominated by large, multinational companies, most of which have their headquarters in the United States or northern Europe. They include the Big Four and the Big Three. They also include companies that primarily offer management services within a specific area such as IT, for example CGI Group and IBM, or public services outsourcing, such as Serco and Sodexo.

A number of large companies that operate primarily in other sectors also have a consultancy arm that constitutes a relatively small proportion of total revenues. They can be an important source of influence or provide access to stakeholders and information that are valuable for the core line of business. In recent years, for example, engineering and construction firms such as Arup and AECOM have become increasingly significant sources of advice in climate adaptation governance.[22] Financial Markets Advisory (FMA), the consultancy arm of the world's largest asset management fund, BlackRock, 'has quietly worked for numerous public institutions, including the UK Treasury and European Central Bank.'[23] By 2021, BlackRock controlled $10 trillion of assets globally. During the COVID-19 pandemic, the Federal Reserve contracted FMA to manage the three vehicles it had created to buy corporate debt from financial markets. These companies have also benefited from the wider reforms to political and corporate governance since the 1980s that encourage contracting out by public sector organizations and company managers, even though providing these services is not their core line of business. Where the Big 3 management consultancies can each count the size of their workforce in the tens of thousands, FMA employs 250 staff.[24]

Around the world there are also tens of thousands of small and medium-sized companies, sometimes referred to as 'boutique consultancies', as well as not-for-profit organizations around the world that provide consulting services. In many countries, in recent decades, the number and revenues of smaller, specialist consultancies have increased significantly, tracking the broader growth of the consulting market. The areas that smaller companies tend to work in have also mirrored wider trends. In the wake of Tony Blair's Labour government, for example, 'those who had worked in the public sector for consultancies would often go on to form their own consultancies, thereby facilitating the further supply of consultants'.[25] The names of the small consultancies in particular will likely only be familiar to a reader working within a particular field or based within a particular area; they tend to operate within local geographies and provide services within a niche industry or specialized function. But they include companies that purport to be specialists in managing digitalization processes, developing sustainability strategies, or making public sector services more efficient. They also include consultancies that provide contracts for specific organizations, such as the European Commission or the UK's National Health Service.

In this book we focus on the political economy of the large, multinational consultancies and their relationships to governments,

Heritage	Origins	Key governance structure	Examples
Strategy	1900s–1930s Scientific management and cost accounting (management approaches that were popular in this period)	Partnership	McKinsey Boston Consulting Group Bain & Company
Accounting	1960s–1970s Auditing client networks and perceived objectivity	Partnership, private corporation	EY Deloitte PwC KPMG
IT	1980s–1990s Computerization and need for connectivity through firm growth	Publicly traded corporation	Capgemini Cognizant Cisco IBM Oracle CGI Group
Outsourcing	1990s–2000s Increase in size and scope of public sector contracts	Publicly traded corporation	Serco Sodexo Atos ISS
Boutique	2000s–2010s Growth in opportunities for management consulting	Private corporation, not-for-profit organisation	Putnam Associates Vivid Economics

Figure 1

Types of Management Consultancies

businesses and other organizations. These firms provide a range of consulting services, from strategic advice and management to project implementation and outsourcing. While there are important differences between them and the extent to which they focus on different types of consulting services, they are nonetheless related by the dynamics that have led to the growth in scale and scope of consulting contracts, and are united in their need for the continuation and expansion of those contracts. At times, we look specifically at the role of smaller, specialist consultancies. A summary of the five main 'types' of consultancies by heritage is included in Table 1 below. We will explore their origins and governance in more detail later.

Most of these firms break down the management consulting services they offer into different categories, based on the project area, industry or – in the case of IT consultancies – technology involved. Capgemini offers services across the business areas of 'Finance & Accounting', 'Supply Chain', 'Employee Operations', 'Customer Operations' and 'Intelligent Automation'.[26] McKinsey offers services across 'functions' including 'M&A', 'Operations', 'Organization', 'Strategy & Corporate Governance' and 'Transformation'.[27] The groups of firms that others have described as the 'outsourcing generation' of consultancy firms and 'outsourcing consultancy' focus on managing large contracts in different areas of the public sector.[28] Serco, for example, breaks down its offerings by the 'key market sectors' of 'Defence', 'Healthcare', 'Justice', 'Immigration', 'Transport' and 'Citizen Services'.[29] In many ways, focusing on the various labels that consultancies or even academics use to describe what they do obfuscates what the consulting industry is – what unites these diverse companies. All the companies described above rely for their very existence on other organizations continuing to contract out management, expertise and capacity.

There are many individuals, companies and other organizations that provide expert advice or services that we do not include in our definition of the consulting industry, because they do not have the resources to extract rents through the Big Con. Most of them are also not structurally dependent on these contracts, even though they may charge a fee for their services; their growth or existence is not contingent on other organizations contracting them for consulting services. Examples include public health experts who have provided input on the structure of governments' pandemic responses, retired teachers who sit on school boards, and academics in universities who share insights from research with public, private or civic sector organizations. There are also businesses that solely provide goods, which are known as 'vendors'. Most accountancies are not part of the consulting industry, because they do not provide consulting services at all. The same is not true of the Big Four accountancies, which derive over 40 per cent of their revenue through management consulting contracts – more than they receive from audit and assurance services.

Meet the consultants

Large consultancies operate according to strict hierarchies, and there are different types of consultant within them, depending on the area of business. There are clear pathways for progression within many firms, notably within the Big Three and the Big Four. On the lowest rungs are employees recruited as graduates, sometimes following an internship or summer training programme. We will refer to them as Analysts, though, depending on the company, their title could also be 'Associate' or 'Consultant'. On a typical project, an Analyst will be expected to conduct research and produce 'deliverables', such as slide decks, as instructed by a more senior member of the team. As part of their employment, Analysts are usually required to complete general training in project and stakeholder management, but are not expected to have 'sectoral knowledge'. On the next rung are employees who have usually either completed the consultancy's graduate training programme or a Master of Business Administration (MBA) at a business school. We will refer to them as Senior Consultants, though they are variously titled 'Consultant', 'Project Leader' or 'Associate', depending on the company. They share some responsibilities with Analysts but may be more prominent in client-facing tasks, such as interviewing executives or presenting updates. One former Big Four consultant described Analysts and Senior Consultants as 'the do-ers' in a project team.

Beyond them are Managers, who are usually responsible for coordinating the team of consultants on the ground and engagement with the client but may also be considered specialists in a particular area of management or industry. According to our interviews, it is usually only these Managers and people on the next level – Partners or Principals – who are expected to have and utilize sectoral knowledge or technical expertise, often as a result of long careers in an industry. Partners or Principals are those consultants who have either succeeded in moving up the ranks through a long career within the company or have been recruited from within a specific industry. Often, however, contracting organizations are only able to access a very limited amount of direct engagement with a Partner or Principal, as they tend to advise on multiple projects at once, and are rarely seconded full-time.

The most senior people within a management consultancy are the Directors, who are usually individuals with long consulting careers behind them and are largely responsible for negotiating sales and managing stakeholder relationships. Boutique consulting firms often adopt similar organizational hierarchies and titles, but, depending on the specialism of the firm, specific skills or knowledge may be more important at the more junior levels as well as for the senior managers. Outsourcing consultancies tend also to be hierarchical, though the responsibilities of individuals employed to manage and deliver contracts vary significantly. Depending on the nature of the contract, these organizations tend also to employ frontline or 'blue collar' service employees directly, though many are subcontracted from other firms.

The scale of consulting

Accurately valuing the global market for consulting services is impossible. Few public sector organizations and multinational firms are mandated by governments, in the case of the former, or shareholders, in the case of the latter, to accurately document consulting spend. Many of the largest consultancies also have business structures that mean they do not need to disclose how much revenue they earn, what their profits are, or even where in the world they make their money. The Big Four and the Big Three all operate as incorporated partnerships or other forms of limited private company, and therefore 'enjoy levels of opacity denied to many of their multinational corporation clients'.[30] It is much easier to find out how much oil companies or Silicon Valley giants earn in a given year, because they are publicly traded – they sell shares on stock exchanges – and are legally required to report this information so that potential and current investors and financial market regulators can access it. Estimates of the value of the consulting industry globally nonetheless all suggest that the market has soared in recent decades. In 1999, management consulting revenues globally were estimated to be worth somewhere between $100 billion and $110 billion (£62.6–£68.9 billion).[31] By 2010, one study estimated the market size at around $350 billion (£225.6 billion).[32] Estimates in 2021 ranged from almost $700 billion to $900 billion (£525–£674 billion).[33]

The largest multinational consultancies are very large indeed. In 2021, Deloitte was the third largest private company in the United

States, and was followed closely by PwC in fourth position, with EY following at number six.[34] McKinsey and Boston Consulting Group both ranked in the top fifty, outpacing biotech firms, insurance giants and entertainment titans. Accenture, which earned $17.3 billion (£13.4 billion) in revenue from consulting services in 2019, was the fortieth biggest company in the world in 2021 by market capitalization, ranking higher than global behemoths like Royal Dutch Shell, Boeing and Eli Lilly.[35] Other publicly traded IT consultancies counted among the 100 biggest publicly traded firms include the Indian Tata Consultancy Services, which earned $14.9 billion (£11.6 billion) in revenue from consulting services in 2019.[36]

These firms provide services around the world, and have offices in most countries, employing hundreds of thousands of people. The Big Four have offices in more than 130 countries and employ a total of about 400,000 people.[37] McKinsey alone operates across more than 130 cities in over 65 countries. Despite this reach, their revenues are derived overwhelmingly from just a handful of countries. One study suggests that 96 per cent of consulting revenues come from North America and Europe, and that 70 per cent of consultancy fees worldwide are generated by just five nations – the United States, Canada, the United Kingdom, France and Germany.[38] There are many reasons for this divergence between regions of the world, beyond the simple fact that fees for management consultants in developing countries tend to be far lower than in Western consulting markets.[39] For one, there is a much longer historical precedent of using this source of external advice or capacity in some regions than others; the largest multinational companies today emerged within North America and expanded first to Europe.[40] Some countries, such as Japan, have historically focused on developing expertise by investing internally in existing staff, or drawing on insights from other external organizations, such as universities or trade unions.[41] Other countries have also at different times introduced rules that directly limit the ability of Western management consultancies to access domestic industry clients. In 2014, for example, the Chinese government ordered its state-owned enterprises to cut ties with US-based consulting companies.[42] Local resistance by businesses to international management consultancy firms has also limited their growth during particular periods, such as in South Korea in the early 2000s.[43]

In any case, the financial data alone can only tell us so much. There is plenty that these numbers do not reveal about the scope of the consulting industry's activity – and its influence – in the global economy. This is particularly the case in developing countries, which have actually seen higher growth in recent decades than Western markets, despite only accounting for a small proportion of the total revenues for consulting globally.[44] In many developing countries, demand for multinational management consultancies has also not always been driven by domestic governments and businesses, but rather by intergovernmental organizations such as the International Monetary Fund (IMF) and the World Bank, which have advocated that indebted governments contract consultants to develop and implement the market-driven economic reforms that are a condition of their loans. This use is not accounted for in national management consulting statistics.

Even within countries or regions, the distribution of contract revenues does not always reflect the extent of the consulting industry's work. Quantitative data rarely reveals the nature of a consultancy's contract, and services outsourcing and goods procurement are not neatly separated in the statistics.[45] Data on the revenues of the six largest outsourcing consultancies in terms of UK government contracts nonetheless suggests that spending on their services alone goes well into the billions. Currently, forty companies are included in the UK Cabinet Office's list of Strategic

Suppliers – the private sector companies deemed most significant in government contracting – and they operate across areas of the economy including telecoms, defence, IT and management consulting. Atos, Capita, G4S, ISS, Serco and Sodexo are all among them. Since 2015, these six companies have collectively received contracts worth more than £20 billion ($26.7 billion).[46] Globally, the value of their combined sales in 2020 alone equalled over $68 billion (£51 billion).*

Getting in the room

In the lucrative markets of North America and Europe, when demand has decreased in economic downturns or because of public policy reforms, consultancies have employed strategies to remain relevant, in the hopes that this will improve their chances of securing a profitable contract in the future. Between 2010 and 2015, for example, the Coalition government in the UK introduced measures to reverse the previous government's extensive use of management consultants. However, several multinational consultancies continued to provide consulting services to central government departments pro bono or at a significantly reduced rate.[47] Speaking to the *Guardian* in 2011, the head of public sector at KPMG put his company's strategy bluntly:

> We can't afford to [work pro bono] indefinitely, but we can in the short-term. We're hoping to position ourselves well when the government decides it is willing to pay . . . Firms like ours are always keen to get in on the really big programmes. If you

* Calculated using publicly available company financial data.

can get in at the part of the programme when you are working out how to do it, the hope is you can stay there.[48]

In this case, the low revenues belied the scope of the consultancy's work. To make sense of the role that management consultancies play in economies across continents today, we thus need to look not just at the financial data, but at what lies within their contracts, what they actually do, and how their relationship develops. The wide reach of the consulting industry within government departments, businesses and non-governmental organizations (NGOs) is not just confined to economies in North America and Western Europe. From South East Asia to West Africa, consultants have been brought in not simply as advisors; they *are* the management and deliver core functions; their proposals to decision-makers are adopted as the final word.

In India, for example, annual turnover at consulting firms increased by 10.8 per cent annually on average in the five years to 2018, with industry revenues totalling $64.8 billion (£50.8 billion) that year.[49] Demand in India is driven largely by the private sector, but many government bodies are increasingly turning to consultants to deliver state functions as well. Tata Consultancy Services has been a clear beneficiary of growing demand for consultants. Since 2008, it has been responsible for developing India's passport system, and operating centres where biometric data is collected, documents are checked and passports are issued. Meanwhile, at the central planning commission, budget allocations for professional services increased nearly fivefold between 2016–17 and the following year, and subsequently rose by 30 per cent in 2018–19.[50]

Sometimes, the extensive use of the consulting industry by governments in low- and middle-income countries is justified by politicians because their public sector bureaucracies are incapable of matching the ambitions of newly elected policymakers. In countries that have been forced to service mounting debt piles over many years, for example, or where war or corruption has depleted or undermined sources of government revenue, internal capacity may be very weak. But the outsourcing of management and delivery to powerful, opaque companies on a grand scale so often does not help electorates and businesses achieve their goals – and in fact can undermine them in the long run, stalling development and preventing accountability.

In Kenya, McKinsey has been involved in several economic initiatives. The non-profit journalism website *Rest of World*, which reports on global tech developments, recently investigated the role that the company has played in the expensive failure of Kenya's 'smart city' project, Konza City, which sits forty miles south of the country's capital, Nairobi.[51] Konza City was the crown jewel of McKinsey's *Vision 2030 Strategy*, which it developed on behalf of the Kenyan government in 2008. With promises of economic growth, job creation and technological innovation, Kenya's *Vision 2030 Strategy* purported to offer a blueprint for attracting investment from multinational tech companies. But in 2021, thirteen years after construction began, Konza City remained deserted and devoid of investors – much like the McKinsey *Vision* projects that preceded it in Andhra Pradesh, Mumbai and Malaysia.[52]

Similarly extensive 'involvement' in national economic policy can be found in Indonesia. In 2020, the Indonesian government appointed McKinsey and Boston Consulting Group to guide an overhaul of the country's 114 state-owned enterprises, with a combined revenue of $172 billion (£129 billion). Although the value of this contract remains hidden, its scope was unprecedented in the country. This was not a case of a handful of expert advisors sharing insights with ministers and civil servants. Rather, the contract made the two multinational consulting giants responsible for developing the restructuring 'roadmap'.[53]

Interrogating the omnipresence

Many citizens, politicians and media platforms have now started to challenge governments relying on the consulting industry, and the assumption that large multinational consulting firms will create value through their contracts. In May 2021, Boston Consulting Group was summoned to an inquiry by the Australian Senate into issues with the country's postal service, having received AUD$1.32 million (£710,000; $980,000) contract from the Australian government to report on the service's future viability. Senior managers employed by Australia Post had repeatedly raised concerns about the consultancy's work. During the inquiry, BCG Managing Directors were unable to explain what new analysis they had provided, with the inquiry chairwoman stating emphatically: 'It's hard to know what [the money] delivered actually.'[54] In the UK, amid wider criticism of the government's spending on management consultants during the COVID-19 pandemic, the parliamentary Public Accounts Committee pushed the government to investigate £2 million ($2.65 million) spent on management consultants to assess bids made by charities for emergency funds.[55] South Africa's newspapers have scrutinized McKinsey, KPMG and Deloitte after contracts with them were linked to alleged corruption in state-owned enterprises under the presidency of Jacob Zuma. McKinsey reached an agreement with the South African government to repay R1 billion ($67.3 million; £57 million) for work it did at Eskom, the state power monopoly, alongside a company linked to the Gupta brothers who were accused of using their close ties with the former President to secure major public contracts.[56] A January 2022 report published as part of a government inquiry into 'state capture' suggested that prosecutions should be considered into the awarding of contracts with Bain & Co., which has been accused of enabling Zuma to weaken the tax authority. In response, the consultancy said the report 'mischaracterizes' its role, though it also agreed to pay back the fees earned from the contract in question.[57] In August of that year, the UK government imposed a three year ban on Bain & Co bidding for public sector contracts because of its "grave professional misconduct" in South Africa, with the consultancy launching a legal challenge to the decision the following month.[58] Although the allegations against the consultancies in South Africa in many ways constitute a unique case, they have prompted extensive public debate about the role of the consultants in business and government.

As important as government inquiries and investigative reports are for raising awareness about the problems consultancies so often help to bring about, they rarely question whether the crisis is indicative of deeper contradictions in contemporary capitalism and the role of the consulting industry. Instead, their questions tend to focus on poor management by executives at the consultancy, or shoddy procurement processes in the government department, or the corrupt behaviour of individuals on either side of the contract. The solutions they propose correspondingly call for replacing the consultancy's senior executives, perhaps with a more representative group of people, tinkering with procurement structures, or improving transparency. The origins of and harms posed by the consulting industry are nonetheless structural, going deep into the heart of capitalism and politics – and so must be met with a far more ambitious response than governments or commissions have offered so far.

3. Where Consulting Came From: A Brief History

In July 1971, Chilean engineer and politician Fernando Flores was working for the Chilean Production Development Corporation, a public organization responsible for fostering economic development in the country. Following the election of the new government under President Salvador Allende the previous year, Flores faced a difficult task: how to manage the newly nationalized sectors of Chile's economy. Party leaders had never been able to deliver their economic policy goals, which included economic growth and income redistribution, and, despite the ambition, the Chilean public sector simply did not have the capabilities to deliver the mandate on which it was elected. But it was also not afraid to draw on relevant expertise in the private sector.

This was how British management consultant Stafford Beer came to advise the newly elected government – a partnership that ultimately developed one of the most innovative computing systems of the time: Project Cybersyn. Beer, a former steel executive with a lavish lifestyle,[1] was not a socialist, but he saw in the collaboration with the socialist Allende government an opportunity to put his ground-breaking management research and ideas into practice. The government wanted to develop a computer-assisted system that would aid its economic decision-making by using real-time data to forecast different scenarios. At the heart of the project was a central operations room from which politicians could view projected simulations of the Chilean economy under different conditions, supporting them to make economic policy decisions. Initially, it had also aimed at providing workers with a channel for democratic input into those decisions. It is no exaggeration to say that Project Cybersyn was an ambitious undertaking. At the time, total computing power in the country was less than an iPhone.

Nonetheless, with the advice of Stafford Beer, Project Cybersyn went some way to achieving its technological goals, before political unrest subverted any hopes of long-term industrial strategy, culminating in the violent military coup by General Augusto Pinochet two years later.[2] Although short-lived, the relationship worked for everyone involved: the Chilean state was able to learn new approaches to meet its democratic mandate, and Stafford Beer was able to develop his theory of 'management cybernetics'. He had found the project so rewarding that he eventually left the UK to work for the Chilean government full-time.

The Pinochet coup prevented Chile from further evolving the knowledge it had gained through working with Stafford Beer and Project Cybersyn. But around the world there are plenty of historical examples of partnerships with consultants that helped to create knowledge and capabilities to achieve democratic goals. Consultants came to play a valuable role as governments in Europe and North America worked to build welfare state programmes in the wake of the Second World War; for instance, advising among other things on 'more efficient use of utilities and cleaning practices in hospitals for the Ministry of Health' in the newly established National Health Service of the United Kingdom.[3]

For much of the twentieth century, consultants were sought by governments and businesses as a source of knowledge when they lacked capabilities. Although there were also risks of undue political influence in their work, the scale and scope of consulting contracts was much smaller than today. This began to change from the late 1970s, when new economic interests reconfigured many societies following the election of politicians such as Margaret Thatcher in the United Kingdom and Ronald Reagan in the United States, who did not believe governments could create value. They ushered markets into the delivery of public services and introduced policies that transformed corporate structures. A shift took place, making consulting firms key actors in both politics and business, and in the delivery of important functions across the economy.

In the 1990s, for example, the changes management consultants oversaw in the NHS were 'largely driven by the efforts of hospital trusts and health authorities to find ways of surviving in the face of constant financial shortfalls'. One academic study found that 'because NHS regional offices no longer provide [hospital trusts and health authorities] with planning expertise, they instead rely on private management consultants'.[4] Consultants were contracted to provide management services, because internal management had been diminished as a result of 'downsizing' measures, rather than as a source of information or expertise, as was more often the case previously.

In another example, following the passage into law of the 2012 Health and Social Care Act, the NHS was forced to hire management consultants to help manage health services. The Act had mandated that the local authorities responsible for commissioning health services, Clinical Commissioning Groups (CCGs), would be led by local physicians – known as General Practitioners or GPs in the United Kingdom – on the grounds that local GPs are embedded in patient populations and thus could represent the interests of patients. This change was challenged from the outset by civil society and professional bodies, which argued that, despite their close contact with patients, GPs do not necessarily have the time or knowledge to negotiate suitable contracts with providers, and so would likely turn to private management consultants for advice, thus undermining the reform's democratic claims.[5] For its part, the Royal College of General Practitioners contended that 'CCGs would be able to outsource the majority of their commissioning functions to private providers'.[6] We now know that millions of pounds have been spent by CCGs on management consulting services from firms including McKinsey, PwC and Deloitte since the implementation of the Act.[7] Ironically, the Health Secretary who oversaw the introduction of the Act, Andrew Lansley – a Conservative politician – had criticized the Blair government only a few years earlier in 2006 for 'reaching for management consultants in a desperate bid to compensate for their management failures'.[8]

What explains the transformation of the role of consultants in the NHS from the 1950s to the turn of the millennium? To what extent did this change reflect a broader transformation in the consulting industry – and in governance? Was the consulting industry merely a passive actor within broader developments in capitalism, or did it play an active role in shaping them?

When consultants counselled

Rulers – kings and queens, high priests and spiritual leaders – have always had advisors, but the establishment of extensive markets for consulting is a development particular to the industrialization of production in Western societies. Historians generally suggest the birth of modern consulting can be situated in one of three periods: the late nineteenth century, with the appearance of 'consultant engineers' in Europe and the United States; the popularity of 'scientific management' and the ideas of Frederick Taylor two decades later; and the development of 'cost accounting' methods, which gave rise to McKinsey in the 1920s.[9] Each of these periods is critical for understanding, respectively, the emergence, entrenchment and expansion of consulting as it exists today.

The historian Christopher D. McKenna's account of 'the world's newest profession' begins in the 1870s with the Second Industrial Revolution. At this time, companies such as General Electric and Standard Oil had started to employ some engineers on a short-term basis – as opposed to as employees who were fully integrated in the company. They did this in an attempt to 'control the pace of innovation within their science-based industries'.[10] These early engineering consultants were true experts in their field – they were often graduates of engineering programmes at prestigious universities, and were equipped with the latest scientific knowledge. Eventually, some engineers who had been contracted in this way decided to formalize their work and establish what became known as engineering consulting firms. They included Arthur D. Little, a chemist based at MIT, who founded his eponymous firm in 1909 after working on various contracts in Boston, Massachusetts. The company still exists today, under the same name, and its website in fact describes Little's firm as the 'world's first management consultancy'.[11]

There were nonetheless other developments occurring across other new industries that would come to shape consultancy practices in the early twentieth century. In 1911, Frederick Taylor published his essay 'The Principles of Scientific Management'. He'd been developing the ideas it contained over decades working on the shop-floors of manufacturing companies.[12] Taylor had held several machine-based jobs across various manufacturing firms before joining the ranks of the engineering consultants. It was this shopfloor work that most inspired his thinking – not that it put the interests of shopfloor workers first. Indeed, the American Federation of Labor, the largest group of trade unions, opposed scientific management, objecting that it 'looks upon the worker as a mere instrument of production and reduces him to a semi-automatic attachment to the machine or tool'.[13]

From Taylor's perspective, though, scientific management offered the 'development of a true science' in management. He advocated that the 'one best method' for manufacturing should be found to replace the old 'rule of thumb' method, whereby individual workers could use what they felt was the best way to complete a task based on their own experience, and which Taylor contended was less efficient.[14] He argued that although there were many different ways to complete a task, 'among the various methods and implements used in each element of each trade there is always one method and one implement which is quicker and better than any of the rest'.[15] Over a century later, in 2022, many people are familiar with one of Taylor's key ideas outlined in 'The Principles of Scientific Management'. Namely, that the most efficient way of running a factory shopfloor could be discovered by breaking up a process into individual tasks, and timing how long it takes to complete them in order to find the most efficient means of producing goods. The other three principles were also concerned with improving efficiency. Taylor's second principle was that the most efficient worker for a task should also be selected by managers 'scientifically'; this involved observing all workers and selecting from them those who had the most suitable characteristics for the particular task. This person would then be trained to fulfil that task, 'whereas in the past he chose his own work and trained himself as best he could'.[16] His third principle was that managers should supervise workers to ensure the tasks are completed in the 'scientific' way. And finally, that there should be a division between managers and workers that Taylor described as 'equal': managers should be responsible for planning and supervising the work, and workers should carry it out, but both needed to cooperate, which required managers to 'assume a much larger share of the responsibility for results than under usual conditions is assumed by the management'.[17]

Taylorism and the wider movement of 'scientific management' became very influential across manufacturing industries in the United States and Europe in the early decades of the twentieth century, largely because it spawned a torrent of management consulting firms and independent consultants that promoted it far and wide. It even found support in the Soviet Union, which was generally opposed to American ideas. After initially rejecting Taylorism as a ' "scientific" system of sweating . . . to squeeze out of the worker three times more labour during the working day',[18] by the mid-1920s, both Lenin and Trotsky had embraced it, contracting US-based consultant Walter Polakov for advice on developing its national industries and the first five-year plan, working in Moscow, Tula and Kovrov.[19]

In many ways, Taylorism was a product of the technological developments that had also made possible rapid industrialization in the United States. The desire to speed up manual work in the factory and increase production to increase profits was facilitated by the introduction of new machinery. But Taylor and the consultants who preached his ideas also transformed popular understanding of what makes a 'good' company and, ultimately, how value is created in production.

Taylorism treated workers less as human labourers and more as 'resources' in the factory. It was the first theory adopted en masse by consultants. But more than that, it was an early case of top-down firm restructuring based on a management consulting idea and it represented a turning point in industrial development.

From engineering to the matrix

Throughout the twentieth century, consultancies would go on to develop and commercialize many ideas and tools, often in collaboration with business schools. Among the best-known of these is the 'Growth Share Matrix' launched by Boston Consulting Group in 1970, which, according to the company, was at one point used by about half of all Fortune 500 companies (*Fortune* magazine's annual list of the 500 biggest US companies measured by revenues).[20] The matrix is a table, divided into four quadrants representing varying degrees of profitability (see Figure 2 below). The 'cash cow' quadrant is assigned to business areas that are low growth but have a high market share – businesses should milk them for cash that can be reinvested elsewhere. The 'dog' quadrant is designated to business areas that companies should divest from because they are unprofitable or risky. The 'star' quadrant represents those areas that have high growth and high market share, meaning that companies should invest in these areas, as they have high future potential. Finally, the 'question mark' quadrant is for the parts of the company where there is a large degree of uncertainty about their future.

The Growth Share Matrix was developed in the United States within a context where businesses were increasingly facing financial pressures. Under conditions of crisis and constraint, it 'spread like wildfire' in the 1970s. Just two years after its launch, the matrix was being used by over 100 major US firms, and would be widely taught in business schools around the world for decades to come. Business academics throughout this time nonetheless remained sceptical. Criticism of both the Growth Share Matrix and trends in investment portfolio planning that it emerged within included that it was not comprehensive and ignored important factors in

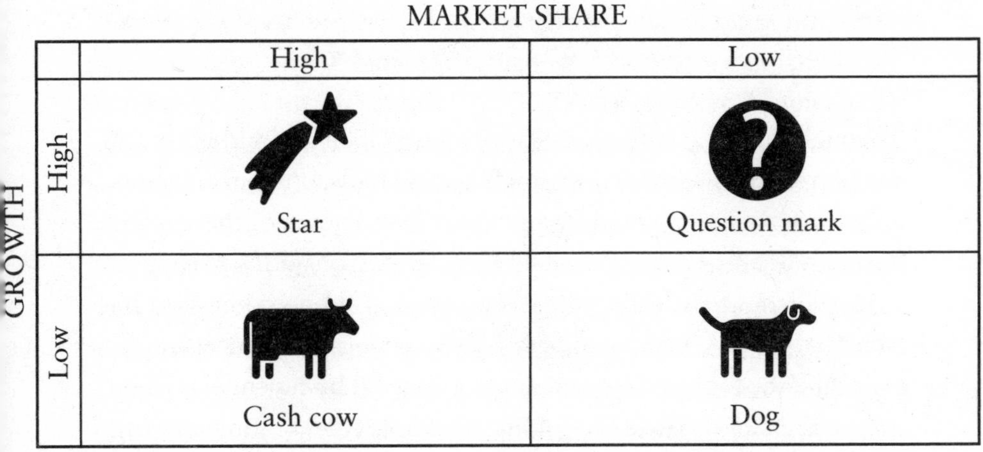

MARKET SHARE

	High	Low
High	Star	Question mark
Low	Cash cow	Dog

GROWTH

Source: BCG, 2021.

Figure 2

Boston Consulting Group Growth Share Matrix

corporate strategy, such as the relationship between market share and cash flow.[21]

In any case, it wasn't primarily the ideas and methods of consultancies that led to the widespread growth of management consulting contracts in the United States of the 1930s. Rather, it was the unexpected consequence of legislation introduced in the wake of the 1929 Great Depression.[22] The Glass-Steagall Banking Act of 1933 aimed first and foremost to limit the power of banks by forcing them to separate commercial and investment activity. Previously, commercial bankers had been permitted to conduct the 'financial investigations' that would later be carried out by management consultants, but the Act forbade them from providing these consultative services. Introduced in the same year, the Securities Act mandated banks' financing of companies to be preceded by 'the investigation of the subject firm by a firm of competent consultants'. Large accounting companies, which, like banks, had previously conducted 'financial investigations', were also required by the Securities and Exchange Commission (SEC) to 'restructure their professional practices around corporate audits', owing to concerns about conflicts of interest. At this time, audit contracts were far more lucrative for those firms than consulting. This left an open goal for management consulting firms, which were now the only advisors still legally permitted to provide management advice to companies. Consequently, 'Management consulting did not grow through a gradual process of linear evolution, but instead emerged from a competitive equilibrium shattered by regulatory change in the early 1930s.'[23]

Consulting by numbers

One such firm was McKinsey & Company. James O. McKinsey was a professor of accounting at the University of Chicago at the time he founded his firm in 1926. McKinsey was an early developer and proponent of the method of 'cost accounting', which sought to give managers advice based on evaluations of their company's variable and fixed costs. Cost accounting evolved with wider developments in neoclassical microeconomic theory, which would come to fundamentally transform the way that the state, businesses and financial markets act. Today, such methods of analysis are standard practice across the private sector, but at the time they were revolutionary – loved by some and loathed by many others, including the mainstream accounting profession.

McKinsey's business had benefitted from the Great Depression, offering financial advice to struggling companies. Clients during the 1930s included the department store firm Marshall Field &

Company. Founded in the mid-twentieth century, Marshall Field & Company had flourished in the roaring twenties, but quickly found itself in trouble after going public in 1930. The company 'had lost $12 million over the previous five years and was faced with an impending loan repayment'.[24] Chicago, where it had its biggest department store, had also been one of the most heavily unionized cities in the United States since the late nineteenth century, and Marshall Field & Company had long been a target of industrial action – to which it had usually responded brutally, firing workers for even being in the company of a union member.[25] The proposals that McKinsey made to the firm offered a means of not just tackling the financial challenges, but curbing the options of organized labour once and for all. McKinsey advised Marshall Field to 'specialize: unload its wholesale business, sell its 18 textile mills, focus entirely on retail, and cut, cut, cut'.[26] In the end, more than 1,200 employees were let go – and James O. McKinsey was offered the post of chairman and chief executive of Marshall Field, which he accepted. The advice that McKinsey & Company provided in the case of Marshall Field attests to the political uses to which the consulting industry was often put, even in the twentieth century. By recommending job cuts at such scale, during a time of organized labour opposition and immiserization, McKinsey provided the executives of Marshall Field with an ostensibly impartial and external actor to blame for the decision.

McKinsey & Company continued to grow in the following decades, even after the founder's untimely death from pneumonia in 1937.[27] The growth of many American management consultancies during this period was aided in no small part by the availability of contracts in the expanding world of defence, as the country prepared for conflict with and then engaged in drawn-out Cold War with the Soviet Union, which would endure for the best part of the century.

Government agencies facing budgetary constraints and technological demands turned to management consultants for support. For example, the consultancy Booz Allen, which had been founded in 1914 and would go on to become one of the largest contractors for the US military in the twenty-first century, was contracted to advise on the restructure of the entire US Naval organization.[28] Large consultancies were also contracted to advise on converting companies for wartime production – and then reconvert them after the war.[29] In fact, the Second World War saw not just increased use of consulting advice, but also the direct employment of consultants into military positions: consultants became a source of military capacity. A Partner of Booz Allen, Richard Paget, for example, was 'named head of the navy's Office of the Management Engineer, and Mark Cresap (also a Booz Allen consultant) was appointed to a similar position in the army'.[30]

The role of McKinsey in the early years of the National Aeronautics and Space Administration (NASA) during the Cold War exemplifies how consultancies' advisory services could be wielded in internal political struggles. In 1958, NASA was established with an unprecedented budget of $300 billion. The directors of NASA recognized that it would need to work with technical contractors; new technologies had to be procured, and building capabilities would by necessity entail learning from other actors.

There were disagreements, however, about the role that management consultants should play in NASA's development. The agency's first director, Keith Glennan, had an ideological inclination towards involving management consultants in NASA's development and operations,[31] once describing himself in an interview as 'a person who relies to a considerable extent on outside counsel'.[32] One of the first contracts that Glennan oversaw was for an evaluation of the organizational structure that senior administrators had implemented at NASA. Glennan wanted 'to have someone come in and study us and what we thought we were going to do, or what the staff thought we were going to do, the top people . . . and suggest changes if necessary in the NACA-proposed [National Advisory Committee for Aeronautics] structure'.[33] That contract went to McKinsey. McKinsey would continue to be a key advisor during Glennan's tenure, providing a source of external – and purportedly disinterested – justification for his ambitions to increase the use of contractors, rather than internalize the agency's technical capabilities, because he wanted 'to avoid excessive additions to the federal payroll'.[34] McKinsey more than satisfied Glennan's desires, recommending that America's 'free enterprise society dictates that industry should be given as extensive a role as possible'.[35] The approach that Glennan and McKinsey advocated would nonetheless be challenged with the publication of a report by Budget Director David Bell in 1962, a year after Glennan resigned from NASA. Although NASA continued to rely to a large extent on technical vendors for building its systems, the Bell Report, as it became known, stated in no uncertain terms that the management and control of programmes had to remain in-house, and that the maintenance of internal capabilities for managing contracts was of utmost importance.[36]

Shaping post-war capitalism

In the wake of the Second World War, management consultants continued to advise the US federal government and took on contracts across welfare services and administration in an effort to help realize ambitious goals. In 1947, President Hoover launched a Commission aiming to integrate structures of the various agencies and improve effectiveness of the administration; management consultants were commissioned to 'lead fifteen of its thirty-four policy studies'.[37] One scholar suggests that the growth in use of consultants in state and local government was a consequence of the increased adoption of business practices, logics and structures in the public sector during this period, describing how the consulting industry played an active role in promoting these to government bodies, while also benefitting from those changes. Projects for which consultancies were contracted to work on ranged from city-wide strategy initiatives, such as the 'Model Cities' programme in New York, to local restructuring tasks, such as Booz Allen's contract to reorganize Pasadena's school budget.[38] They were similarly recruited to advise on developments in healthcare systems, as new organizational forms were adopted.[39]

Consulting firms also influenced the development of economies in Europe during this period. The role of American management consulting firms there was part of the broader spread of American management ideas and models, where 'the Marshall Plan, in particular, facilitated the expansion of US consulting firms to Europe'.[40] Introduced in 1948, the Marshall Plan was an economic recovery programme led by the United States that provided aid to European countries following the devastation of the Second World War.

As the value of consulting contracts grew in the post-war decades, two other types of consulting company that would come to dominate the market in the twenty-first century were gaining ground. Although they remained restricted in the types of services they could offer in the United States, some accounting firms – notably Arthur Andersen – began to take on contracts for advice on information systems management in the 1950s. These companies were dramatically expanding the geographical scope of their accounting activities, tracking the growth of their major clients – a trend that would continue into the later decades of the twentieth century. This was achieved largely through acquiring and merging local accounting firms across countries. In Canada, for example, the national branch of KPMG 'was formed from merging "more than 115 firms in communities across Canada" '.[41] Waves of mergers and acquisitions within accountancies would continue throughout the twentieth century, such that by 1996, '93 per cent of the revenues earned by the top eighteen accounting firms in the US in that year went to the Big Six',[42] – Price Waterhouse, Peat Marwick McLintock, Coopers & Lybrand, Ernst & Young, Deloitte Touche Tohmatsu and Arthur Andersen – and they audited 494 of the Fortune 500.[43] Like many other sectors by the end of the twentieth century accounting had become very concentrated.

Having earned a reputation for quantitative rigour and meticulousness, it is perhaps not surprising that accountancies became popular sources of advice as government departments and businesses adopted IT.

Ever since the introduction of computers in civil service departments – as early as the 1950s in both the UK and the US – governments had largely maintained IT infrastructure in-house. In fact, public sectors were the source of many key innovations in computing throughout the twentieth century, partly because of military developments, but also because of reforms to bureaucratize the civil service and make communication processes more efficient.[44] But administrative technologies that had been developed in the private sector were also frequently sought by governments, especially after they had proven to be effective in business. In such cases, long before digital computing technologies, government departments would turn to the technology companies to both implement the new systems and provide advice on how to use them.*

---

* A lesser-known fact about IBM is that through its contracts with Nazi Germany it provided a technology that was used in the Holocaust. The scope of IBM's

Historians have explored why the British state, in particular, lost its in-house capabilities in IT during the twentieth century. Mar Hicks, for example, argues that the loss of 'state computerization competence' occurred as computing jobs in the civil service became male-dominated in the 1960s and 1970s.[45] Previously, women had carried out the bulk of computing tasks. Antonio Weiss argues that it was the growing gap in skills between the state and consultants from Arthur Andersen that led to the civil service outsourcing IT infrastructure and expertise in the UK.[46] Data on the gendered make-up of the consulting industry during the twentieth century would suggest a third hypothesis, synthesizing both the above arguments: that the consulting industry was overwhelmingly dominated by men throughout those decades,[47] and so the 'masculinization' of IT in the state and elsewhere likely went hand-in-hand with the growth of computing consultants in the state. The loss of capabilities that occurred as a result of the increasing reliance on consultants was nonetheless a gradual process until the later decades of the century, when the election of neoliberal governments in the United Kingdom and the United States led to an unprecedented transformation of the global economy, radically reconfiguring the relationship between states and the private sector.

Consultancies' success in IT in the US was also aided by rules introduced in 1956 that forbade computing contractors from providing advice on their systems to clients, owing to antitrust concerns.

---

involvement with the Third Reich has been contested. For example, 'it is not entirely clear that IBM's New York executives knew the ultimate use to which their machines were being put'. Nonetheless, according to the *Guardian*, IBM 'has not denied the role of its subsidiaries in aiding the Nazis' management of the Holocaust' (Burkeman, 2002), and there is no doubt that the IBM Hollerith machine, a punch card tabulating device, was used in the tracking of people, trains and logistics during it (Black, 2012).

Specifically, the Department of Justice prohibited IBM from offering consulting advice on installing and using computers.[48] Over the course of the twentieth century, auditing gradually became a low margin activity for the large accounting consultancies, and by the 1970s and 1980s they were increasingly focusing efforts on securing contracts for these IT consulting services, which were far more lucrative. Some accounting consultancies legally split their accounting and consulting divisions, though the entities were never fully separated because auditing continued to be subsidized by consulting. Arthur Andersen, for example, spun out Andersen Consulting in 1989, the firm that would eventually be renamed Accenture.[49] In the United Kingdom, there were no rules preventing IT companies from providing consulting advice, which partly explains why during the second half of the twentieth century the largest IT consulting companies, such as Capgemini Sogeti, International Computers Limited (ICL) and Computer Sciences Corporation (CSC), were either UK-based or very well established there.[50]

Neoliberalism's opportunities

No period has ushered in a greater transformation in the nature of consulting than the 1980s. In this decade, the size of the industry and the roles it played in government and business would be forever changed by the introduction of 'neoliberalism' – an economic agenda that included market liberalization, state enterprise privatization and public sector management reforms. Each of these reforms would create unparalleled opportunities for management consultancies, as the private sector came to be viewed by many in power as more effective and *efficient* than government.

The elections of Margaret Thatcher in the United Kingdom in

1979 and Ronald Reagan the following year in the United States were preceded by a decade of turmoil in the global economy, beginning with the disintegration of the institutions that had helped to maintain monetary stability since the 1940s. As spending on military efforts in Vietnam placed ever greater fiscal pressure on the federal budget, President Nixon decided unilaterally in 1971 to end the convertibility of US dollars into gold. This led to the immediate devaluation of the dollar, contributing to a slowdown in economic growth, soaring unemployment and a rise in commodity prices – a phenomenon known as 'stagflation' that characterized the economies of many countries throughout the 1970s. The effects of this breakdown of the post-war global financial institutions were further exacerbated by the 1973 oil crisis, which led to a recession in the United States and the withholding of capital by potential investors there. Across the Atlantic, economic instability was also taking its toll on the population of the United Kingdom, culminating in the 'Winter of Discontent' in 1978–79, which saw mass strikes by trade unions and heavy criticism across the media of the ruling Labour Party – itself also beset by internal battles that crippled economic decision-making.

It was in this context that the first elected neoliberal governments came to power. Throughout the post-war decades, economic strategies in the United States and the United Kingdom had broadly followed an approach named after the British economist and politician John Maynard Keynes. Keynesianism was a form of capitalism that advocated the use of counter-cyclical monetary and fiscal policies to maintain economic stability, as well as increased investment in public infrastructure and spending on welfare services, such as healthcare and education. Following their elections, the Conservative Party in the United Kingdom and the Republican Party in the United States wasted no time in declaring that this approach lay at the heart of the struggles that their populations were experiencing, proposing instead a neoliberal economic agenda that was also being tested during the Chilean military dictatorship of General Pinochet.[51]

Developed by a group of academic economists based at the University of Chicago, neoliberalism can be understood as a theory that views the market as the sole creator of value in society. The role of the state in this paradigm is reduced to ensuring that the right 'conditions' exist for the market to function properly, such as through enforcing antitrust laws to maintain competition among companies. Neoliberal policies are usually understood as measures that shrink the state in order to enable market actors to grow through increased competition.[52] Indeed, similar terms were used by the Conservative Party in its 1979 manifesto to describe its proposed economic policies. But while in some countries public budgets were slashed following the introduction of a neoliberal agenda, particularly in the Global South, it is more accurate to understand neoliberalism as the reconfiguration of state institutions and the redirection of state spending as a means of transferring greater responsibility for producing goods and services to market actors. Neoliberal policies in fact neither led to a significant shrinking of public spending, nor to increased competition in key industries in the long term. Under Thatcher, total managed government expenditure in real terms increased by 7.7 per cent between 1979 and 1990.[53] Federal spending also grew in the United States under Reagan — by 9 per cent each year on average. While this was carried significantly by the President's 35 per cent increase in defence spending, public programmes such as Medicare were also expanded. Rules constraining mergers between two firms in the same industry were relaxed; the 'takeover wave' that ensued was also facilitated by liberalizing changes in financial regulation, which made certain types of finance more easily available to firms.[54] The process of becoming increasingly reliant on equity and debt for delivering operations, which leads to higher distributions of profits to investors, is known as 'financialization'.

Privatization and the growth of consulting giants

For the consulting industry, neoliberalism created fresh possibilities for expansion across business and government. In the private sector, the emergence of unprecedentedly huge companies that resulted from the mergers, acquisitions and easier access to credit led management consultancies to develop advisory arms specializing in multinational strategy. Because consultancies had established offices around the world, many leaders took their claims to local expertise at face value. They were also frequently sought for insights and analysis in the run-up to merger and acquisition deals. Increasingly, as the risk of liability loomed ever larger over company boards due to the sheer size of firms and their use of riskier forms of finance, directors turned to management consultants for help – and someone to point the finger at should things take a turn for the worse. From the mid-1980s in the United States, consultancies and other professional firms were occasionally named as co-defendants in shareholder lawsuits against corporate boards, a practice that only ended with the introduction of the Private Securities Reform Act of 1995 that abolished joint and several liability for professional firms. The large consultancies 'increasingly found themselves selling legitimacy, not simply knowledge transfer'.[55] The financialization of many companies during this decade also brought with it even greater pressure from shareholders for companies to improve productivity, further increasing demand for the new ideas and techniques that the consulting industry promised would lead to improved profit margins.[56]

Meanwhile, in the public sector, spending on consulting exploded, marking the beginning of an expansion in markets for government services that has continued to grow ever since. Data from the United Kingdom illustrates the scale of this growth, though it would find parallels in governments from Canada to Australia by the 1990s and 2000s. At the time of the 1979 general election in the United Kingdom, the government was spending around £6 million on consulting services annually; when Margaret Thatcher stepped down as prime minister eleven years later, the amount was more than forty times greater at £246 million.[57] In France, the market for management consulting increased steadily from 1 billion to 7 billion francs in the decade from 1982 to 1992.[58] In Canada, annual expenditure on 'other professional services' across government showed a continuous increase from C$239 million in 1981–82 to C$1.55 billion in 2000–2001.[59] Describing how 'managerialism' in the mid-1980s ushered in flexibility for managers in the allocation of 'running costs' between in-house staff and outside procurement', one academic paper notes that in Australia an average of AUD$142.635 million was spent by government departments between 1987 and 1999.[60]

The increased role of consultants in government was also related to their growth in the private sector.[61] While their roles in the public sector were enormously varied, management consultancies were central to two key reforms. Firstly, the privatization of state-owned enterprises and the introduction of new competition rules for the public sector, which led to increased outsourcing of public services, created new sources of revenue for consulting companies. From the side of governments, consulting firms were contracted to provide advice on transferring companies into private hands. In 1992, for example, consultants from McKinsey were brought in to assist the British Transport Commission with its 'privatization strategy' of the railway system.[62] Consultants from

Coopers & Lybrand, KPMG and Deloitte Haskins & Sells were contracted to advise on a host of issues related to rail privatization.[63] Under Reagan, private consultants were contracted to conduct evaluations that would help determine if a good or service should be privatized or contracted out, based on whether or not it could be considered an 'inherently government function'.[64] For example, the Environmental Protection Agency's (EPA) Office of Administration and Resources Management awarded a contract worth $9 million for a broad range of tasks related to management issues, including the establishment of a framework and criteria for assessing when in-house commercial activities should be contracted out. A 1991 report conducted by the United States General Accounting Office on the use of consultancies in federal agencies raised concerns about the conflict of interest arising from consultancies being contracted to establish the criteria for outsourcing: 'a contractor's involvement in determining which activities may be done under contract places the contractor in the position of possibly becoming associated in the future with some of the activities he identified as being appropriate for contracting'. The report's authors also noted that the EPA case was potentially inconsistent with the rules governing procurement at the time, because the contractor had also 'appeared to take the lead in shaping important agency policy'. When questioned, the agency officials conceded that 'this work probably should have been done in-house. However, the agency did not have sufficient staff available and also did not have staff with sufficient expertise.' Crucially, they also acknowledged that 'there was not sufficient in-house capability to adequately direct, supervise, and monitor this contract'.[65]

The companies that sought to take over state-owned enterprises would also turn to the consulting industry for advice on succeeding in their bids, drawing on the knowledge of the workings of government that consulting companies had developed through public sector contracts. Those companies that were successful in a bid would then seek advice on managing their newly acquired enterprise from management consultants, given that they were usually entities with complex organizational structures that were bound by specific regulations and often operating as natural monopolies. These dynamics followed a similar pattern in the new markets for public services contracting. Reagan adopted the Competition in Contracting Act in 1984, requiring US federal government agencies to arrange 'full and open competition through the use of competitive procedures'. The equivalent in the United Kingdom was 'Compulsory Competitive Tendering', which created an external market for public services.

Given the potential lucrativeness for management consultancies of state enterprise privatization and public services outsourcing, it is perhaps not surprising that they also often actively championed these policies in the governments where they worked. Once again, we see that the consulting industry was in this way both shaped by and actively shaping developments in government. During the postwar decades, public sector bureaucracies in Europe and North America had been guided by a model of government that hierarchically linked civil servants within a department to the minister with political authority for that policy area. Public administration was governed by strict procedural rules that sought to ensure the actions of civil servants aligned as closely as possible with the instructions of elected officials. From the 1980s, neoliberal politicians began to call for the introduction of a package of public sector reforms known as New Public Management (NPM). Although a controversial term when it was first introduced, NPM is accepted today as shorthand for a policy agenda that sought to make public sector practices more 'business-like'. Under NPM, civil servants were instead guided by performance measures that evaluated the public sector on the basis of its cost-effectiveness, efficiency and customer (citizen) satisfaction, drawing directly on approaches from the private sector. NPM policies included the introduction of performance-related pay for civil servants; the application of financial metrics used in the private sector, such as cost accounting and profit and loss statements; moves to decentralize the bureaucracy and give public managers greater discretion; and the shift towards viewing citizens as 'customers' whose 'satisfaction' with public services could be measured as an indication of effectiveness.[66]

Management consultants were contracted by governments to implement such administrative reforms, owing to the perception that they had expertise in these business practices. But in their contracts with governments more widely, they also acted as 'diffusers' and promoters of NPM, notably in the United Kingdom.[67]

In 1991, the academics Christopher Hood and Michael Jackson coined the term 'consultocracy' to describe what they recognized as the increasing influence of management consultants in the public administrations of governments. The consultocracy was understood as a 'self-serving movement designed to promote the career interests of an elite group of New Managerialists' (senior managers and consultants) and a 'vehicle for particularistic advantage'.[68] But consultants were also increasingly sought not merely as a source of advice or legitimation for controversial reforms. In many countries, the scope of their role evolved, as spending on them also grew.[69] One study of the UK public sector published in 2001 found, for example, that the use of consultants 'as an extra resource to act as a substitute for internal staff' had been reported as being of increased importance, vis-à-vis their recruitment 'to work on a particular problem/introduce a new technique'.[70] In other words, consultants were increasingly being contracted as outsourced management capacity – as the examples from UK NHS regional offices to the United States' EPA also attest.

By the final decade of the twentieth century, the term 'consultocracy' was already too narrow. Public sector departments in the UK, the United States and many other countries had indeed become increasingly influenced by the advice of consultants, and their use as advisors in the private sector was also growing. And through contracts for delivering government functions, significant power was transferred to the consulting industry, ensuring it would continue to serve as not just a passive intermediary but an active agent in broader economic and governance changes, shaping reforms as it benefitted from them. Crucially, from the 1980s, this economic system – and the influence of consultants within it – ceased to be confined to the borders of Europe and North America. Consultancies would become the 'foot soldiers' of international governance organizations dominated by these developed countries in their attempts to export neoliberal reforms around the world.[71]

Consultants without borders

The economic disruptions of the 1970s in the Global North – the wealthier countries in Europe, North America, Australasia and parts of Asia – would over the course of the decade produce ripples in the economies of the Global South – developing countries in Africa, Latin America, the Caribbean and parts of Asia. When combined with local challenges arising from the struggles for independence from colonial forces, these events culminated in a series of sovereign debt crises that have stalked low-income economies ever since. Throughout the 1960s and 1970s, particularly after the oil crisis of 1973, many developing countries seeking to grow their industries had taken out loans from creditors based in the Global North, such as the World Bank and New York-based banks. In Latin America, for example, total outstanding debt from all sources rose from approximately $29 billion in 1970 to approximately $159 billion in 1978, with approximately 80 per cent of this debt owned by national governments, government agencies, or by private firms with public guarantees.[72] Creditors were more than happy to lend such high amounts because they (incorrectly) believed that the growth those countries had experienced through investing in infrastructure would continue. But as interest rates soared in the United States towards the end of the decade, developing countries (among them Mexico, the Philippines, Nigeria, Morocco and Côte d'Ivoire) found it increasingly hard to service debt. By the early 1980s, debt in many countries had grown so vast that it became clear many would be unable to continue to meet agreed debt obligations, leading to 'sovereign default'. In the attempt to recover their economies, these countries were forced to seek new loan agreements from the World Bank and the International Monetary Fund.

Having once advocated that governments take the lead on developing industrial capacity, by the late 1970s the World Bank and the IMF were advocating neoliberal policies. Loans to developing countries that were facing economic crisis required that they adopt reforms to privatize state-owned enterprises and liberalize trade and finance. These were known as 'Structural Adjustment Programs' (SAPs). Consulting firms helped to implement these reforms via their direct involvement with businesses and governments. Nigeria, for example, was forced to take a loan from the World Bank worth $452 million in 1987 on the condition of a SAP that included 'efforts to limit government spending, downsize the public sector, improve the management of publicly owned assets, improve allocations to infrastructure and social sectors and rely more on market forces'.[73]

As part of this, the government established the Technical Committee on Privatisation and Commercialisation by decree to oversee the privatization of 110 state-owned enterprises, which was 'staffed by professionals from the private sector who are well motivated and well paid . . . including merchant banks and issuing houses, accounting and legal firms, and general management consultants'. According to one 'privatization specialist' of the World Bank writing at the time, who had previously worked as a management consultant, one lesson from Nigeria's experience of privatization concerned 'the need to make full use of specialist consultants':

> There is a growing body of experience in privatization worldwide. Where the expertise is available in-country it should be used, but governments should not hesitate to use expertise from other countries which have successfully implemented privatization programs. International donors are normally willing to help finance such assistance.[74]

The use of external consultants was in fact also sometimes a condition of loans to developing countries. For example, the conditions of the World Bank's loan to Guinea-Bissau included an article stating: 'In order to assist BNG [National Bank of Guinea-Bissau] in carrying out its responsibility . . . the Borrower, acting through BNG, shall: (i) employ a team of project management consultants and experts; and (ii) assign adequate numbers of qualified local professional and support staff in BNG to work with such a team in discharging such responsibility.'[75]

Mexico was the first country to default during the 1980s debt crisis. The restructuring of its economy as mandated by its loans from the IMF continued throughout the 1980s and 1990s under presidents Miguel de la Madrid and Carlos Salinas, who were themselves also proponents of neoliberalism. The privatization of state-owned enterprises and public banks in Mexico involved numerous foreign consulting firms, as well as private banks that were based in Europe and North America. McKinsey and Booz Allen prepared the sales prospectuses on more than half of the eighteen bank privatizations, with Price Waterhouse also providing input. Mercer, which is today best known as an asset management firm but was, at the time, primarily a management consultancy, was contracted to advise on the restructuring of the Mexican National Railroad.[76] Neoliberal policies may have been designed by academics, states and financial institutions in the Global North, but consulting firms helped to deliver those changes on the ground in the Global South and ensure that the neoliberal transformation of capitalism was global.

Lucrative transitions

In Hong Kong, management consultants had been deployed by British colonial rulers to 'modernize' the administration as early as 1974, when McKinsey was contracted to lead the restructuring of government machinery, and they continued to be brought in for input on the reform programme of the 1990s.[77] In Angola, Arthur D. Little was contracted for advice on managing the country's state-owned oil company following independence from Portugal.[78] After the fall of the Berlin Wall in 1989, the consulting industry also benefitted from the political upheavals that would lead the academic Francis Fukuyama to declare famously that humanity had reached 'the end of history' with the hegemony of Western liberalism.[79] The dissolution of the Soviet Union was viewed as a new market by large multinational consulting firms, such as Ernst & Young, McKinsey,

Bain, PricewaterhouseCoopers and BCG, which quickly established themselves in Central and Eastern Europe. New domestic players could also be found in most former countries of the Soviet Union. The transition from communism to capitalism gave impetus to large-scale privatization, and the sale or merger of many domestic firms to large foreign entities created plenty of opportunity for consultancies.[80] Within government, new human resources, technology and operational problems had to be solved: 'Bain, BCG, Berger, Kearney, McKinsey, and others were ready to assist and advise'. Countries including Bulgaria, Hungary and Slovenia established national associations for management consulting.[81]

But it is China's experience with the consulting industry that perhaps most closely tracked the tectonic shifts under way in the global political economy. The emergence of Western consulting firms there can be traced back to the liberalizing reforms introduced in 1978 under Deng Xiaoping. Prior to their entry into the country, business advice had been provided primarily by academics from universities and research institutions, and was often provided free of charge.[82] But as North American and European multinational companies increasingly moved into China, the consultancies they used in their home countries followed suit, establishing local offices in the large cities where subsidiaries had set up shop. Early movers included Boston Consulting Group, Bain & Company, McKinsey, A.T. Kearney and Booz Allen Hamilton. The strategies that Western consultancies employed in China at this time mirrored those used in emerging markets elsewhere. Services were provided pro bono or at far below global market rates. Although this meant that profit margins remained low in the beginning, the companies anticipated these early costs would lead to expanding market share as purchasing business advice became standard practice and global capitalist production norms spread in the country. And indeed, in the decades that followed, as foreign direct investment soared and Chinese state-owned businesses globalized, fresh opportunities for the Western consultancies were plentiful. They were not, however, always popular. One example is McKinsey's 2001 contract with the Chinese company Start Computer Group.[83] McKinsey had been contracted to restructure its client's organization in 1998. But by 2001, Start Computer Group had been under scrutiny from investors for posting losses for two years running. In a televised interview that was broadcast nationwide in April of that year, executives at the company explicitly tied its losses to the advice McKinsey consultants had given. The wider Chinese media subsequently attributed the perceived failure of McKinsey to its 'ignorance of the special Chinese context and business culture'.[84]

Much as the merger wave of the 1980s had spurred consultancies to create new specialist services in multinational organization management, the ambitions of China's state-owned enterprises – combined with pressures from above to innovate management practices – also fostered the consulting industry's growth in China. Andersen Consulting even 'collaborated with the Chinese central government in organizing a three-week training program for executives such as Party secretaries from high profile Chinese state-owned companies'. By 2007, over 70 per cent of the consultancy's revenues in China came from local Chinese companies.[85] In the late 1990s, the Chinese government's liberalization reforms intensified, as the ruling Communist Party sought to spur private sector growth in its bid to accrue power in the global economy. Once again, the ready availability of commercialized advice reinforced broader changes to the structure of the economy.

In one recent ethnographic study, a multinational consultancy based in China, was found to 'pla[y] a vital role in making [Chinese SOEs] into viable investment targets':

By shaping the objectives, the processes and the operations of Chinese SOEs, [the consultancy] helps to create a narrative that these entities are professionalized, modernized entities with "good management."[86]

The case of China attests to the differences in how, when and to what extent consultancies became accepted in different countries. National divergences in the use of consultancies have been documented extensively,[87] and it is clear that differences between economies, the conception of the role of the state, culture and ideology, industrial relations and education within a country affect both demand for and supply of management consultancies.[88] Consulting services are used more in liberal market economies, such as the UK, than in coordinated market economies, such as Germany.[89] In some countries, foreign consultancies failed to garner interest from local client markets, and have only ever achieved limited reach – and even then, it has been through multinational clients with branches in those countries. In South Korea, for example, 'western management consultancies received only short-lived prevalence in the aftermath of the 1997 Asia economic crisis, after which the appeal of western "best practice" decreased'.[90] Today, although some Western companies have a base in the country, their ability to maintain clients is far from guaranteed. In December 2020, Oliver Wyman announced it had closed its office in Seoul after almost two decades, following years of declining revenues and projects. This loss of business was due in part to the rising trend in South Korea of recruiting in-house consultants in key client markets, including the financial services sector.[91]

By the end of the millennium, nonetheless, few countries in the world had been untouched by the consulting industry in some way, as economic developments that originated in Anglo-America extended beyond its borders. But while the reach of the consulting industry had expanded dramatically, with many new firms also being established within formerly colonized and ex-Soviet countries, the market continued to be dominated by a handful of giants based in North America and Europe. It would take the Enron scandal in 2001, which led to the largest bankruptcy in US history, for governments in those countries to recognize how structurally significant the consulting industry had become – and that, in the hands of powerful interests, this influence could also have grave consequences for their own economies.

Taming a Goliath?

By the end of the twentieth century, consulting advice had become a huge source of revenue for many different types of horizontally integrated companies. In no sector was this more apparent than in the large accountancies, which increasingly relied on revenue from non-auditing contracts more than their purported 'core' line of business. The largest accountancies 'began to view themselves primarily as high-level business advisors rather than as accounting firms focused primarily on auditing'. Between 1982 and 1990, audit's share of Big Six revenues dropped from 62 per cent to just under 50 per cent.[92] Although these companies continued to provide auditing, it was a low-margin activity and was offered largely 'because of the spin-off benefits that an audit could produce' – namely:

> An audit allowed an accounting firm to enter the client's business, and to discover how the client's various business systems operated. If the accounting firm tangentially detected aspects of the client's systems that could be improved, then there would be

an opportunity for the selling of consulting services to fix the client's problems.[93]

By the turn of the millennium, auditing had declined further and now accounted for less than a third of the Big Six's fees.[94] In large part, this was because revenue from consulting in the companies had skyrocketed. From 1996 to 1998 alone, Ernst & Young's revenues from management consulting grew over 30 per cent, while its audit business grew by just 10 per cent.[95] Consulting would remain critical to the profit margins of these companies until the collapse of energy giant Enron brought the accounting profession to its knees in the United States.

The companies were employing various strategies to 'cross-sell' their many services, using existing connections and claims to organizational knowledge. The former Arthur Andersen consultant Barbara Ley Toffler described the process of cross-selling as follows: 'Typically, the auditor – the keeper of the sacrosanct relationship – would set up the meeting with the client, and then would call as many consultants as he could to come and strut their stuff.'[96] Accounting consultancies had become one stop shops that provided core professional services across operational and governance areas. Unfortunately, the systemic risks of these dynamics were not recognized before it was too late.

At the time that its executives committed accounting fraud, Enron was one of the largest energy companies in the world and a key supplier of natural gas in the United States. It had grown rapidly during the 1990s – but this growth was owed in no small part to the company's high stock price, which itself was only possible thanks to a combination of legal accounting tricks and illegal fraudulent financial statements. The deregulation of the energy market in the United States that had been pursued under Reagan had made it possible for

Enron to transfer some of its liabilities 'off the books', meaning that investors were not aware of the scale or nature of all of Enron's debts. And the company also went far beyond what the lax regulation permitted, transferring some losses to shell companies held offshore, which allowed it to avoid paying taxes: a *New York Times* investigation found that Enron paid no income taxes in the United States in four of the years between 1996 and 2001, using almost 900 subsidiaries based in tax haven countries to effectively hide the true nature of its profits, losses and debts.[97] Eventually, shareholders, journalists and Wall Street analysts began to realize that something was amiss. Then, the new CEO resigned after just six months – though not before he had cashed in shares in the company worth $33 million. The company's share price plummeted, and no other company would agree to a merger deal with Enron. Before long, Enron had no choice but to declare bankruptcy, leading to thousands of job losses overnight and power outages that would endure for weeks.

Executives at Enron eventually pleaded to or were found guilty of charges including fraud, money laundering and insider trading. But Enron's executives did not act alone; they were enabled by the company's auditor, Arthur Andersen, which failed to alert appropriate bodies about the financial gaming of Enron employees. On top of this, Arthur Andersen's actions immediately after Enron's collapse became the subject of a criminal investigation. Accountants at the firm spent the night following Enron's bankruptcy shredding documents and deleting emails that could prove their involvement in the Enron audit – a scene that would be reported widely across national media over the coming days and weeks. Although the resulting conviction of 'obstruction of justice' for these actions was later overturned by the Supreme Court, the reputational damage to the company was so great that the accounting division of Arthur Andersen ceased functioning altogether. Operating under a new name, Accenture, the company's consulting entity would nonetheless go on to become one of the largest consulting firms in the world.

The collapse of Enron and the involvement of Arthur Andersen were widely depicted as the doing of a few criminals, and a few more bad apples. But subsequent analysis suggested the case had much more structural origins. In the wake of Enron's bankruptcy, public officials would learn of the 'inherent conflict of interest between the firm's $27 million in management consulting fees and the $25 million that Andersen earned from Enron for its audit work'.[98] Like many other companies, Arthur Andersen had effectively been using its audit services as a 'loss-leader' product to secure management consulting contracts. Auditing had become structurally important for the future revenues of the other half of Arthur Andersen's business. During this time, audit clients had also begun not just to seek out price quotations for audits, but were engaging in a practice known as 'opinion shopping', whereby they 'would also attempt to ascertain the degree to which each firm might interpret accounting standards so as to present the client's financial statements in the manner that management most preferred'.[99] Both of these features of the sector – cross-selling by auditors and opinion shopping by clients – created incentives for an auditor to make judgements that were favourable to the executives of its client – in this case, Enron.

The Economist had anticipated the risks of these emerging dynamics of accounting services in a 1990 article, amid wider scrutiny of the profession in the United Kingdom:

All the accountants' problems have a common origin: they are no longer seen to be impartial . . . Like advertising agencies and investment bankers, they fell for the 1980s fad of the service conglomerate. The big eight firms became the big six as they merged and remerged, struggling to push under one roof a whole range of business services, like tax advice, management consultancy, corporate finance, and, yes, insolvency. This left them woefully dependent on non-recurring fee businesses like consulting; it also encouraged them to cut auditing fees to win other business. When auditing becomes a loss-leader it is hardly surprising that it gets done badly or misleadingly.[100]

It was this conflict of interest produced by the structural dynamics of the sector that led to the inclusion in the Sarbanes-Oxley Act of 2002 of rules explicitly barring accounting firms in the United States from providing management consulting services to companies they were auditing.[101] The Sarbanes-Oxley Act was developed directly in response to Enron and other financial scandals where similar patterns of auditing behaviour could be found. The collapse of telecommunications company WorldCom in the summer of 2002 was another example where criminal activity among executives had been overlooked owing to a conflict of interest of the company's auditor, which again was Arthur Andersen. The revenue split between Arthur Andersen's consulting and audit revenues at World-Com had been three to one – even greater than at Enron. In a speech made in January 2003, Securities and Exchange Commissioner Cynthia A. Glassman described how the law 'was enacted in July in response to financial frauds at Enron, WorldCom and other corporations and the realization that many of the "gatekeepers" responsible for preventing fraud had fallen down on the job'. She noted how, during the 1990s, 'changing business conditions [had] placed pressure on auditors to diversify the services they offered public companies', which had, in turn, 'placed pressure on auditors to go along with whatever it took to meet Wall Street expectations'.[102]

Despite the risks that they were developed in response to, the provisions in the Sarbanes-Oxley Act were not introduced in other countries. Lawmakers in the United Kingdom considered adopting equivalent legislation, but ultimately abandoned plans to do so. Even in the United States, the provisions were limited. Although lawmakers had identified the conflicts of interest inherent in the services provided by the large accounting firms at the time, there was nothing in the Act to prevent accounting firms from providing consulting services to non-audit clients that were in the same sector or shared investors.[103]

Large consultancies were also using a strategy of lowballing in tenders to secure consulting contracts. In this way, some consulting contracts – particularly for new clients or in emerging markets – had also become 'loss-leaders', incentivizing the provision of advice that satisfies the contracting client in the short term, but that may not be in the long-term interest of the company or indeed wider society. Where consulting services play a legitimating function, staving off regulatory intervention, this tendency further incentivizes the creation of tools that will enable the client to achieve short-term financial or political goals, at the best possible price.

From the spread of American business models and ideas during the Cold War, to the structural adjustment policies of the World Bank in the 1980s, management consultancies rode the waves of key transformations in economies around the world – aided by reforms to government introduced in the wake of neoliberalism. Despite the fall from grace of Arthur Andersen, the consulting industry would continue to grow and to shape economies.

4. The Outsourcing Turn: Government by Consultancy and the Third Way

Tuesday 1 October 2013 should have been a momentous day in American history. After decades of campaigning, the federal government had at last signed into law legislation that would ensure citizens could access basic medical care. The Affordable Care Act, passed three years earlier and dubbed 'Obamacare', included three key provisions: expanding eligibility of the public health insurance programme, Medicaid; requiring all citizens to have a form of health insurance; and reforming delivery systems to make healthcare affordable, including for those with pre-existing conditions. In short, Obamacare was a bold mission to bring healthcare to more people who needed it in the United States.

Healthcare reform had been at the heart of Barack Obama's 2008 election campaign, and in the years after his victory there had been tense debates and negotiations about what that should entail. Dozens of contractors were brought in to manage the delivery of core parts of Obamacare. This included HealthCare.gov, the website through which individuals could purchase subsidized private health insurance via an exchange market platform and sign up for Medicaid. HealthCare.gov was central to Obama's reform. At the end of every meeting with his White House staff ahead of the website's release on 1 October 2013, the president would say, 'I want to remind the team that this only works if the technology works.'[1]

It was an unusually warm Tuesday in October when the website launched. With a few clicks, residents of the United States who had previously been unable to afford insurance would soon be able to change that. For Matt Warren, speaking to *CBS News*, the day couldn't come soon enough. With a wife and two children, the Warren family's insurance cost almost $5,000 a year – and Matt himself wasn't even included in the policy. His high cholesterol and case of skin cancer made it too expensive. But when he tried to get onto the platform, he was met with an error message that told him to wait. And wait. And wait. Eventually, he gave up.[2]

Matt was not alone in his disappointment. By 7 a.m., millions of people had tried and failed to access HealthCare.gov. The website had crashed. It would soon be revealed that just six people had succeeded in signing up for health insurance on that first day.[3] Within hours of the website launch, Republicans were calling for the entire Affordable Care Act to be scrapped. News of the failure dominated the headlines. Two and a half weeks later, the White House even considered shutting the website down indefinitely.[4]

This was supposed to be the landmark reform of Obama's first term – the thing that his administration would be remembered for in the history books. So how did it go so wrong?

Most criticism of the HealthCare.gov failure has centred on some form of perceived government incompetence. Writing for the IBM Center for the Business of Government – a private think-tank established by consultancy PwC in 1998 and later acquired by IBM – Gwanhoo Lee and Justin Brumer list a charge sheet of failures by the Centers for Medicare and Medicaid Services (CMS), the federal agency responsible for HealthCare.gov. It includes poor scoping and project planning, a lack of clear leadership from federal top administrators, and a time frame that was impractically short for developers.[5] Others have focused on inadequacies in the procurement process, arguing that it was 'overly burdensome and bureaucratic' and that 'the operational units within each agency responsible for managing contracts and implementing reforms are too far removed from the procurement process'.[6] In essence, they assume that HealthCare.gov would have been successful, had the government been smarter – that bumbling public officials and clunky bureaucracy were the weak links on which the entire project collapsed.

But beyond the public sector was a matrix of business actors, including some very large companies. The platform's development was not a case of bringing in a few experts and programmers to advise on or assist with a policy reform. Rather, contracting out key parts of the project became *the* strategy for achieving what amounted to the most ambitious health policy reform of Obama's administration. Technology contractors and vendors were brought in to do almost everything related to the development of the website, software and integrating systems. These included the military technology giant Lockheed Martin, as well as companies that specialized in providing digital technologies for the federal government, such as Aquilent – which has since been acquired by Lockheed Martin – and a host of other smaller IT and software engineering firms. In total, over fifty-five companies were hired to work directly on the project.

As has become typical across many governments, huge contracts were also given to companies to help plan and coordinate the project – and even processes for contracting other companies for various goods and services. The military technology firm and IT consultancy Booz Allen Hamilton was awarded a contract worth over $25 million 'to provide technical and operational guidance' for setting up a data centre for the HealthCare.gov market exchange platform and 'to support exchange vendors in the ongoing development and propagation of essential exchange capabilities and traceability reporting'. HP Enterprise Services – an IT consultancy that was at the time a subsidiary of Hewlett-Packard – received a wide-ranging contract that included 'all necessary aspects of planning, implementing, transitioning, operating, and maintaining the CMS's applications and all related hardware and software within the Virtual Data Center environment'. That contract was estimated to be worth $208 million at the time of its award in July 2013. Deloitte was granted a contract to help manage the process of evaluating HealthCare.gov's performance, even developing the metrics used to measure success. A number of smaller consultancies also received large contracts for services critical to the project: a health policy consultancy was brought in 'to conduct appropriate qualitative and quantitative research' on consumers' experiences of HealthCare.gov, and derive insights from this to aid the website's development; a small design consultancy was contracted 'to purchase online marketing consulting services' for HealthCare.gov.[7]

From planning to procuring vendors and specialist skills (i.e. contracting), implementing and integrating different parts, evaluating, and using insights from those evaluations to guide future decisions, external consultancies were at the core of HealthCare.gov.

Contracts at scale and scope

A government review in 2014 revealed that the costs for delivering HealthCare.gov had soared to $1.7 billion – multiples of the original budget. The scale and scope of tasks outsourced to companies is exemplified in the contracts to CGI Group, which describes itself as 'among the largest IT and business consulting services firms in the world'.[8] At the time it was awarded its first contract for HealthCare.gov in 2010, over a third of the company's revenue came from government and healthcare contracts globally. The Canadian company was dependent on continuing to secure the types of contracts federal bodies such as CMS provide, and which were on offer through the HealthCare.gov platform. The value of CGI Group's work for the US federal government had increased from 10.3 per cent of total revenue to 13.7 per cent following the acquisition of another federal contractor and increased success in tender bids across various departments.[9] On the day that HealthCare.gov was supposed to launch, CGI Group had a market capitalization of $8.9 billion, with annual revenues of around $4.8 billion.[10] One of its founders, Serge Godin, was a multi-billionaire. CGI Group was not just some specialist IT company staffed by passionate and geeky programmers, but a powerful economic actor.

In total, over $200 million was set aside for the Canadian firm. In the end, the cost overrun for its five HealthCare.gov contracts reached $28 million.[11] Across them, the company was responsible for managing the technical build of the market exchange platform, as well as the processes for procuring other contractors and vendors. CGI Group managers, technical staff and subcontractors were deemed critical to the reform's success.

In 2016, an investigation by the Office of Inspector General identified many failings by CGI Group across its HealthCare.gov contracts. On numerous occasions, the company failed to communicate problems with work that it was delivering and the risks of launching the project. It did not 'adequately increase staffing and expertise when changes were made and progress began to deteriorate'.[12] There were also many technical issues throughout. An independent review determined in February 2013 that there were 'a high number of coding defects' in CGI Group's work.[13] Internal staff in CMS discovered that the company's developers 'did not follow some best practices for making last-stage coding changes, resulting in code conflicts between some systems'. In the end, these all proved critical to HealthCare.gov's botched launch. But despite these failures, as far as the Office of Inspector General was concerned, responsibility for the calamity that unfolded on 1 October 2013 ultimately lay with CMS for failing to provide leadership and oversight. The recommendations it put forward to 'avoid future problems' addressed the federal agency's management, and its 'organizational structure and culture'.[14]

To assume that HealthCare.gov would have been successful if only CMS senior managers had 'declared a clear "business owner"'[15] or improved communication among its own staff ignores the systemic problems with an approach to government that relies on outsourcing core functions and parts of their management to consultants. Even with the best public managers in the world, and with an organizational culture that 'promoted acceptance of bad news' and 'continuous learning' – as also recommended in the Office of Inspector General's report[16] – the size and complexity of the contracts exacerbated the risk to the whole healthcare initiative – and to the government. To believe that these organizational tweaks would even be possible after decades of outsourcing across government departments was wishful thinking.

CGI Group's failures were in many ways inevitable within this model. Its biggest contract for the exchange market was structured as what's known as a 'cost-plus-fixed-fee', meaning that it was able to bill for additional labour and material expenses as it incurred them. This type of contract is common in large and complex tenders, because it transfers the costs of failure away from the contractor to the government, and so incentivizes companies to bid for them: they can reap the rewards without taking on the risks.[17] But it also 'provides the contractor with less incentive to control costs and provide high quality products'[18] – because they can just bill the client for any additional items. This is exactly what CGI Group did. CMS paid

CGI Group for charges associated with the extra work needed to correct the defects with the platform that were a result of its own failures up to four months after the original launch day.[19] These issues could not have been resolved simply by structuring the contract differently in the beginning; the cost-plus-fixed-fee model was used because CMS would have struggled to attract companies if it did not take on the risks of failure itself. But in taking on the risks of failure and using the cost-plus-fixed-fee contract, CMS opened itself up for CGI Group, either purposefully or due to negligence, to extract financial value from the contract far beyond what its efforts created or the contract originally stated.

HealthCare.gov represented a broader trend across many governments and businesses: consultancies are hired not just to advise public managers or provide well-defined specialist services, but *to do* government. In the Anglosphere, where this outsourcing mode of government emerged, entirely new consulting companies specializing in contract management have sprung up, such as Serco and Sodexo, extracting huge rents through government choices. The parallel growth in government spending on more established consulting firms cannot be separated from this development.

'Reinventing' government

In January 1993, when Bill Clinton was inaugurated as US President, the Republican Party had been in power for twelve years. The radical reforms to reconfigure the government adopted under the Reagan administration had continued under Clinton's predecessor, George H.W. Bush. Throughout the period of their presidencies, government bureaucracy had taken a bashing – not just in terms of its funding, but also in the public sphere. Along with Margaret

Thatcher in Britain and Brian Mulroney in Canada, Reagan and Bush Senior had 'found that there was plenty of political capital to be made from publicly castigating the public sector'.[20] By the time Clinton was elected, opinion polls showed that confidence in the public sector had plummeted, and disillusionment among government employees was at an all-time high. After the extreme anti-government rhetoric and practices of the 1980s, as far as the Clinton campaign was concerned, there had never been a better moment for the Democrats to articulate an alternative approach and distinguish itself from the incumbent party.

The approach endorsed by Clinton during his campaign and subsequently adopted by his administration was inspired in large part by a book published in the run-up to the election in 1992. *Reinventing Government: How the Entrepreneurial Spirit is Transforming the Public Sector* was written by two independent consultants, David Osborne and Ted Gaebler, and its proposals would soon form the basis of wide-reaching reforms across federal government via the National Performance Review (NPR), of which Osborne also became the chair. The book sought to reclaim a role for government in society and the economy, challenging the widely held views of neoliberal presidents about its inherent harms. But crucially, its programme also diverged dramatically from earlier Democrat visions of the state, viewing government as the vehicle for delivering 'a new customer service contract with the American people', echoing the rhetoric of earlier New Public Management.[21] The function of government, under this vision, was to ensure the services that citizens wanted were available – but not necessarily to provide those services itself through the public sector. Instead, NPR envisioned a government that would 'steer more, row less'.[22] As well as advocating for even greater deregulation of internal administration – or removing 'red tape', as the NPR report put it – and decentralizing functions, the programme of

Reinventing Government championed 'creating market dynamics' and 'using market mechanisms to solve problems', giving examples of 'how public bureaucracies can compete with private firms and win the bid to provide a particular service',[23] such as garbage collection. It pledged that the trend among neoliberal governments 'to contract services competitively . . . will not be reversed', asserting that 'By creating competition between public organizations, contracting services out to private organizations, listening to our customers, and embracing market incentives wherever appropriate, we can transform the quality of services delivered to the American people.'[24] In other words, although the approach was adopted by progressive politicians, its fundamental assumptions about the appropriate role of the government in the creation of goods and services shared much in common with that of the earlier neoliberal politicians.

This new vision of government as responsible for meeting public needs without necessarily providing services itself 'reinforced the belief that a middle way could be found between the market and the state'[25] – or 'beyond left and right', as another important figure in this emerging governance paradigm would soon put it.[26] Anthony Giddens was a professor at the London School of Economics who became an advisor to both Bill Clinton and Tony Blair in 1997, after the latter was elected in a landslide victory. Like Clinton, Blair was keen to emphasize the Labour Party's plans to reform the public sector. The ideas that Giddens espoused became known as the 'Third Way', because they purported to offer a middle ground between what Giddens viewed as the state socialism of the 'Old Left' and market reforms of the 'New Right', which lacked notions of social justice. The term 'Third Way' had already been used to describe similar policies adopted by the Australian governments of Bob Hawke and Paul Keating, and it quickly became associated with the reform programmes of Bill Clinton and Tony Blair.

The consulting industry played an important role in shaping and then diffusing the Third Way agenda across the bureaucracies of the Anglosphere, and then to other governments around the world. Given that this was an approach to government that emphasized the importance of market actors, such as consultancies, the enthusiasm with which consultancies themselves promoted the Third Way is hardly surprising. Following its endorsement by the Clinton administration, *Reinventing Government* became critical in this in several ways. Management consultancies quickly co-opted the language and ideas contained in the book, deploying them in marketing material to the growing public sector clients it had established during the 1980s. KPMG advertised its 'success at Reinventing Government', and Price Waterhouse established 'Reinvention Teams', even developing its own 'methodology for Reinvention'.[27] Meanwhile, Coopers & Lybrand, which was later merged with Price Waterhouse, promoted *Reinventing Government* in the UK as the 'most influential bible of the new movement in public management'.[28] The book's authors, Osborne and Gaebler, also established the Reinventing Government Network, a group of 100 management consultancies with branches in the United States, Canada, Australia, the United Kingdom and the Netherlands, membership of which 'provide[d] a useful marketing tool for consulting firms who want to be seen at the cutting edge of "entrepreneurial" public sector management'.[29]

Beyond spreading the gospel of *Reinventing Government*, consultancies were also hugely influential in shaping the economic policies of Third Way politicians within government. Arthur Andersen, for example, was contracted by the UK Labour Party to develop future economic and fiscal policies while it was still in opposition, before it was elected. Patricia Hewitt, who would become Economic Secretary to the Treasury in 1998, had also been head of Andersen Research, part of the consulting arm of Arthur Andersen.[30] But it was the consulting industry's involvement in establishing new contracting models that perhaps had the greatest impact in the Third Way reform agenda.

Who contracts the contractors?

Under the Republican presidencies in the US, and Thatcher and her Conservative Party successor John Major in the UK, while contracting out public services had increased a great deal, contracts had tended to be for single services.[31] For example, a local hospital might outsource its cleaning to a private cleaning company. But under Third Way governments, new commissioning models were developed and forms of 'public-private partnership' (PPP) were introduced that required much bigger and often much longer contracts.

These included the Private Finance Initiative (PFI), other forms of public-private partnership, and contracts for aggregated services, such as 'strategic' or 'joint' commissioning and 'prime contracting'. PFI is 'a procurement method where the private sector finances, builds and operates infrastructure and provides long term services and facilities management through long term contractual arrangements'.[32] PFI was initially developed for construction contracts, and entailed a company or consortium (a group of companies) taking on responsibility for financing the project. The company or consortium would lease the building or infrastructure back to the government, which would then make payments for the capital cost of the project over the life of the PFI contract. In the UK, PFI had been introduced by John Major. In opposition, the Labour Party had described PFI as 'totally unacceptable' and as 'the thin end of the wedge of privatisation'.[33] But once in power, the party became a staunch proponent of this form of contracting. One important reason why PFI was popular under Blair's government was that although 'future unitary payments represent a liability to the public sector, this liability is usually recorded off balance sheet and is thus excluded from public debt calculations'.[34] PFI constituted a way to reduce current government spending and thus prevent growth in public sector net debt or public sector net borrowing by transferring responsibility for financing to the private sector – albeit while many risks of failure remained with the public sector.[35] It was thus a paragon policy for politicians seeking to implement the *Reinventing Government* playbook, and prove it was possible to 'do more with less'[36] by 'using market mechanisms to solve problems'.[37] Subsequent analysis published by the UK Treasury in 2015 showed that the costs of servicing debt accrued through PFI was by then double that of government borrowing.[38]

The consulting industry was influential in the growth of PFI contracts under the Blair government. Once in office, Blair's government appointed personnel from Andersen Consulting as political advisors, establishing a taskforce with them to explore how to increase the use of PFI.[39] This body then became Partnerships UK, a public limited company that was majority owned by private investors. While technically a public body, it was staffed primarily by management consultants, accountants and procurement specialists, and even those staff coming from the public sector often had close ties to the consulting industry. They included, for example, the head of PFI policy at the Treasury, Richard Abadie, a former PwC Partner specializing in PFI, who returned to the consultancy within a few years.[40] Notably, Partnerships UK was also tasked with promoting PFI internationally, and claimed 'to have provided "high-level" support for the design and structure of PPP programs being designed by other governments . . . eg, to the Czech Republic,

Mexico and South Africa'. The consulting industry, and large accountancies in particular, also provided advice to private sector firms that tendered for PFI contracts. PwC 'took by far the largest share of the PFI advisory market in terms of both the number and size of the projects'.[41] PFI contracts were widely used in the construction of new hospitals in the NHS; the first fifteen such contracts alone generated £45 million in fees for their advisors in contracts across the public and private sector, worth 4 per cent of the capital value of the deals.[42]

In the realm of public services, 'strategic' or 'joint' commissioning and 'prime contracting' were developed as contracting models that aggregated multiple services within single contracts. In

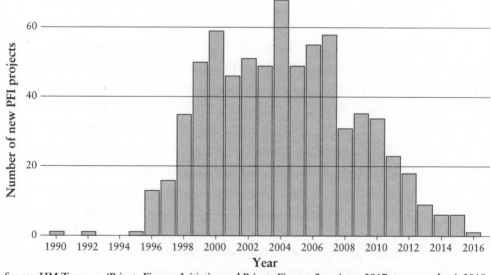

Source: HM Treasury, 'Private Finance Initiative and Private Finance 2 projects: 2017 summary data', 2018. By year of financial close. Expired or terminated projects are not included in the data.

Figure 3

PFI projects in the United Kingdom, 1990–2016

strategic commissioning, single companies that provided a range of services would be contracted to deliver them all. For example, in the early 2000s Somerset County Council in southwest England contracted IBM to provide a range of back-office functions for revenues and benefits, establish call centres and provide core services such as HR and payroll.[43] In joint commissioning, multiple public sector bodies come together to commission a private company – or occasionally a third sector organization – to provide the same service for all of them. For example, the Greater Manchester Health and Social Care Partnership established in 2016 brought together the local NHS organizations and councils of ten boroughs to commission services that would benefit shared population groups across the region. It was hoped this would reduce costs by stopping duplication and siloing of work.[44]

In prime contracting, a public body, or sometimes a group of public bodies, contracts a single company (the prime contractor) to become the main point of contact and manage the (sub)contracting of a range of services and functions across a specific area. The prime contractor does not necessarily deliver services itself beyond the contract management. An early example of this is New York City's reforms of its public assistance programmes in the late 1990s. The Human Resource Administration was responsible for delivering most income support benefits, job search and placement services, and work experience programmes. Until 1999, 'these services were delivered through multiple contracts with "dozens" of local non-profit agencies. By early 2000 all these services were consolidated by HRA into 17 multi-million dollar "prime contracts" awarded to 13 for-profit and non-profit organisations'.[45]

All these forms of aggregated contracting led to a proliferation of very large contracts in the public sector. Third Way politicians thought aggregated services contracts helped to streamline procurement and reduce the administrative costs associated with managing contractors, as well as reducing the direct costs of delivering services by harnessing capabilities of the private sector. As with PFI, the growth of these types of contracts in many countries was aided in no small part by the advice of the consulting industry – often as a result of its very direct involvement in the development of policies. Another taskforce established under Blair, for example, was the 'Delivery Unit', which worked in partnerships with government departments and the Prime Minister's Office to 'assess delivery and provide performance management for key delivery areas'.[46] Launching in 2001, during Blair's second term, it was headed by a former advisor to the Prime Minister, Michael Barber, who subsequently joined McKinsey as a Partner. It was staffed by consultants from firms including McKinsey and Accenture, who worked alongside civil servants, and 'consciously partnered state and non-state actors in the management of public services'.[47]

Crucially, these large contracts also brought with them a new potential source of income for the consulting industry. Consultancies were often themselves the prime contractors. The 'privatisation of contract governance' through the mainstreaming of these types of 'larger and longer-term complex contracts' led to the 'wider use of management consultants for reviews and procurement'.[48] In PFI, consultancies succeeded in 'advocat[ing] for governments to go ahead and finance public infrastructure through schemes from which they themselves would benefit'.[49] More generally, aggregation was not only 'attractive to larger private sector consultancy firms as it increased the contract value' but also because the scope of the contract was not always defined completely in the beginning, allowing later for 'contracts to include additional services that would not be subject to separate tendering processes'.[50] A key area where this occurred was public sector digitalization.

Digital era outsourcing

PFI and prime contracting were at the heart of IT reforms known as 'e-government' that were implemented across the Global North throughout the 2000s.[51] By this time, personal computers had become more affordable and user-friendly. Employees at firms in the private sector were using them widely. The invention of the internet also offered the possibility of faster and more effective communication across public sector departments; no longer would instructions need to be sent via memo or letter. Email was becoming the norm. Information or data about processes and citizens could be accessed by public managers at the click of a button.

It was in this process of technological change that many governments adopted e-government reforms, aiming to bring the 'digital era' into the public sector. It was hoped that the digitalization of government would not only lead to greater efficiency in the public sector, but that citizen needs could more readily be met. Following the initial National Performance Review report, Vice President Al Gore launched an initiative called 'Access America' through what was then the National Partnership for Reinventing Government, pledging that citizens would have electronic access to government by the turn of the millennium.[52] Crucially, from the outset, e-government reforms entailed shifting from IT systems that were largely centralized and maintained in-house, to ones that were provided by private contractors. Today, it is hard to believe that governments once managed and serviced much of their IT infrastructure in-house, but that was the case throughout the twentieth century in many countries, including those already mentioned in the Anglosphere. The expansion of federal IT outsourcing from the mid-1990s marked an acceleration of longer-term trends; between 1982 and 1993, commercial services as a proportion of IT expenditure had already risen in the United States from 39 to 49 per cent.[53] Governments across the Global North soon followed with similar IT reform programmes, though the extent of outsourcing varied significantly between countries, broadly tracking the scale of New Public Management reforms.[54] For example, the Netherlands, Japan and Scandinavian countries retained extensive capabilities in-house until relatively late. Denmark maintained its own central IT systems management and development company, Datacentralen, in-house until its privatization in 1996.[55]

There were many drivers of this shift. The broader tendency towards contracting among Third Way governments was important in shifting the responsibility for IT infrastructure and management to private hands. Governments also struggled to recruit and retain the IT specialists necessary to deliver digital transformation in-house. Not only were government salaries uncompetitive with those available in the booming private IT sector,[56] but by this time, the rhetoric of public sector incompetence had rendered government employment less attractive than what was available in the private sector. Narratives about the supremacy of the private sector in digital innovation had proliferated, in part because of the rapid growth of California-based, venture capital-funded, start-up technology companies, such as Apple and Google, and the wider IT industry.[57] Often led by alluring and intelligent media-friendly personalities, these firms contributed to the idea that innovation and digital technology were the proper domain of the private sector. The potential lucrativeness of government contracts for these hardware and software companies spurred fierce lobbying of politicians and public managers. In an alternative history where the public sector had been equally recognized, celebrated and remunerated for its contributions to technological innovation, there is every chance that government would have continued to be the career par excellence for IT specialists.

The digitalization of government administration and services was a hugely profitable advisory market for the consulting industry. From the early days of the World Wide Web, consulting firms positioned themselves as sages of the digital era, offering advice to governments on IT procurement and management. From the 1990s, firms that had originally started out as computing developers, such as IBM, focused efforts on IT consulting, securing large contracts for digital government advice.[58] In the decade before 2002, IBM's total revenue grew by 26 per cent from $64.5 billion to $81.2 billion, but during the same period services revenue at the company grew by 492 per cent from $7.4 billion to $36.4 billion.[59] By 2006, around two thirds of all spending on consultants in the UK public sector was estimated to be for IT systems consultants, with the largest contractors being IBM, LogicaCMG, Accenture, PA Consulting and Capgemini.[60] Accenture 'increased its staff by around 20 per cent in 2004'.[61]

The consulting industry encouraged the government to outsource public sector digitalization just as it did in all parts of government. E-government and digitalization contracts became targets for prime contracting, with IT infrastructure frequently falling under PFI arrangements in countries such as the UK and Australia. The consulting industry became a key beneficiary of these arrangements. For example, Accenture and PwC were prime contractors in a number of the UK government's IT contracts under Blair, including for projects in sensitive areas of government such as the Benefits Agency and the Ministry of Defence.[62] In the US, the scale and scope of contracts across government civilian bodies grew in the wake of the tragic events of 9/11 with parallel developments in the defence agencies. The 'War on Terror' created ample opportunity for the expansion of IT consulting services in the state, as a digital security bureaucracy was built from the latest Silicon Valley technologies.

In 2013, the whistleblower Edward Snowden revealed that the United States government had engaged in extensive intelligence gathering with his leaks of classified information from the National Security Agency (NSA). The initial reports on the documents that Snowden leaked suggested that the NSA had been collecting the telephone records of millions of customers of one of the largest telecoms providers in the United States, Verizon.[63] The *Washington Post* alleged the NSA and its equivalent in the United Kingdom, Government Communications Headquarters (GCHQ), were also 'tapping directly into the central servers of nine leading US internet companies, extracting audio and video chats, photographs, e-mails, documents, and connection logs that enable analysts to track foreign targets'.[64]

Snowden's revelations also made visible the extent of IT contracting by firms including consultancies that underpinned the government's secretive military and security operations, indicating how, 'in the twenty-first century, more than ever before, government intelligence agencies collaborate with the private sector to counter diverse security threats'.[65] At the time of his revelations, Snowden himself was working for the NSA through a contract held by Booz Allen Hamilton, which has continued to be listed as one of the military's largest contractors ever since. In 2013, the company earned 99 per cent of its revenues from services under 5,700 contracts and task orders with the US government. Thirty-nine per cent of those revenues came from contracts with the Army and intelligence agencies. Ninety-one per cent of revenues were from contracts in which it acted as the prime contractor.[66]

Companies such as Amazon and Google remained, for the most part, strangers to government even at the turn of the millennium. But within twenty years, they would become central to the digital infrastructure of public sectors around the world. Although the scale and scope of big tech companies' involvement in government IT infrastructure is unprecedented, it must nonetheless be viewed as enabled by the growth of earlier IT contracting during the 1990s and 2000s. This is partly because earlier e-government and public sector digitalization created the market for government goods and services that Silicon Valley firms would later capture as they monopolized digital infrastructure across the economy. But also, in so doing, it created technological dependencies, as public sector capabilities failed to keep pace with developments in the private sector and normalized the entrenchment of private sector delivery of government IT.

At the turn of the millennium, a new group of companies purporting to specialize in managing aggregated public sector contracts emerged. In popular discourse, companies such as Serco, Atos and Sodexo are usually understood as service providers, but it is more accurate to describe the function they provide as managing contracts: they are outsourcing consultancies. They may describe themselves today as 'public services companies', but once upon a time companies' annual reports and media coverage about them used the term 'outsourcing firms'. The former suggests the firms exist to provide public services, conjuring benign images of a public health department, or perhaps a local government waste collection service. The latter actually gets to the heart of why these companies exist: the inversion of public provision – the sourcing *out* of services. Their purported expertise lies in bidding for large public sector contracts, and then helping to manage the delivery of those contracts through a combination of internal provision and subcontracting.

During the 2000s, these companies became clients of the more established consultancies, turning to them for advice on how to win bids from the government and manage infrastructure investments, which consultants were able to provide using the knowledge they had built up through their own contracts with the public sector. PwC, for example, acted as the 'lead financial and structuring advisers to Serco . . . on the disposal of their PPP portfolio interests'.[67] But it was only in the wake of the financial crisis of 2008 that the opportunities for securing these lucrative aggregated contracts – and providing professional services related to them – would come to redefine the consulting industry.

Consulting the financial crisis

The collapse of the investment bank Lehman Brothers in September 2008 marked the end of a decade of plenty in Europe and North America. Governments had accrued deficits through extensive public budgets that in many countries helped to line the pockets of contractors.

Consulting firms were by no means the perpetrator of the crisis. In the United States, credit was more easily accessible to more people than it had been for many years. The excessively risky behaviour of banks in their lending to homebuyers would ultimately be the catalyst that brought down the banking system. Caught up in an illusion of seemingly never-ending growth, bankers had taken to offering mortgages to people who would struggle to meet their obligations. These were known as 'subprime mortgages'. The greedy lure of potentially huge profits when these risky mortgages were turned into complex financial instruments and then traded on largely unregulated markets created a monstrous housing bubble that would destroy lives and livelihoods when it inevitably burst.

Few people saw the financial crisis coming. But there was one group of companies whose job it was to identify harmful practices in the financial sector. Wearing their auditor hats, the Big Four accounting consultancies 'signed off trillion-dollar balance sheets, sanctioned increased dividends in bank shares that collapsed months later, blithely assumed markets would function seamlessly and established controversial rules that inflated bubbles and amplified losses'.[68] They okayed the numbers for banks that ran into difficulty including Northern Rock, Landsbanki, Carlyle Capital Corporation, Glitnir, Alliance & Leicester, RBS, Bear Stearns, HBOS, Kaupthing, Bradford & Bingley, and even Lehman Brothers. Beyond providing auditing services, consulting companies also served as advisors to banks in the years running up to the crisis, although in the wake of the Enron scandal and the earlier dotcom recession, there had been some indication that financial firms were using consultancies less. Exact figures on banks' spending on consultants are unknown, though it is estimated that in countries with large financial hubs, financial services represent over 30 per cent of consulting fees.[69] Similarly, little is known about the nature of advice that consultancies provided to banks in the run-up to the financial crisis – though had they offered the kind that might have prevented the crisis, it would be surprising they haven't publicized that.

Media headlines – and subsequent public investigations – were reserved for the reckless behaviour of traders in the weeks and months running up to the collapse of their banks. Before long, fingers also pointed towards the politicians who had let them get away with it. It became clear very quickly that no government had planned for a financial crisis of the scale witnessed in 2008. In the attempt to prevent their economies from collapsing as part of a financial domino effect, governments in Europe and North America quickly bought up the now worthless debt that their banks had accumulated. In the United States, the asset management firm BlackRock was contracted by the Federal Reserve to run the three vehicles that it created to hold assets from the collapsed insurance firm AIG (American International Group) and investment bank Bear Stearns, marking the birth of BlackRock's consultancy arm, Financial Markets Advisory. The Great Recession that followed the financial crisis and the unprecedented intervention of states in financial institutions would transform not just how governments operated but the lives of ordinary people too. Millions of people around the world lost their jobs and were forced to leave their homes, and panic quickly turned into anger. After the financial crisis, voters in many countries ushered in politicians who promised change, politicians who blamed the spending of previous governments for the current turmoil and pledged to rein in the government budget – or 'tighten the public purse strings', as the analogy so often went. They included Silvio Berlusconi in Italy, Valdis Dombrovskis in Latvia and the Liberal Democrat–Conservative Coalition government in the United Kingdom. Citizens wanted life to go back to how it once had been, but – they were told – this would require reductions in government spending in the short term. The consensus across many governments was that recovery required 'austerity'.

Immediately after the recession, the established strategy, accountancy and IT consultancies saw a global downturn in revenues across public and private sector divisions. Nonetheless, in some parts of the world, financial turmoil created fresh opportunities for advising governments and financial institutions on economic recovery. Europe offered a particularly rewarding market, as euro-denominated countries and banks fought ever growing mountains of debt. The 'Troika' – made up of the European Commission (EC), the European Central Bank (ECB) and the IMF – employed external consultants from the consulting industry as well as asset management funds including BlackRock, to determine how much indebted countries and banks would need to borrow to prevent a default.[70] US-based management consulting firm Oliver Wyman could be found in public bureaucracies across Europe, including in Spain, where it was employed to analyse or 'stress test' what remained of the country's banking system. Spain was one of the worst affected countries in the European debt crisis, and its government spent tens of millions of euros on contracts with the consulting industry during the recovery. Deloitte, for example, had served as the auditor for Bankia, a large Spanish bank that collapsed during the financial crisis, but this apparently did not warrant a debarring from the Spanish government's books: the company subsequently received an estimated €1.8 million in government contracts for audit work.[71]

Across the public sector, Deloitte urged governments to 'us[e] the downturn as a catalyst' for reform.[72] Boston Consulting Group lamented that 'many concepts of strategy have been imported from business into government, but few have taken hold'.[73] McKinsey called on the Swedish government to 'improve growth in the local services sector through a second wave of deregulation and regulatory reforms'.[74] Meanwhile, Greece was encouraged to 'eliminat[e] redundant public sector entities and improv[e] public administration efficiency while the private sector builds larger, more extrovert organizations that better utilize resources, investment capital and technology'.[75] Governments throughout Europe were advised to 'improve public-sector productivity by . . . creating competitive conditions in the provision of services where possible (including through the judicious use of outsourcing)'.[76] The pattern was clear: the large consultancies viewed the 2008 financial crisis as an opportunity for public sector retrenchment and private sector growth. Their advice was anything but neutral.

The rhetoric of the political leaders who inherited the global recession nonetheless suggested that these ambitions would not be easily achieved. Politicians' profligate spending on management consultants during the 2000s was criticized by opposition parties and new governments in key national markets after the crash. In 2009, newly elected President Barack Obama slammed the Bush administration's spending on contractors, which had more than doubled since 2001. In 2011, Obama also pledged to reduce federal spending on advisory services by 15 per cent. In Australia, following his election in 2007, the Labor Party Prime Minister Kevin Rudd had similarly promised a crackdown on the government's use of external consultancies, which had skyrocketed under his predecessor, the conservative Liberal politician John Howard. In a 2008 speech, future Conservative Prime Minister David Cameron lambasted New Labour's reliance on the consulting industry, arguing that 'For the last decade or so, in the name of modernisation, rationalisation and efficiency, we have been living under a regime of government by management consultant and policy by PowerPoint.'[77] A few months later, commenting on Blair's reforms of the NHS during a speech at the Conservative Party Conference, he declared that Labour had 'taken our most treasured national institution, ripped out its soul and replaced it with targets, directives, management consultants and computers'.[78] Once in power, the Coalition government that was elected in 2010 with Cameron at the helm promised to halt spending on consultants.

Contracting for austerity

These fighting words were not matched by radical actions.

Obama did achieve his goal of cutting spending on advisory services ahead of schedule. But spending on the consulting industry continued to be eye-wateringly large in the United States throughout the 2010s, even during Obama's tenure. In 2009 – the same year that he committed to reducing spending on contractors – Obama appointed a Director of McKinsey & Company, Nancy Killefer, to a newly created position working with economic officials 'to increase efficiencies and eliminate waste in government spending'. Killefer never made it into the Treasury, after problems with her taxes forced her to resign.[79] Meanwhile, in Australia, a year after the financial crisis, newspapers were reporting that the Rudd government's spending on management consultancies, including BCG, McKinsey, KPMG and Allen Consulting Group, was on par with the previous government's peak of AUD$480 million.[80]

While spending on contracts with the established strategy, accountancy and IT consultancies in central government departments did decrease under the UK Coalition government, the true scale of their influence during this time was considerable. For one, companies reverted to the strategy they had long used to capture emerging markets in their attempts to maintain connections in government: they worked for free or at rates far below what they would normally charge. In 2011, for example, KPMG revealed that it provided 10 per cent of its public sector work free of charge and had even put in bids of £1 for some contracts that were worth millions.[81]

The extent of public sector spending on established large consultancies was also affected by broader public administrative reforms introduced by the Coalition government within its austerity programme. During this time, local government authorities and NHS bodies became simultaneously endowed with greater responsibilities while their budgets were reduced. In these parts of government, spending on management consultants increased dramatically, as spending cuts placed pressure on administrative and management capacity, forcing managers to look to short-term, private sector solutions for support.[82]

Wider austerity measures adopted within the United Kingdom and many other countries across Europe put pressure not only on management capacity, but also on welfare services. Across central and local government, managers were encouraged and often forced to outsource crucial services and critical functions to firms that promised short-term cost savings. Government spending on out-sourcing of services in areas including prisons, hospitals, job centres, schools and waste disposal soared to £88 billion by 2014 – twice what it had been when the Coalition government came to power.[83] The leading beneficiaries of these contracts were the outsourcing consul-tancies that had emerged and secured a growing share of the market for managing aggregated contracts during the Blair government. The firms that dominate this segment of the consulting industry grew out of a hodgepodge of firms working in areas including con-struction, facilities management and financial services. One company, Capita, which manages contracts for governments around the world today, began its life as a management consultancy.[84]

In the decade that followed the financial crisis, the scale and scope of contracts that the outsourcing consultancies received for delivering public services in many countries around the world was unprecedented. They became responsible for core tasks including keeping hospitals clean, delivering school meals and providing security for large public events. But they were also tasked with run-ning the darker parts of government – asylum seeker detention centres, prisons, benefits sanctions, border controls – areas subject to far more critical public debate and contestation from those affected about what the appropriate role of the state should be.

Many people in the UK – and in other countries where they have had a considerable presence – have heard of these companies today not because they are considered national treasures, like many industries of old, but because of their handling of number of very large government contracts, or because of legal issues that have arisen through them. G4S was globally reviled when it was revealed that the company had failed to train enough staff to provide security for the 2012 London Olympic Games – just a few weeks before the events were due to start – prompting the deployment of the British military.[85] The French company Atos became known for its role in administering 'fitness to work' tests on behalf of the UK government's Department for Work and Pensions, when it was revealed a number of people with disabilities had wrongly had their benefits removed.[86] New Zealand-based firm Broadspectrum (previously Transfield Services) has become, along with Serco and G4S, responsible for running the offshore detention centres in Australia that the United Nations has deemed illegal.[87]

Perhaps the company best known across the biggest outsourcing markets for its record in the 2010s is British firm Serco. Originally a division of Radio Corporation of America, delivering services for cinema chains, the company's directors pivoted corporate strategy towards the nascent public services outsourcing market in the late 1980s. Over the course of the next decade, Serco would establish itself in the public sectors of the UK, Australia and North America, holding contracts in areas as diverse as transport, prisons, healthcare, waste, school education and defence. Serco's role in governments was never without scrutiny from the media, trade unions and other interest groups, who questioned how one company could possibly have the necessary capabilities to deliver services across such a vast range of specialized areas. The company would soon make headlines. In 2013 and 2014 Serco was:

- stripped of contracts for failing to sterilize medical equipment properly, leading to delays in the number of operations that could be used at one of Australia's biggest hospitals, and then fined AUD$1 million for poor performance in areas including cleaning, IT and logistics;[88]
- condemned by human rights officials in the country for the filthy conditions of its migrant detention centre on Christmas Island and high rates of self-harm there;[89]
- investigated by the UK's Ministry of Justice for overcharging on a contract for electronically tagging former prisoners. The company subsequently agreed to repay £68.5 million. Following a separate investigation by the Serious Fraud Office, which included allegations of charging for tagging people who were either dead, in jail or had left the country, the company was fined £23 million as part of a settlement;[90] *
- pushed to terminate its contract for out-of-hours GP services in the English county of Cornwall early after failing to provide enough doctors;[91]
- and was even embroiled in the HealthCare.gov calamity after it was awarded a contract worth $1.3 billion to manage paper applications in the implementation of Obamacare.

The scrutiny was not the end for Serco. Although the company did issue profit warnings in both 2013 and 2014,[92] it nonetheless managed to remain afloat. How the company was able to weather the storm is not clear. But in 2013, an investigation by the *Guardian* found that Serco had twenty-three subsidiaries based in tax havens.[93] The

---

* Two former executives at the company who had been charged with defrauding the Ministry of Justice between 2011 and 2013 subsequently had their charges of fraud relating to the electronic tagging contract dropped (BBC, 2021).

Paradise Papers – a set of confidential documents relating to off-shore investments that was leaked a few years later – suggested the possibility that Serco had wanted to make even greater use of tax loopholes, but had encountered consternation from those that could make that possible. At least one offshore law firm was concerned about the risks of working with Serco, according to the *Guardian*. Appleby, which offers specialist advice in tax havens including Bermuda, the British Virgin Islands, the Cayman Islands and Mauritius, was uneasy about Serco's 'history of problems, failures, fatal errors and overcharging' and deemed it 'high-risk'.[94]

Despite this, Serco continued to receive new contracts from other governments around the world throughout the 2010s. In large part, this was because austerity measures would endure throughout this period, but there were also other reasons. Often the capabilities for managing the delivery of a service in-house would be completely lost after they had been outsourced, and so the costs of re-insourcing were very great. Public sector bodies had little choice but to continue using consultants.

Auditing the outsourcers

As the decade wore on, once the promises of post-crisis governments to cut spending on the established consultancies had been forgotten, they reconsolidated influence again. In the UK, spending on management consultants in the NHS trebled between 2016 and 2019.[95] Not only were these consultancies also sometimes named as the prime contractor in aggregated services contracts, creating incentives for them to recommend private sector outsourcing, but many outsourcing firms became an increasingly important group of clients for the established consultancies. This was especially true of those with an audit arm, but it also extended to the non-accounting consultancies. When Serco's shares plummeted in 2014, for example, it was reported that both McKinsey and EY had been contracted to carry out a review of the company's 700 contracts.[96] The conflicts of interest inherent in this arrangement would only come to light in the wake of another corporate fiasco, this time in the UK, whose hardest hit victims would, once again, be ordinary people.

At the time of its collapse in January 2018, Carillion was one of the largest outsourcing companies in the world, holding contracts across a range of government public services, from education to transport, energy and healthcare. It is no coincidence that it was, like many other giants in this sector, a British firm. Carillion had benefitted from the increase in scale and scope of outsourcing contracts in the UK throughout the 2000s. The company directly employed 43,000 people globally, but many more wages than that were tied to it through subcontracting. At the time of its collapse, around 90 per cent of the operations Carillion had been contracted to deliver were subcontracted to other companies. The people who worked to deliver Carillion's contracts were cleaners, caterers, builders, secretaries. They were often on precarious employment terms. Public services outsourcing has been associated with a 'deterioration in terms and conditions of employment, particularly in the United Kingdom', where collective bargaining in the private sector has been weakened.[97] When the news came that Carillion would go into liquidation, thousands of people working for the company learned that their wages would be halted immediately.[98] They included the 1,200 apprentices who were employed by Carillion, around a third of whom would still be out of work by April 2018, after losing access to the training that would provide them with qualifications.[99] Of course, those working on Carillion's front lines played no part in the company's downfall.

Critical to it instead were the huge risks built into the company's business model and the decisions of its directors.[100] For example, managers at Carillion had continuously bid on projects that were low margin, meaning that while the profits could be very large – its contract to build the Royal Liverpool University Hospital, for example, was worth £335 million – they were not significant relative to the costs of a project. They also often secured them through bidding at far below market rates. It appears that managers increasingly did this as the company struggled through its final years because it guaranteed future income that could be leveraged to cover more pressing payment obligations, including dividends to shareholders – something the *Financial Times* described as 'a lawful sort of Ponzi scheme'.[101] Crucially, its ability to borrow in this way was aided by the long-term nature of the government contracts it continued to secure around the world, becoming one of the twenty-five most significant contractors in the UK. Accounting professor Adam Leaver has described how large contracts enabled Carillion to effectively '[pull] income from the future' by booking profits based on forecasts and estimates: 'In other words, annual profit was imputed as a proportion of the imagined future profit of each contract.' Part of the estimated value of the company, an accounting line known as 'goodwill', which enabled it to access debt and would not have hurt its contracting prospects, was similarly based on these potential future profits:

> Carillion . . . borrowed money – secured against assets the value of which depended on the accurate forecasting of future cashflows and discount rates – and paid out dividends, which were affordable according to profit figures calculated as a percentage of expected total contract value. Carillion were in effect 'levered on the future'.[102]

This extremely risky financing structure left almost no room for hitches in the delivery of contracts. But crucially, the model of deriving profits from aggregated services contracts made hitches inevitable: so much rested on the success of subcontracted companies over which Carillion had little control. When problems emerged in a handful of building projects, resulting in unplanned expenses and capacity pressures, there was no buffer. The coffers were more than empty – Carillion had debts worth an astounding £2 billion and a pension deficit of over £800 million at the time of its liquidation, putting the future livelihoods of thousands of employees in jeopardy.

Former directors of Carillion have denied wrongdoing, and in 2022 are also disputing legal action by the Insolvency Service, a government agency, to ban them from running other companies in the UK.[103] In the years since Carillion's collapse, scrutiny of the companies involved has largely centred on the potential shortcomings of its external audits. The Financial Reporting Council (FRC), the UK's accountancy watchdog, launched an investigation into KPMG's audits of Carillion, and subjected it to a disciplinary tribunal, alleging that the company 'provided false or misleading information in connection with its routine quality inspections of the audits of Carillion for the financial year ending December 2016'.[104] In July 2022, the FRC announced that KPMG had been fined £14.4 million in relation to its audits of Carillion and another company, Regenersis. Four auditors were also fined and excluded from membership of the Institute of Chartered Accountants in England and Wales for between seven and ten years.[105]

KPMG has been accused of 'failures' in its duty as Carillion's auditor.[106] In February 2022, the Insolvency Service, acting as liquidators of Carillion, sued KPMG for £1.3 billion, contending that the auditor 'missed "red flags" that the UK outsourcer's accounts were misstated and that the group was insolvent more than two years before it collapsed'. The Partner responsible for the audit was alleged to have 'failed to respect the proper boundaries of the auditor-client relationship'.[107] In a statement to the *Financial Times*, KPMG has said, 'We believe this claim is without merit and we will robustly defend the case. Responsibility for the failure of Carillion lies solely with the company's board and management, who set the strategy and ran the business.'[108]

Analysis following the collapse of Carillion has found that each of the Big Four had also received contracts from Carillion for both consulting and financial services. PwC had provided advice on the company's pension system since 2012, which ended up recklessly indebted. Deloitte had conducted the company's internal audit. E Y had been awarded £10.8 million to 'provide advice to the Board about options for rescuing the firm' dating back to July 2017. In addition to its audit work for Carillion, KPMG had provided advisory services including reviews of PFI finance models and reporting on debt-to-equity swaps. All four companies had also been awarded contracts worth millions of pounds by the British government for services relating to its contracts with Carillion. In every facet of outsourcing – from government demand to market supply and the contractor audit – the Big Four were there.

The case has prompted widespread calls for the Big Four to separate audit practices from their other operations to reduce the risk of conflicts of interest. The FRC has set a deadline of June 2024 to decide whether the UK should adopt legislation like the Sarbanes-Oxley Act, introduced in the wake of Enron's demise.[109] In May 2022, it was reported that E Y was considering spinning off its audit business into a separate company following the downfall of Carillion, with its global chair and chief executive claiming that the move would also increase consulting fees by up to $10 billion from US tech companies that it is currently unable to provide consulting services to while acting as auditor.[110] At the time, EY was also under investigation by the FRC into its own audits of the failed travel firm Thomas Cook, and of two further companies that collapsed amid claims of fraud. In 2021, it had been fined £2.2 million for failing to properly scrutinize the claims of bosses at the transport company Stagecoach during an audit in 2017.[111] In an interview with the *Financial Times* in July 2022, PwC's global chairman stated that it would not follow suit, and that continuing to offer both auditing and advisory services would offer PwC a 'competitive advantage'.[112] Total fines for accounting firms in the UK reached a record £46.5 million in 2021.[113]

The introduction of laws mandating companies to separate auditing and consulting practices in the UK would reduce the potential for conflicting interests in these areas. But the case of Carillion is indicative of deeper conflicts in the consulting industry. The firms also bid on management outsourcing and public service prime contracts themselves. In the years since the collapse of Carillion, KPMG has been subject to investigation for issues with its audits of other large companies – including the car manufacturer Rolls-Royce and the logistics firm Eddie Stobart. Amid growing public scrutiny, in December 2021, the consultancy pledged to temporarily stop bidding for public sector contracts, pending the results of a review by the government's Cabinet Office. However, just four months later, the *Financial Times* revealed that the company had continued to win government contracts worth £10 million in total with various government departments and 'vital work with NHS England', the precise details of which remain unknown at the time of writing.[114]

The conflicts of interest that arise from consultancies' role not only as advisors and auditors of government contractors but as

outsourcers of government functions have received far less attention, but suggest they have an interest in the continued outsourcing
of public services at scale and scope. The growth of accounting consultancies also depends at least in part on the continuation of this
form of governance.

To understand why the consulting industry has become so vast
requires understanding the client–consultant relationship and
consulting practices in more depth. How do contracting organizations understand the value of consultancies? As we will see in the
next chapter, it turns out that the growth of the consulting industry
over the past century may have little to do with improving other
organizations.

5. The Big Confidence Trick: Consultology and Economic Rents

In his first fifteen years working for large manufacturing companies in Britain, David rarely encountered management consultants.[1] He had joined the telecoms sector in the 1990s, after deciding that his passion for vinyl could be pursued as a hobby, rather than from behind the till of the record store where he had been working. In the beginning, David told us, when the senior managers identified inconsistecies in production processes in different parts of the company, or wanted to improve how something was done, technical employees from the factory shopfloor through to the engineering offices would be brought together, and their insights harnessed for improvements that were grounded in experience. In these situations, short-term cost savings were usually viewed as secondary to more effective ways of achieving the company's goals in the long run – and ultimately better technologies. Toyota's rapid growth and the Japanese approaches to employee involvement that had been a part of the company's success had become influential within many Western manufacturing firms. According to David, these approaches not only drove significant improvement but also gave every employee the opportunity to make their mark on the business. It was an inclusive means of improving performance.

But over time, as he gradually moved up the ranks of management, David sensed something was changing. The small improvements regularly made by people on the shopfloor were no longer enough for leaders with an eye to the share price looking to make the biggest improvement possible in the shortest time.

Although CEOs still enthused about employee-derived improve-ment and internal capabilities, it was clear that driving growth through acquisition and pushing for profit by slashing costs were the new gods. Now, executive directors – or, more often, the senior managers to whom they delegated responsibility for strategic objectives – would contract teams of management consultants to conduct analyses of the organization and come up with the improvements.

David's experience reflects broader trends in the 2000s, where it was reported that increasing numbers of corporate managers were encountering consultants.[2] According to him, 'Sometimes this was done so that the senior management had someone else to blame if targets weren't hit.' But often, the decision to contract a consultancy was driven by the belief that the management consultants' methods for understanding the organization were superior to anything that existed internally. It was hoped that the proposals they developed through their analyses would lead to process innovations that ultim-ately produced improvements in the technologies that gave the firm 'competitive advantage' – the watchword of Michael Porter, a busi-ness professor and corporate management guru, who developed the term in the 1980s.

This aspiration, however, was only ever achieved occasionally. As often as not, the consultants' proposals could not be provably shown to 'add value' – and sometimes would not be implemented at all. From time to time, the proposals of the management consult-ants were identified as being completely flawed before they were implemented. In one instance, when David was working for an air-craft manufacturing firm, a senior manager wanted to conduct a review of the manufacturing processes in place within the compa-ny's factories across Europe. Rather than bring together the local factory managers to share insights and experiences, the senior manager put out a tender for a management consultancy to conduct an organizational review. The Big Four company that won the contract was successful because its bid also promised that the analysis the consultants produced would be able to identify immediate operational cost saving opportunities. Under pressure from the company's shareholders and his own line manager to increase margins, the senior manager found this offer irresistible.

After a number of weeks, the team of management consultants presented their analysis and proposals to the aircraft manufacturer's most senior leaders. Reviewing internal data and organizational charts, the consultants proposed an entirely new organizational structure for the company's factories, based on analysis they had conducted of data about one of the factories in Germany. At no point in their investigation, it appeared, had the management consultants actually consulted with those working in the German factory. If they had, it would have become obvious that the organizational chart that they had access to was not only outdated, but missing entire layers of employees. Unfortunately, these shortcomings in the consultants' methods and practical knowledge were not immediately clear to the leadership team at David's company, which moved to implement the new organizational structure. It was only when the reform was challenged by relatively junior members of staff who were able to cite their own experiences that the proposal was eventually scrapped. Its introduction would almost certainly have led to huge losses and many pointless redundancies.

Why bring in the consultants?

The dominant theory of why consultancies exist in capitalist economies has historically been that they serve a 'functional' purpose, enabling other organizations to increase profits or achieve other objectives.[3] According to this view, consultants are experts whose role is to transfer knowledge between organizations, use particular management frameworks to help clients to achieve their objectives, or provide additional skilled capacity. In other words, they are 'experts, extras and facilitators'[4] who create value by leveraging expertise and brokering technical or managerial knowledge.[5] In economic terms the corollary would be that consultancies exist because they create 'economies of scale' in types of managerial, sectoral or technical knowledge, which others have called 'economies of knowledge'. The consulting industry – the 'supply' – is a response to a 'demand' from other organizations in the economy, which choose to contract consultants in order to improve processes and increase efficiency, thereby reducing their own 'transaction costs'.[6] This theory suggests that the scale and scope of the consulting industry today is a consequence of the real value that it creates across the economy. In other words, the extraordinary growth of consulting contracts since the 1980s is a natural response to the benefits that consultancies have provided for their clients across the public, private and third sectors. The additional value they help to create is equal to the value they extract.

David's case attests that consultancies do not always meet their client's objectives, and they do not necessarily possess knowledge that they are able to put to productive uses. The example is straightforward: the consultants were evidently not experts in the area they were contracted to work in, and they did not offer managerial techniques that enabled the client to come up with its own solutions. They did not 'reduce transaction costs' and they did not create value, either in strictly financial terms or otherwise.

The question of to what extent value has been created for an organization is rarely so clear cut, and other factors play into a client's perception of the consultancy's contribution. Many in business, academia and journalism have long argued that 'the real value of consulting is very difficult to ascertain and, hence, consulting is concerned mainly with creating an impression of value'.[7] Challenging the functional theory of consulting, these views contend that consultants are instead 'impression managers', who 'deliver images, impressions and rhetorical acts'[8] through 'analyses, presentations and theories'[9] to convince potential and existing clients of their legitimacy and ability to create value. Consequently, the productive contribution of consultancies to the economy and society is far more modest than the market value of the consulting industry would suggest.

These critiques imply that the scale and scope of the consulting industry today reflects the success of the rhetorical tactics that its consultants employ, which instil confidence in clients – much like the confidence men of the Gilded Age of capitalism. As well as giving rise to the first 'engineering consultants', America's Gilded Age was also marked by vast inequalities, because although technological innovations made production processes more efficient, the wages of workers remained, for the most part, very low. By 1897, 'the richest 4,000 families in the US (representing less than 1% of the population) had about as much wealth as the other 11.6 million families all together'.[10] For the financiers and owners of factories, it was possible to accumulate riches on a scale never witnessed before in history. Where previously the highest pillars of wealth were reserved only for the aristocracy and others who had inherited land and vast sums, business and finance were increasingly populated by self-made individuals. The nouveaux riches, as they became known in North America and Europe in the nineteenth and twentieth centuries, were ostentatious in their tastes, and unafraid to flaunt their status through luxurious clothing and flashy accessories – what the sociologist Thorstein Veblen called 'conspicuous consumption'.

With this new class of elites came also new forms of criminality that targeted their wealth and its excesses. The techniques of tricksters targeting the nouveaux riches exploited the feelings of trust that existed between the wealthy. This was also the golden age of scamming, the period that gave us such cunning figures as David Lamar – the original 'Wolf of Wall Street' – who swindled well-heeled denizens of New York out of millions of dollars. His victims included the son of business magnate John Rockefeller Senior, who had made his money investing in the oil wells of Pennsylvania, and subsequently became the country's first ever billionaire. Using his connections in the world of the wealthy, David Lamar cultivated a relationship with Rockefeller's secretary, George Rogers, feigning to have information that promised a windfall on the stock market: a well-known trader had taken a huge position in US leather stock. Keen to curry favour with the Rockefeller family, Rogers shared this detail with John Rockefeller Junior – precisely what Lamar had hoped for – who subsequently bought $1 million of the stock himself. (Today, that would be worth $17 million.) In fact, the well-known trader had never invested in the stock, but Lamar was able to liquidate the shares he owned as quickly as the Rockefeller son bid it up, causing him to lose it all.

A less notorious but similarly rapacious character who became the subject of much media intrigue at this time was Victor Lustig, an Austro-Hungarian who became known for his 'Romanian Box' scam. This trick preyed on the widespread fascination with and paradoxical ignorance about the era's new technologies among the elite class. Lustig would present victims with a mahogany box that he claimed was in fact a machine that could create exact copies of any banknote the user wished to duplicate. The box had two slots – one where users could insert their bills, and another where the duplicated copies would appear. The process, his victims were informed, took six hours. Along with various levers and pulleys designed to make it appear machine-like, the box also had a secret compartment that Lustig had stuffed with actual banknotes of all denominations. To test the veracity of the contraption, Lustig would ask his victims to insert any banknote into the box along with a blank piece of paper. When, after six hours, the box churned out an apparently duplicated banknote, much to the astonishment of his victims, Lustig would accompany them to a bank, where it would invariably be authenticated. The new note was of course simply just one of the many notes that Lustig had hidden within the box, but by the time his victims realized this, many, many hours later, after purchasing the box from him for thousands of dollars, Lustig was long gone.

Both Lamar and Lustig were masters of aplomb, but it was an earlier figure of the Victorian era that gave rise to the term 'confidence trick' — eventually shortened to 'con'. William Thompson also operated in New York, with his last-known scam before his arrest in 1849 taking place on William Street, which cuts through Wall Street. Donning the attire of that period's elite, Thompson targeted the newly wealthy in the area, approaching them congenially, as if they were old friends. After making small talk and polite conversation, he would ask to borrow the stranger's watch until the next day, saying something along the lines of: 'Have you the confidence in me to trust me with your watch until tomorrow?'[11] The victim, no doubt a little bemused, but nonetheless believing they were acquaintances, would then hand over his watch. And of course, Thompson would never hand it back. The popular media in New York came to refer to Thompson as the 'confidence man', because his scam was premised on persuading targets that they were kin.

These tricksters used offers of proprietary information, awe-inspiring technology and linguistic prowess to instil confidence in their promises – similar to the ways critics of the functional view of consulting describe the methods of consultants.

Extracting rents

The consulting industry's growth is not a measure of the value of its knowledge assets and their uses, but nor is it purely the result of rhetorical tricks by consultants, as some critical perspectives suggest. For one, this view of consultants doesn't explain why clients work with them in the first place. Public sector managers and business executives are not idiots. The idea that consultants secure contracts primarily by duping these employees would nonetheless imply as much. Some critical accounts 'have exaggerated a sense of power asymmetry between client and consultant that has almost had the effect of blotting out the client as an independent agent'.[12] Any depiction of clients as monolithically 'passive victims of rhetorical strategies' is ahistorical, and ignores the mounting evidence from academia[13] – and indeed anecdotal experiences of many in business and government – of individual employees' scepticism towards the consulting industry.

They also often don't consider how governance reforms across business and government constrain the choices and behaviour of their employees. Both government and business organizations often face resource constraints which mean that the contracting manager has little choice but to recruit a consultancy as a source of (short-term) capacity – whether as 'expert, extra or facilitator'. The pressure on existing employees can also affect the client organization's ability to assess appropriately the value promises of a consultancy. More generally, the tumultuousness of the economy and the precariousness of even managers' employment in many workplaces has increased 'managerial anxieties', which the *Economist* journalists

John Micklethwait and Adrian Wooldridge once described companies selling management 'fads' as thriving on: 'To these anxiety-ridden men and women, management books offer a rare source of security.'[14] In a world where managers are under more pressure than ever to deliver greater profit margins (in the case of the private sector) or efficiency (in government), the lure of a well-written bid delivered by a team of high-flying consultants who have previously worked for a partner organization can be very tempting. The long shadow of narratives depicting the public sector as incompetent and sluggish and the private sector as innovative and supreme – epitomized in Ronald Reagan's famous claim that 'outside of its legitimate function, government does nothing as well or economically as the private sector' – must also be seen as contributing to managerial anxiety in government contracting.[15]

And perhaps most importantly, the critical perspective overlooks the structural power of the industry and how this influences the perceptions of potential clients. The difference between the value they create and the wealth they take can be understood as 'economic rents'.[16] These rents do not necessarily stem from the ownership of scarce valuable knowledge assets, but from the possession of the means to create an impression of value. The scale and scope of the consulting industry today endows it with immense resources and networks that help to instil confidence in the value of a consultancy and the consulting profession. It is this ability to create impressions of value that enable consultancies to secure lucrative contracts. In this way, the Big Con does not just describe discursive tricks, but also how the practices of the consulting industry – what we call 'consultology' – combine with the broader structures of our political economy to extract rents from clients – often by enabling those clients to extract rents themselves. Ultimately, this entrenches businesses' and governments' reliance on consultancies.

The best and brightest

Writing in 2005, Christopher D. McKenna described how, by the end of the twentieth century, top graduates viewed a career as a consultant as the most sought-after job. 'Just how had it come to pass that nearly one-third of the top MBA graduates and one-sixth of all elite undergraduates (whether at Oxford or Yale) now began their working lives as management consultants?' he ponders. 'What explained the remarkable dominance of the world's newest profession?'[17] During the 1960s, McKinsey was famed for its recruitment of Harvard 'Baker Scholars' (those graduating in the top 5 per cent of its MBA programme).[18]

There is some data suggesting that the elite selectivity of new recruits may be changing. According to one survey from the UK's Management Consultancies Association (MCA), the proportion of consultants who had attended a Russell Group university – high-ranking, long-established and research-intensive institutions – declined between 2011 and 2019 from 73 to 44 per cent. The proportion who were graduates of the country's top universities – Oxford and Cambridge – also dropped in this period, from 13 to 3 per cent. The MCA has suggested that this is a 'reflection of the number of initiatives MCA member firms are undertaking to increase social mobility'.[19]

There may be other reasons for these statistics. One former consultant, who had worked at both a Big 4 and large IT consultancy, suggested that clients were often more interested in hearing that a consultant had experience in tackling similar problems than what their alma mater was. The industry's growth is also increasing demand for new recruits, as other booming sectors including financial services and Big Tech compete for similar applicants. The

Financial Times reported in August 2022 that, in the United States, these conditions had pushed McKinsey, Bain & Co and BCG to 'increase annual base salaries for MBA graduates in the US from $175,000 to between $190,000 and $192,000'.

As the largest firms and the industry as a whole expands, perhaps it is simply no longer possible to recruit only from top universities. And as firms move into new client markets, a more diverse pool of recruits also increases the likelihood of finding consultants that meet the client's expectations on paper. Indeed the MCA has increasingly counted outsourcing companies among its members; these companies derive most of their income from contracts with government services, and do not rely on contracts with finance and business. Indeed, the differences between the types of organizations that the Big Four and Big Three consultancies on the one hand, and outsourcing consultancies on the other hand, predominately contract with might reveal deeper reasons why the former has historically pursued a strategy of recruiting from globally top universities. It is undeniable that many of those employed by management consultancies have been very academically successful. But intellect alone does not lead to contracts; beyond the behaviour of consultants, credentials from a top university can instil confidence in a consulting team. The final decision about which consultancy to award a contract to often rests, at the final stages, on how the consulting team presents itself. It certainly doesn't harm a bid to include in the application roster that one of the team has a degree in PPE (Politics, Philosophy and Economics) from Oxford in addition to their seven years with the firm, another has a UC Berkeley PhD, and, for good measure, that the two most junior members are data-savvy engineering graduates with MBAs keen to build up their portfolios in the real world of business. The desire to project competence in the form of qualifications was at the heart of the consulting industry's highly selective recruitment practices throughout the twentieth century, and was viewed as helping to create an impression of legitimacy around the profession.[20]

Although it may not be an explicit objective of consultancies' recruitment strategies, employing graduates from top universities may also aid the growth of business relationships in another way. As has been documented extensively ever since the 1956 publication of C. Wright Mills's sociology classic *The Power Elite*, those in powerful positions tend to have acquaintances in powerful positions. Graduates from top universities are more likely to have networks in the places that pay for consultants. They studied with people, whether at university or even before that – for example, at private school – who are more likely to be in high-ranking jobs in society. A 2019 report by the Sutton Trust and the Social Mobility Commission in the UK found that two fifths of people working in the most powerful positions across politics, business and the media had attended private school for their childhood education – which, in the UK, is often a gateway to a top university.[21] Just 7 per cent of the wider population is privately educated. Over a quarter of FTSE 350 chairs were educated at either Oxford or Cambridge, as were 12 per cent of tech firm CEOs, 56 per cent of permanent secretaries in the civil service (the highest-ranking non-elected bureaucrat) and 40 per cent of public body chairs. In the general population, fewer than 1 in 100 people attend these universities. In other words: people educated at top universities work for the organizations that become the clients of the consulting industry. When a consultancy's employee is able to reach out to their former classmate for a word about a contract that is out for tender, or just recognizes the name on a bid from their social circles, it can make the process of securing it a whole lot smoother.

Others have made similar arguments about the 'up-or-out'

structures of career progression that exist in many consulting firms, in which 'either people clearly improve and get promoted or are expected to leave the firm'.[22] The management scholars Andrew Sturdy and Christopher Wright have described how this creates a 'consulting diaspora':

> The 'up or out' promotion policies of large consulting firms have assisted a process of personnel diffusion in which former consultants are seeded into client organizations. This has created powerful 'alumni' networks, which provide a ready source of future business for consulting firms . . . [and] the potential of ex-consultants to act as promoters of management knowledge and organizational change in their own right.[23]

One former consultant described this promotion structure as 'survival of the fittest', because many young consultants do have ambitions to reach higher positions in the consulting hierarchy or have positive references when they leave. As well as being effective tools for disciplining people keen to have a long career – young consultants will work long hours in order to be viewed positively – up-or-out structures ensure there are always contacts to reach out to across organizations in business, the public sector and beyond. In some consultancies, the up-or-out model means there is a wildly disproportionate ratio of junior consultants to Partners or senior executives. But that is part of the design. Few who have previously worked as a management consultant will have difficulty finding work once they leave, especially if they have been employed by a well-known consultancy. In 2013, more than seventy past and present CEOs of Fortune 500 companies were former McKinsey employees.[24] The hundreds of former management consultants now working across the most powerful companies and public sector bodies become the contacts who survivors within the consultancies reach out to when a contract is up for renewal. Indeed, a number of large consultancies have come to recognize the potential value of their former employees and have established 'alumni networks' to ensure the chains that bound them as colleagues never break – much like many universities do. McKinsey's Alumni Center, for example, is described as 'help[ing] our global network of alumni remain engaged with one another, and with the firm'. It regularly hosts events for its former employees. In 2021, these included a discussion with Hubert Joly, a former McKinsey Partner who went on to become CEO of Best Buy, on his new business book; a Q&A with four alumni who were also former Olympians; and an event about the 'nineteen alum-founded unicorns' – start-ups valued at over \$1 billion that 'may have already changed your life'. Recruiters are encouraged to post job adverts for alumni, who can also be head-hunted via the company's 'Find an alum or firm member' widget.[25]

Talent drain

Popular media depictions of the consulting industry, such as in television shows like *House of Lies*, tend to depict consultants as ruthless, cocky and borderline sociopathic individuals. As the audience, we are supposed to believe that there is something fundamentally different about these people that makes them calculating and manipulative not just in their day job, but also in their personal relationships. But while this might make for gripping entertainment, the great majority of people who join the consulting industry are, of course, not borderline sociopaths who thrive on others' distress. No individual becomes a consultant because they want to wilfully dupe clients into handing over cash to their employer.

There are many good reasons why individuals turn to a career in consulting that are important to reflect on. For one, although graduate salaries in the consulting industry are rarely as high as in some other private sector industries, such as financial services or law, they are usually above median incomes and can cover housing rent comfortably. At more senior positions, pay becomes multiples of the median income, with some Partners in countries such as the UK earning hundreds of thousands of pounds a year.

Secondly, as was also true of graduate consultants of the 1960s and 2000s,[26] consulting promises an interesting diversity of (white collar) experiences – something that is particularly attractive for graduates of non-specialist academic university degrees who have no clue what they really want to do. Many hope that the variety of work environments encountered during a graduate training pro-gramme at a management consultancy will not only be intellectually stimulating, but will also help them to discover their true interest and develop general management skills. In no other industry is it possible to work on a research project in an NGO for six weeks, then a merger deal in a bank for three months, followed by an IT project in local government for another two months.

Relatedly, they also promise candidates something that young people increasingly seek from work: meaning. According to one survey by PwC, 'Millennials want their work to have a purpose, to contribute something to the world and they want to be proud of their employer.'[27] The recruitment pages of large consultancies are lit-tered with promises of meaningful work. Apparently heeding its own advice, for example, PwC's graduate jobs portal highlights 'purpose and values' at the top of the page for potential applicants: 'Our values define how we do things, what we should stand for, now and into the future,' reads the website. 'And our purpose is why we exist – to build trust in society and solve important problems.'[28]

There are some indications that many who have joined consultancies may now be leaving precisely because 'they feel they add little value to the world and lack a sense of personal growth, community and purpose', as one recent article in the *Financial Times* put it.[29] One young consultant interviewed for the article, Laurie, who had graduated with a first-class degree from a top university and joined a midsized consulting firm in 2017, was described as being initially 'excited about enacting real change, but three years later feels unfulfilled and wants to switch career'. Amid wider mass resignations during the global COVID-19 pandemic, management consulting was found in a study published in *MIT Sloan Management Review* to have the second highest attrition rate of any sector, with '[company] failure to promote diversity, equity, and inclusion; workers feeling disrespected; and unethical behavior' found to be the strongest predictor of industry-adjusted attrition.[30] The study included employees who left their employer for any reason, including quitting, retiring or being laid off.

A final important reason why so many set their sights on a career in management consulting – and why graduate schemes continue to be astonishingly competitive to get into – is that, in addition to general management skills, many consultancies promise to inculcate specialist knowledge and provide opportunities for building expertise about a particular function or sector. Graduates in these roles are people who want to continue learning. Indeed, the big consultancies all recognize this. BCG pitches its graduate programme to those who 'Never Stop Learning: You've always been the one who seeks the extra challenge, the extra credit, and the extraordinary opportunities.'[31] McKinsey tells its US MBA applicants: 'We invest heavily in support and training – more than $100 million per year – for all of our firm members. Programs run the gamut from our proprietary e-learning to office- or practice-based sessions to our formal global training curriculum.'[32] KPMG promises to be 'a place where the curious come together . . . Wherever you join us, you'll find yourself in an intellectually stimulating environment.'[33]

Graduate training programmes can provide general skills that may be useful in white collar work environments. Former consultants have reflected that the courses they had in 'storytelling' with PowerPoint and data analysis in Excel have been valuable in subsequent roles in other sectors. They learned how to manage projects using planning tools and to maintain relationships with 'stakeholders'. But proficiency in these skills is not the same as developing the expertise that many hope for. One former consultant said that:

> The thing – *the* thing – that you hear all graduates on these programmes say is: 'I'm not developing enough technical knowledge'. I cannot emphasise that strongly enough. A lot of people join because they want to build – this is literally the phrase – 'technical knowledge'. But it is so secondary. It is basically nonexistent for the first couple of years that you work there, and it's actually quite disillusioning.[34]

In many ways, the kind of training consulting graduate schemes offer is a crash course in the general skills of a white collar career: 'ultimately it is only "management knowledge" in the broadest sense that consultants possess and transfer, the same basic knowledge that clients have'.[35] One person whose work with the UK public sector has involved lots of engagement with large multinational consultancies described, for example, how although some consultants he has worked with have relatively strong project management skills, 'the good ones felt like they were people who had some level of common sense from just working on projects before'.

But he noted how this project management competence was rarely on par with that of in-house employees: 'Even the best one I've worked with, I can one hundred per cent say I have worked with civil servants who could manage a project that well.' These skills can nonetheless be important in convincing a client of a consulting team's value-creating capabilities.

Beyond helping to create an impression that a team of consultants know what they are doing, the skills of consultology also serve another purpose. At least until a consultant finds the space to reflect and question the role of their industry – which seems more common among former consultants than is usually assumed – the various courses, workshops, seminars and lectures that consultants gain access to help to inculcate a sense that what they have to offer is truly valuable, despite their lack of context-specific knowledge or expertise. After all, why go through so much training, if not because what they were learning was useful for organizations? There is evidence that consultants do believe their skills are needed. The International Council of Management Consulting Institutes, a global professional body, once conducted a survey that found 75 per cent of consultants 'agreed that public servants do not have the required expertise that consultants have' and '71 per cent believed that consultants provide a better quality of service'.[36] Graduate consulting programmes instil confidence in the practices of consultology, and in the value of the consulting industry to society.[37]

Case-savvy and PowerPoint-ready

The consulting industry's own 'knowledge management' systems are a good place to examine how these companies claim to create value. In the consulting industry, companies have sophisticated systems for collating and distributing information about previous contracts. Work with a previous client is usually recorded internally and stored digitally so that other consultants are able to access them.[38] These records are often referred to as 'cases', a concept that is used widely across business, as well as in management academia.

In large consultancies such as the Big Four, the internal data depositories of 'project histories' are very large and are usually held on special client management software. Consultants have access to these systems, and, in this way, they can be a valuable source of knowledge for a particular client. They might, for example, include a copy of the tender and the consultancy's bid application, as well as information about how the consulting team approached the client's needs and what the impact was. But the information they provide may also be shallow; there is only so much that will be written up at the end of a contract. The breadth of cases that a consultant might be able to read about or role play on training courses should not be confused with the kind of in-depth insight and 'tacit' knowledge that employees working within a company, field or sector are able to build up over a long career. Project histories and other superficial sources of learning do not, in other words, necessarily constitute economies of scale in knowledge – though they are implied to be such by consultancies and proponents of the functional view of consultants. The idea prevails that a team of consultants a few years out of graduate school can offer supremely intelligent advice in part because they are able to tap into the written-up experiences of their colleagues.

These systems do nonetheless serve other ends beyond storing knowledge for the purpose of winning contracts and new clients. In contract bids and sales meetings, having information about work with previous clients can be very useful. Although it can be difficult for the wider public to find out who a consultancy's clients

We have supported the development of new governance strategies with clients across sectors		
Biotech after IPO	**Ministry of Health**	**Fareshire County Council**
Approach: • Supported a biotech firm to review their governance model following an unsuccessful IPO • Assessed the 'as-is' through internal focus groups • Evaluated best practice in biotech governance through research	**Approach:** • Conducted a review of the framework assessing the governance of hospitals • Mapped stakeholders and partners of hospitals across five regions • Conducted interviews internally	**Approach:** • Supported council officers in restructuring of departments following budgetary changes • Developed and implemented new organisational structure
Impact: • Developed new governance model • Proposed changes to core business	**Impact:** • New framework adopted • Performance of 12 hospitals reviewed	**Impact:** • Council operating under new organisational structure

Figure 4

Example of how project histories are used in marketing material

are, in tender applications and marketing material consultants will share favourable examples of how they have helped other organizations in the same sector or facing similar challenges. An individual consultant may know very little about their company's relationship with an organization or its sector in the beginning, but can access cases to pique the interest of a potential client. An example of how this information is recycled when consultancies bid for new contracts is included in Figure 4 below. It is based on a real-life example.

But this archive of cases may undermine a consultant's ability to provide tailored solutions for a client – the productive part of consulting. Consultants are often themselves very stretched for time, particularly if their consultancy has underbid for a contract, purporting to require fewer hours to deliver the contract than are in fact necessary. Copy-and-pasting anecdotes from a handful of cases is much quicker than conducting research via other channels. One former Big Four senior management consultant expressed this challenge well:

> Theoretically, the value of large consultancies is that you are able to accumulate knowledge, develop sectoral expertise and create a cross-company view of what works best. Consultants can then go into a company and develop tailored, specific approaches to client problems. But in reality, only a generalized knowledge base is used and these are applied to most companies. For example, in reality, when we put together proposal decks, or we put together the final report, I would say that 50 per cent of the slides we used were already used on other clients, which showed a strong sense of superficiality.[39]

Of course, other organizations in business and government also recycle material. And in instances where consultancies are contracted to provide general insights about other companies, it could make sense for whoever is creating the slide deck to copy and paste information that is useful to the client, if it has already been written elsewhere. But consultancies are not contracted merely as knowledge depositories. They are often brought in to advise and deliver tasks that require them to *use* particular skills and knowledge. Recycling slides using the superficial case-based insights that were likely put together by another consultant is at odds with the promise of expertise.

The case-based approach of consulting knowledge can

contribute to the superficiality of insights in other ways. In fact, this is true right at the recruitment stage of a consultant's career. The 'case interview' has come to be considered the recruitment tool par excellence of the consulting industry in recent years, with many books now available purporting to offer aspiring consultants ready-made responses and 'case interview secrets'. Business schools and the consulting student societies of universities produce their own 'case-books' full of examples so that students can prepare ahead of interviewing for a graduate job at a consultancy. During a case interview, the interviewee is told about a real or fictional problem that a real or fictional client has encountered, and then asked what they propose as a solution. They must then 'solve' the case by verbally formulating a plan. Success in such exercises can be summed up as the ability to use superficial knowledge. And crucially, interviewers for such positions are not just looking for cognitive dexterity in a candidate's responses. They are often most keen to see self-assurance and conviction in the solutions that the candidate proposes. As one popular case interview handbook written by a former McKinsey consultant and interviewer puts it:

> Clients often interpret nervousness as a lack of conviction about a particular recommendation, which is why answering a case perfectly but nervously will get you rejected. For example, if a consultant were to recommend nervously that the client lay off 2,500 employees, the client would second-guess the recommendation. Even if the recommendation were 100 per cent correct, the client would sense some degree of hesitation, uncertainty, or reservation from the consultant based on *how* the message was delivered, not the content of the message itself. As a result, consulting firm interviewers assess the level of confidence you project while solving a problem analytically.[40]

In other words, even if laying off 2,500 employees has the potential to harm the client company, the ideal consulting candidate will behave as if that proposal is the strongest. Of course, an element of bluff can be found in the recruitment rooms of many graduate schemes – few people leave university with true professional expertise. But the case interview approach actively encourages it. In few other sectors is such performed confidence in giving advice on something you have just learned about – and disregard of the potentially disastrous consequences – valued so much in the job application process. The case interview weeds out those who would be unable, or perhaps unwilling, to try to convince a client that they know what they are talking about even if they don't really. The hope is that the client won't be able to see through it, and will believe the consultant understands the challenge well.

Particularly at senior levels of the consulting industry, individuals are recruited into a consultancy or promoted because they have what is perceived as 'sectoral knowledge'. They may, for example, have had a long career within a niche field of industry, or, during their career as a consultant, they may have spent substantial time working on projects within that field. These people are usually referred to as specialists. While years of experience and commendations from other sectoral leaders can be a useful, if fallible, measure of 'sectoral knowledge', it is in practice almost impossible to define or measure, as it is 'constantly negotiated and constructed by a number of actors, including clients, consultants, business journalists, and academics'.[41] This means that even when a consultant possesses this subjective expertise that may create value for a business, they still need to rely heavily on other methods to convince a client that they will add value. This is not least because the client is similarly in possession of general sectoral knowledge.

The wider structures of the industry also serve to instil

confidence among clients of the value of contracting consultants. Their investments in what are nominally research institutions can play an important role in this.

Quasi-academia and fast fashions

Alumni networks are not the only idea the consulting industry has borrowed from academia. In their struggle to gain popular legitimacy in the twentieth century, several management consultancies established what looked on the outside to be academic institutions. By the late 1990s, companies including IBM had 'dignified their in-house training programs with the title of "university"'.[42] Deloitte University was launched in 2011, and its main facility is based within an impressive campus-like area thirty miles northwest of Dallas. Its website describes the facility as 'part learning center, part ranch-style retreat', offering 'multiple venues for learning, eating, networking, and well-being'. Other Deloitte University sites can be found in Brussels, Hyderabad, Mexico City, Singapore and Toronto. 'Learners' take part in interactive role-playing sessions, and outside the classroom they are surrounded by new technologies including a 'holographic concierge', a 'kinetic touch plane' and 'Pepper the humanoid robot'.[43] Capgemini University has a 'campus' set in the heart of a 130-acre wooded park in Gouvieux, an hour north of Paris, where employees can take part in seminars on 'hot topics'.[44]

Other academic-sounding institutions established in the twentieth century included several publications, such as *McKinsey Quarterly*. Founded in 1964, this non-peer-reviewed publication had a title conspicuously like that of a peer-reviewed academic journal. In 2007, Deloitte followed suit with the launch of *Deloitte Review*, now *Deloitte Insights*. Many companies also set up research centres, led by individuals who had had a successful career in academia, and staffed by others with PhDs in economics and other impressive academic credentials. The best-known of these is the McKinsey Global Institute (MGI), established in 1990, which is described on McKinsey's website as 'the business and economics research arm of McKinsey' and a 'private think tank'.[45] To date, MGI has published reports covering dozens of countries and industries. Most of its Partners have PhDs from prestigious universities, and its promotional material highlights the role of its external 'academic advisers' who include Nobel laureates. Deloitte has similarly established several research 'centres', which produce reports and insights across diverse areas of the economy. They include the Deloitte Center for Health Solutions, the Deloitte Center for Government Insights, and the Center for the Edge, which purportedly 'develops original research and substantive perspective on new corporate growth' and 'helps senior executives make sense of and profit from emerging opportunities on the edge of business and technology'.[46]

Several consultancies have also provided funding to academics, journalists and NGOs via research arms. In 1998, PwC established the Endowment for the Business of Government to issue grants – before it was acquired by IBM in 2002 and renamed the IBM Center for the Business of Government. The Center today not only provides research stipends, but also commissions reports, publishes books and hosts a podcast featuring interviews with government executives. Previous guests have included various directors of defence agencies and even Dr Anthony Fauci, Chief Medical Advisor to the US President. Curiously, the Center's website does not share IBM's branding or even feature its logo. Beyond its name, there is in fact nothing on the website to explicitly link the IBM Center for the Business of Government to the consultancy that owns it.

Beyond in-house publications, many individuals working for management consultancies have published books that have gone on to be bestsellers in popular business and management categories. Historically, many of these books described a framework that had been developed in-house by a consultancy for a non-technical audience. McKinsey consultants alone published over fifty books between 1980 and 1996.[47] One book, *In Search of Excellence: Lessons from America's Best-Run Companies* by McKinsey consultants Tom Peters and Robert H. Waterman Jr., went on to sell more than five million copies. The book has been described as one of the 'most influential sources' of ideas in the development of New Public Management,[48] outlining an approach its authors had come up with called the 7-S Framework (they describe themselves as 'co-inventors' of it). It purported to offer business and public sector organizations an evidence-based model for understanding factors that influence an organization's ability to change – the seven 'S's of 'shared values', 'style', 'skills', 'systems', 'structure', 'staff' and 'strategy'. The book was panned by many academics for lacking rigour and nuance.[49] One empirical study in the influential *Journal of Management* comparing the 'excellent' firms with 1,000 companies evaluated by *Forbes* as high-performing found 'that the excellent firms are not as superior as Peters and Waterman have suggested'.[50] Even complimentary reviews conceded that 'the data presented to develop and support the eight characteristics would, by most scientific standards, not be admissible evidence of valid knowledge'.[51] The book was nonetheless generally very well received across business, with its authors heralded as management 'gurus' – and their own academic credentials paraded in the popular media. Both held an MBA from Stanford University, and Peters also held a Stanford PhD.

Consultancies choose to adopt terms and language usually found in academia to describe these businesses and promote what John

Micklethwait and Adrian Wooldridge described as a 'quasi-academic' image.[52] Certainly, some knowledge developed within them can be valuable to clients. Management books written by consultants, as well as the many, many reports that management consultancies publish via their research arms every year, can be interesting and useful sources of information. Reports on specific sectors can provide general insights into business trends and shifts in practices. Given that the consulting industry is granted inside access to so many companies, and that large consultancies such as McKinsey reportedly spend $100 million annually on research,[53] it would be astounding if there wasn't some value created through them.

Indeed, many people working across business and government will have drawn on reports produced by MGI or other research arms in their work. But this is also precisely why the analysis conducted by management consultancies and published in their reports and 'thought leadership' pieces should not be taken at face value: they are powerful marketing tools for promoting a consultancy as a pioneer in a particular area, and can increase demand for a consultancy's services by projecting confidence.

Individuals working to develop a company's strategy for integrating artificial intelligence (AI) into manufacturing processes, for example, will be able to find countless free reports from the big consultancies, many of which will be available via simple Google searches for related terms. Later, if the company opts to outsource its AI strategy development, or aspects of it, those employees are more likely to remember that PwC or Bain & Company or Accenture had produced interesting reports in this area, and so should be considered during the tender process. The consultants that researched and wrote the report are unlikely to be those deployed to fulfil a contract on the ground. McKinsey was successful in securing contracts within a particular global climate policy area because it had 'cultivated a reputation for "thought leadership" through its journal *The McKinsey Quarterly* and, subsequently, through the McKinsey Global Institute which published freely available reports on a variety of issues'.[54] Lobbying organizations similarly produce quasi-academic reports that they distribute to politicians, not necessarily to directly influence a law or public policy that is in development, but to be thought of as an important stakeholder in that policy area. Later, it is hoped the politician will turn to that lobbyist for advice should the need arise. Reports produced by consultancies are no different.

Rubber stamping

But is it always the contracting manager in the client organization that needs convincing of the value that the consulting industry promises to create? There is often another actor involved. Sometimes, the contracting manager harnesses the Big Con 'as an instrument to further their own objectives by involving consultants in the micro-political games'[55] of their own organization. In other words, consultants are contracted because doing so can help to legitimate the contracting manager's decisions or improve their standing within an organization. As one former consultant put it:

> Often, c-suiters – the people making the decisions at the top of organizations – have already made up their mind, but they really need an external independent arbiter to validate their position or make the case on their behalf. They can then go to the board and say, 'Oh, Deloitte or McKinsey or EY said we should do this.' It's the consultancy credibility stamp of approval. And for me, I saw that on so many of my projects.[56]

In this way, invoking the large consultancies – and the structural power of the consulting industry that they foster – becomes a means of securing internal influence within an organization. Consultants become 'agents of agents, and consultants' dominance vis-à-vis members of the client organisation as an extension of . . . managers' hierarchical' – or political – 'power'.[57]

This dynamic can also play out in a client's relations with other actors beyond the walls of its organization. From the late 1980s, with the rise of shareholder value-maximizing forms of corporate governance, 'corporate boards hired management consultants to defend themselves against potential claims that corporate officers had failed to act with due diligence in their oversight of company policy . . . consultants, in practice, became the independent outsiders who endorsed the "internal" board's previous decisions'.[58] Consultancies became a tool for protection against the new risks their clients faced. And at the same time, many also adopted business models to ensure they would maintain the ability to extract these growing Big Con rents without taking on the risks of failure either.

6. Evading the Risks, Reaping the Rewards: The Business Model

> Initially, all the Partners were like: 'This will be terrible for our clients', especially for financial services clients. But even within six months after the referendum, they were licking their lips at the business opportunities.
>
> *Former Big Four Senior Consultant on Brexit*[1]

Few votes in recent memory have divided a country in the way Brexit divided the UK. On 23 June 2016, citizens took to the polls with a binary choice to either remain within the European Union's single market and its political structures or withdraw from them completely. In the end, 51.9 per cent of the population voted 'Leave', and 48.1 per cent voted 'Remain'. It very quickly transpired that despite the rhetoric of a 'simple in or out choice',[2] leaving the EU would be anything but straightforward. It was an unprecedented and inherently uncertain endeavour. In a world where politicians wanted the UK to remain part of the global trading system, continue to foster scientific collaborations between universities and laboratories in Europe, and cooperate with geographic neighbours on present and future cross-border challenges, such as the climate crisis and the COVID-19 pandemic, there was plenty that needed to be resolved.

From the outset large consultancies viewed the complexity of Brexit as a fresh opportunity for expansion – a new wave they could ride. Companies began investing heavily in Brexit divisions. The Big Three and the Big Four positioned themselves as experts that could assist government bodies and businesses with their withdrawal responses, promising to reduce the uncertainty that many feared. McKinsey published a series of reports for businesses on issues including supply chain management, talent recruitment, UK exports and digital services, encouraging potential clients to look at 'the bigger picture'.[3] Boston Consulting Group followed suit, with Brexit-related publications targeting some of the biggest spenders on consulting services – the pharmaceutical industry, aerospace and defence, and financial services.[4] Deloitte established a Global Brexit Hub, made up of 'Brexit subject matter specialists' based around the world, from Malta to Brazil.[5] PwC developed a proprietary 'Brexit Customs and Trade Impact Assessment' tool that purported to model the impact of Brexit on businesses' global and EU supply chains.[6] The company also launched a dedicated digital platform where clients could access ready-made insights, as well as a podcast series called 'Beyond Brexit'.[7]

These efforts would prove fruitful. Some companies, such as Oliver Wyman and Capita, initially warned of lower profits and revenue growth in the wake of Brexit, but in general Brexit transpired to be very lucrative for the consulting industry. In 2016, the UK consulting market grew by 7.5 per cent to £7.3 billion – four times faster than the UK economy. In one survey of companies that contract consultants, '24 per cent said they were increasing their use of advisers in response to Brexit, and 82 per cent said they expected to call on the so-called "Big Four"'.[8] One senior management consultant was quoted in the *Financial Times* in March 2017 as saying, 'We expect the impact to be positive to us, assuming Brexit doesn't come off the rails completely.'[9] The following year, total fees across the consulting industry in the UK rose again by 7 per cent to £10.6 billion, 'as companies and government departments sought help with their Brexit planning'.[10]

The contracts that consultancies secured with businesses were wide-ranging – as the reports described above indicate. These were areas and industries where consultancies saw most potential for new contracts. In the public sector, Brexit-related tenders for consultancies mushroomed. Between 2017 and 2020, government annual spending on consultants soared to £450 million, with growth related in large part to Brexit. Profligate departments included the Home Office, which increased consultancy spending by 788 per cent during this time, with a number of contracts dealing with issues of security, immigration and border preparations for leaving the EU.[11] In 2019, the government announced a further round of Brexit-related contracts totalling almost £160 million. Some of these related specifically to planning in the case of a 'No Deal' scenario, in which the UK government would fail to reach an agreement with the EU regarding the terms of its withdrawal.

According to a report by the government's National Audit Office (NAO), consultants had been brought in not just to provide 'expert' advice, but also as a source of additional capacity, 'where the time available has constrained departments' ability to recruit or train civil servants to carry out that work'.[12] The examples of contracts included in the NAO's report suggest consultants were central to developments across a wide range of policy areas related to Brexit. The Department for Environment, Food & Rural Affairs contracted Boston Consulting Group in 2018 to 'review the scope, prioritisation and accountabilities of its EU Exit Programme'. The Department of Health and Social Care brought in Deloitte to 'provide programme management support for its work ensuring the supply of medical devices in case the UK leaves the EU without a deal'. PwC was recruited by the Home Office from August 2018 'to design and deliver communications about the EU Exit settlement scheme for EU nationals living in the UK'. From analysis to communications and project management, across policy areas including agriculture, healthcare and transport, consultancies had found their way to the heart of Brexit. More accurately, six consultancies were central to the UK government's withdrawal from the European Union: Deloitte, PA Consulting, PwC, EY, Bain & Company and Boston Consulting Group received 96 per cent of the value of the contracts.[13] If history is anything to go by, the contracts secured by large consultancies in particular are also likely to turn into more contracts in the future; the UK's legislative, financial and trade relationship with the European Union will continue to bring challenges, for which managers will look to the consultants they have previously worked with – and which now have a claim on 'EU Exit advice' – for support.

And crucially, across all these contracts – in both the public and private sector – the rewards that consultancies have reaped in no way reflected the risks of their advice being flawed or otherwise harming the economy. The risks were borne overwhelmingly by the public sector and businesses – with residents of the UK ultimately liable to suffer the consequences of the economy or parts of it tanking, or communication being wrong, or new agreements with the EU undermining a broader democratic mandate, or the consultants not delivering whatever they were supposed to.

Consulting risk

The specific terms of public sector consulting contracts tend to remain under wraps, protected by confidentiality clauses. Since the advent of large-scale contracts in governments including the UK, there have nonetheless been efforts to ensure the private sector contractor becomes responsible if it fails to fulfil a contract. For example, in addition to demonstrating that a PFI contract provides value for money, contracting departments from the 1990s have also been mandated to ensure the private sector genuinely assumes some risk.[14] Legally, there are also some clear instances where contracts must ensure that consultancies bear the risk of failure, such as if qualifications to perform have been misrepresented fraudulently.[15] Unlike in accounting, however, consulting practices and contracts are not tightly regulated. Auditing firms and individuals can be sanctioned by regulators for failing to meet the standards required for an audit, but this is not the case in consulting.

Some risks are easy to identify and account for in consulting contracts. In the case of public services outsourcing, for example, a firm can be made liable to pay a penalty for failing to provide a service for a period within the agreed contract term. But often, the risks of outsourcing are impossible to identify in advance. In PFI contracts for construction, which stipulate clear outputs, such as a hospital building or a bridge, many risks are not known; the collapse of Carillion, which was under many PFI contracts, attests to this. In its role as an advisor on PFI projects, KPMG once described how the 'extent of risk description is . . . limited by the imagination of the parties involved'.[16]

Even when the nature of the risks is anticipated in a contract, quantifying the costs to the client of them coming to fruition represents a further challenge. A government department may identify the risk that a contractor fails to procure the materials to build a new hospital wing and ensure that they are liable for this in the contract. But they may not accurately quantify the financial costs of this correctly in advance, meaning the contractor does not end up paying the full additional costs of sourcing the materials from elsewhere. And what about the social and political costs of this failure? Patients in need of the new facilities may be harmed and will certainly not look fondly on construction delays and extra costs. In large or complex tenders, such as in prime contracting and PFI, where the potential costs of risks are very high, often the public sector ends up assuming them, as this is the only way to incentivize consultancies to bid on them in the first place.[17] We saw this in the example of HealthCare.gov.

In the case of many consulting contracts, these issues become even more complicated owing to the ambiguous nature of the contracted services. Contracts for advice or policy analysis, for example, may stipulate outputs in the form of recommendations or a report, but clients often know very little about the means the consulting team will use to provide such services; their knowledge, methods and data are, after all, what's on offer. Clients therefore cannot know how likely it is that the dataset the consultancy is drawing on contains flaws, or that the consultants working directly on the project do not possess the expertise their firm's bid promised. They don't have access to that information. This differs from contracts for the general procurement of specific goods that have already been produced, such as office equipment or software.

Perhaps most importantly, much as the true value of consulting is often very difficult to ascertain, the qualitative and interactive nature of consultants' relationships with clients can make it challenging for clients to convincingly pinpoint blame when something goes wrong. Consultants are often embedded within or work with teams employed by the organization and take direction from a senior manager. If a strategy that has been designed by a consultancy does not yield greater profits as promised, the manager might point the finger at the consultancy, but the consultancy might equally point to problems with the instruction it received, the behaviour of other employees, or changes in the market outside their control. There is no higher authority in consulting who can judge definitively who is to blame.

This skewed risk-reward relationship is at the heart of the consulting industry's business model. The rewards reaped – the rents – usually far exceed the financial risks of taking on the contract or the costs of creating an impression of value. Unlike Arthur Andersen twenty years ago, large consultancies today can survive knocks to their reputations in the wake of public scandals with the help of their extensive resources, employing savvy legal and PR teams to respond to newspaper exposés and government inquiries. Because consultancies generally do not bear the costs of contract risk – and can withstand reputational risk – there is a conflict between the need to act first and foremost in the client's interest and the need to ensure the profitability and growth of consulting contracts. The absence of an incentive to guard against risk because an individual or organization will not be affected by its consequences is known in economics as a 'moral hazard'.[18] In other words, consulting has proven to be a very promising vehicle for rent extraction not just because the value of contracts is often high, but because the risks consultancies assume relative to the potential rewards are low.

With its inherent uncertainty, lack of precedence and depleted existing capacity in the public sector, Brexit was the perfect storm for companies to extract extraordinary rewards while the risks of failure remained with the public sector, businesses and citizens.

The art of limited liability

In the history of capitalism, some business models have helped to ensure that those responsible for advising or acting on behalf of clients are financially responsible for the costs of their decisions. In fact, that approach to corporate governance pre-dates the modern stock exchange by a few hundred years to fourteenth-century

Renaissance Florence, with the emergence of partnership-based companies.[19] Twelve of the fifty largest companies globally by consulting revenue in 2021 are registered as a form of partnership, including the Big Three and the Big Four, and other large firms such as Grant Thornton, Kearney and Arthur D. Little. In legal terms, a partnership is a company established by at least two people who agree to manage the organization together and share its profits and losses. Outside of the professional services industries, partnership forms of corporate governance have become very uncommon in business. This is particularly the case in sectors that require (or at some point have required) significant capital for investment, such as in IT or manufacturing, which have used equity as a source of funding. All the biggest IT consultancies are in fact publicly traded.

Almost all consultancies that have retained a form of partnership model have their roots in accounting or law. This is because historically, professional services firms were constrained by regulation from trading as public companies, owing to concerns about conflict of interest for their clients. They were mandated to be partnerships, because in this model, Partners were personally liable for any losses incurred by the firm; regulatory bodies viewed incorporation as risking the subordination of clients' interests to the commercial interests of others outside the firm.[20] Partners directly bore the risk of company failure – and investor losses – resulting from poor advice to clients, given as the Partners' other interests were pursued. Partners' salaries were tied to the value of the company, and salary increases linked to growth were also viewed as justified because Partners personally assumed the risk of failure.

In recent decades, however, the rules governing both these professions have been relaxed in many jurisdictions, and it is now possible to have a partnership that limits the liability of Partners, meaning their personal assets are not affected if the company becomes insolvent. In accounting, individuals can be fined by regulators, but in legal terms, Partners no longer bear the risks of company failure. Both the UK and US branches of PwC operate as a limited liability partnership (LLP), for example, and each have hundreds of Partners, as well as thousands of junior staff, who do not have the same stake in the company. Some companies that began as partnerships have continued to mimic the hierarchical structure of partnerships, even though they are technically private companies that have distributed shares to senior employees.

Consultancies large and small can also be wholly owned subsidiaries of larger companies, though some formal control by senior staff and performance-based pay are often retained in these circumstances. Oliver Wyman, for example, is a subsidiary of the professional services giant Marsh McLennan. Thirty-three of the top fifty global companies by consulting revenue in 2021 are private corporations, with nine of them being subsidiaries of conglomerate firms, including other management consultancies and asset management firms.[21]

Across the seventeen publicly traded consultancies in this group, the two largest asset management funds globally – BlackRock and Vanguard – hold around 13 percent of the total shares, reflecting the rise of what one academic has termed 'asset manager capitalism'.[22]

Shareholder value in public firms

In publicly traded consultancies, the compensation of executives is also tied in part to the growth of the company – in the form of stock awards, incentivizing behaviour to grow the rewards even as the individual and the firm take on limited risk. The theory behind giving executives stock-based compensation dates back to the 1980s, when some management theorists began to argue that a manager was more likely to make decisions that would increase the profits of the company if they themselves would directly suffer the consequences of poor performance, and would directly benefit from its growth.[23] This was part of 'agency theory', which assumes humans act primarily in their own economic interest and so require particular incentives to ensure the broader economic interests of the company or its owners are prioritized in their actions. By this time, external shareholders had become central to the financial structure of many companies, and the view that maximizing value for shareholders was the most effective driver of company growth had become prominent. According to the economist William Lazonick, this view is based on an assumption that 'of all participants in the business corporation, shareholders are the only economic actors who make productive contributions *without a guaranteed return*'.[23] In other words, it assumes that in a publicly traded company, it is the shareholders that take on the most risk because they have invested in the company by holding stock, and therefore have the greatest claim on the rewards – the profit, if and when it occurs.[24] Agency theorists argued that the relationship between corporate managers and shareholders was 'fraught with conflicting interests' because 'payouts to shareholders reduce the resources under managers' control, thereby reducing managers' power'.[25] To minimize agency risks (i.e. the misalignment of shareholder and manager interests) managers should receive part of their compensation in the form of stock awards.

Agency theorists understood that this would mean profit objectives would more often trump other interests, such as moral concerns of those employed as executives. In other words, they understood that the potential for increased financial rewards could shape the behaviour of employees in ways that benefitted the company's bottom line. Nonetheless, their view that these increased rewards (i.e.

stock-based compensation) were justified because these actors also took on increased risk was based on a very narrow view of what constitutes 'risk' in the first place. In business and government, employees 'bear risk when they exert effort . . . with a view to sharing in the future gains' – whether those gains are economic or social value.[26] The collective exertion of effort by individual workers is at the heart of value creation in any organization.

There are many actors and individuals involved in contracts with management consultancies that could be viewed as taking on far greater risk than losing share value-based rewards. In government contracts, citizens bear the risk of a consulting firm failing to deliver what it promised. In businesses, a company's employees bear the risk that the advice given by a consulting team results in restructuring and layoffs. Those employed directly or subcontracted by outsourcing consultancies bear the greatest risk internally of the company failing owing to the risky behaviour of executives – their contract is usually their only source of income, and losing it could jeopardize the ability to pay their mortgage or rent, for instance. These are just some examples, but they show that the agency theorists' assumptions about who takes on the greatest risks are shaky.

The performance of some outsourcing consultancies during the COVID-19 pandemic highlights these flaws. By the autumn of 2020, for example, Serco had emerged as one of the biggest winners of contracts for governments' responses to the pandemic. One of its deals with the UK Department of Health and Social Care was estimated then to be worth up to £410 million. Some people working for Serco to deliver COVID-19 contracts were employed in call centres on a short-term basis for low wages. Others worked in testing roles that brought them into close contact with people who were potentially infected with the virus. These employees risked their livelihoods and health. Citizens bore the huge public health risk of

Serco failing to help successfully provide a functioning contact-tracing service, which at the time was at the heart of the government's COVID-19 prevention response. Ultimately, they also bore the financial risk of it failing; Serco's contracts were paid using public money. These possible failures did all, to varying extents, come to pass. The rewards for Serco shareholders were nonetheless unaffected; in fact, they increased significantly. In October 2020, as towns and cities across Europe and North America prepared for renewed lockdown restrictions, shares in the company soared by 18 per cent after it announced profits vastly greater than forecast earlier in the year.

As agency theorists recognized only too well, being a Director or Partner in a company does not just create opportunities for wealth accumulation via stock-based or other company performance-based compensation. By having these positions, individuals are given greater control over the strategic decisions of the company. Which brings us back to why we should not take for granted the functional view that consultancies create value for clients. In no other area of business do we overlook the risks of such a 'moral hazard' between individual consultants and their clients quite so much as in the consulting industry.

Imagine a rapidly expanding fresh local produce company that wants to improve the IT infrastructure it relies on in its operations. The IT infrastructure is critical to the company – it's how it manages the logistics of collection and delivery, working to very tight time frames to prevent the food going off before it reaches customers. So far, the executives have employed several tech-savvy staff to develop and manage the systems that other operational employees use. Those systems have worked well, beyond a few glitches here and there. But the company's directors want to take things to the next level and start offering local produce to a wider range of customers via a new digital platform. So, they open a tender for a contract for advice on the company's IT strategy. The successful firm – a large multinational consultancy, well known for its IT services – sends in a team of five people, led by a 'Senior Executive'. Because the IT infrastructure is central to the food company's operations, most of the consulting team believe that the best thing for the company and its customers would be to expand the in-house department of software developers and IT managers, and occasionally draw on external specialists for specific ad hoc needs. But they also know that the consultancy that they work for has an annual goal to increase its revenue in IT services. If they succeed in convincing the food company to outsource its IT to their consultancy – i.e. cross-selling – not only will it contribute to the growth of the Senior Executive's stock-based compensation for the year, but the junior consultants will be commended for their skills, perhaps even in the form of a bonus and certainly at their end-of-year appraisal. The food produce company executives are none the wiser – after all, they only brought in the consultancy because they didn't feel competent evolving their IT services without external advice. In this instance, everyone benefits from the ability to extract greater rents, even if this approach does not create value for the company and may actually be riskier than opting for an in-house solution. The desire to secure additional rewards through new contracts wins out over the exchange of honest advice and expertise – exactly what we're told is the raison d'être of the consulting industry.

Risk shifts after acquisitions

It is often assumed that smaller or 'boutique' consultancies are more likely to behave in the interest of the client and create value. For boutique firms, which secure far fewer contracts and do not have the resources of large companies, convincing a potential client of their ability to create value is more likely to depend on the (perceived) success of previous contracts and the actual capabilities of consultants within the firm. Many small consultancies do inculcate specialist expertise, such as, for example, consultancies that have been established by individuals who have years or decades of experience working within a niche field in a particular industry, policy area or geographical location.[27] Many are also set up by individuals with highly specialist skills. In these instances, the small consultancy's expertise can be a valuable source of learning for a contracting organization. Indeed, there are many such firms that claim their business objective is to help other organizations to learn and ensure they do not require help in the same area in the future.

This expertise nonetheless cannot be taken for granted. 'Consultant' is not a protected profession and there is no universal accreditation for individuals who use the title. This means that, technically, anyone can set up a business and call themselves a consultant, even if they have no or only limited experience working in the area in which they are trying to sell advice. Of course, someone who has no experience in an area is unlikely to find success – and someone who out-and-out lies or exaggerates their professional background may find themselves accused of fraud. In the case of small consultancies established by individuals who have had long careers in a particular field, those consultants may be a legitimate source of 'sector knowledge' in the beginning, but as technologies, practices and knowledge in the field change, the firm's capabilities may not keep pace. Capabilities are always specific, to a degree, and they evolve over time. Expertise has a half-life. The value proposition of firms run by people with extensive, on-the-ground experience may not hold up in the long run.

As with large firms, boutique consultancies do not necessarily need to create value to be hired again in future. Ultimately, the consultants only need to ensure that the client perceives that value has been created. Satisfying clients may well entail the sharing of actual expertise or knowledge, but it may also involve simply instilling confidence in the value of what has been created. Regardless of size, all consultancies must secure contracts in the future, whether from current clients or others in the sector. A boutique consultancy specializing in UK National Health Service operational delivery depends on organizations within the health system continuing to need it as a source of expertise or capacity. A consultancy offering digitalization strategy or system integration management services requires that those functions remain outsourced. In the end, the consulting organization – and by extension, the consultant – must give the impression its services are necessary and valuable. This imperative exists within both for-profit companies and non-profit organizations. Non-profit organizations are, of course, unable to make a profit, but many have an incentive to remain in business all the same. Without contracts, there are no salaries.

For small firms with limited resources, the reputational risk of failing to fulfil a contract can nonetheless be fatal, perhaps incentivizing genuinely value-creating activity. At the same time, however, there is evidence that large consulting firms have been acquiring smaller firms at a growing rate in recent years, as they seek to consolidate a share of the market in particular geographical regions or for new technical skills and emerging sectors. Companies that McKinsey, Boston Consulting Group and Bain & Company acquired between 2013 and 2021 included a raft of consulting firms operating across data analytics, design and digital marketing, and cultural transformation. Among the acquisitions were BCG's purchase of 'human-centred design' agency AllofUs in 2019; McKinsey's purchase of the Belgian risk analytics firm Risk Dynamics in 2016; and Bain & Company's purchase of the Scandinavian boutique strategy consultancy Qvartz in 2020.[28]

Following an acquisition, the risks – as well as the rewards – that the acquired company assumes in contracts become shared with the parent company. This is a key reason why many small firms with genuine capabilities across different fields of innovation, such as bio-techs in drug development or start-ups in digital technology, agree to acquisition in the first place; it transfers the risk of failure away from them, while often also enabling them to scale up production of their good or service.

But what if the parent company – in our case, a large consultancy – is also able to evade risks relative to the rewards they reap? In the end, who assumes the risks of consulting industry failures? What are the costs of those failures – for economic development, democracy and the planet?

7. Infantilizing Organizations: When Learning Is Undermined Across Government and Business

Sweden was one of the first countries in the world to introduce a national pension scheme. In 1913, at 5.6 million people, the population was a little over half of what it is today. Most of them would never reach retirement age, which was set at sixty-seven; average life expectancy at birth was 54.5 years for men and fifty-seven years for women.[1] As the country evolved its welfare state throughout the twentieth century, the number of older people requiring a pension and more extensive health and social care remained low. In 1970, just 127 Swedes were aged over 100. In 2022, there are some estimates that around half of those born in advanced economies like Sweden can expect to live for a century.[2] All the while, although Sweden no longer has a formal retirement age, for most people the norm is sixty-five.

The fact that in many parts of the world people are living longer than ever before is a testament to astounding progress in medicine, healthcare systems, education and social services during the twentieth century. But it also poses challenges for the ways of life that we have become used to – and the welfare state models we continue to rely on. This is particularly true in northern Europe and North America, where state and private sector-based structures of care for the elderly are favoured over traditional family ones. In such societies, the more people who reach old age, the more resources are needed to support the population, as demand for pensions and health and social care increases. But in most countries the resources to support these growing needs has not kept pace, and the welfare state model is under pressure.[3]

One statistic that is often used to demonstrate the challenge of ageing populations is the Old-Age Dependency Ratio (OADR). It describes the relationship between the number of people who are 'economically active' and the number who are not, and is usually calculated by dividing the total number of people aged under twenty plus those aged over sixty-five or more by the sum of the population aged between twenty and sixty-four. It is a far from perfect metric, not least because it assumes that everyone in the latter age group is employed and paying taxes, ignores tax income derived through other means, such as wealth tax, and overlooks the role of monetary policy in public spending. But it can nonetheless give an indication of the scale of demographic change within a country.

In Sweden, the OADR has steadily climbed since the early 2000s, with some estimates suggesting that due to the ageing population it is expected to rise to 0.92 by 2060. In other words, there will be almost as many people of working age as there are out of work. Compounding Sweden's growing older population is the declining fertility rate in the country. In 2030, the number of people aged over sixty-five is anticipated to exceed the number aged under nineteen, which would be unprecedented.[4]

The demographic changes under way around the world as populations not only age but also become more urbanized require us to radically rethink how we provide care. It means ensuring we are constantly able to improve health systems by innovating technologies and defining what are the most effective ways to ensure everyone can access a good quality of life. In some cases, it means overhauling existing infrastructures and processes entirely.

In 2008, Sweden's Stockholm County Assembly did just that, choosing to completely reimagine the region's largest hospital. Setting the mission of creating a hospital explicitly 'to meet future challenges for health delivery', politicians across the party spectrum agreed to rebuild most of the Karolinska University Hospital, which had been established at the dawn of the country's modern welfare state in 1940. The new hospital, Nya Karolinska Solna (NKS), would develop and implement ground-breaking medical technologies, all in a building designed to minimize the risks of infection, harness the benefits of natural light and materials, and foster interdisciplinary research across departments. Public art, understood as key to patients' holistic well-being and recovery, would adorn the hospital's walls. Acutely aware of the environmental costs of hospital care, Stockholm County Assembly also aimed for NKS to become one of the most sustainable hospitals in the world, with most of its energy coming from renewable sources.

It is hard to overstate the boldness of this vision. But while there was consensus around the need to meet future healthcare demands in a radical way across party lines, from the outset there was also biting contestation about how to achieve that.

Throughout the 2000s, the Swedish public sector had been subject to widespread transformation, with welfare services increasingly decentralized to local authorities and outsourced to third-party providers. Legislative changes had meant that city and county councils were now permitted to hand over the management of hospitals and clinics to private actors.[5] Taking inspiration from Third Way governments in the UK and Australia in particular, the leaders of Stockholm County Assembly proposed a public-private partnership model for building and managing the new hospital. They commissioned reports from Öhrlings PricewaterhouseCoopers (the Swedish branch of PwC) and Ernst & Young to explore the potential challenges of such an approach. Unsurprisingly, both consultancies concluded that private firms would not only offer the 'highest possibility of value creation since it gives incentives to innovation and optimized investments and operating costs over the life cycle' but also 'decreased risk for running costs, since the risk mainly is transferred to the private partner'.[6]

Several contrasting studies had warned about the risks of soaring additional costs in using a PFI for such a complex and ambitious project: it would constitute one of the largest PPPs in the world to date. Many representatives in the Assembly opposed the plans, and the centre-right national government even reportedly attempted to stop the project going ahead, fearing the high long-term costs of private financing.[7] There were also growing concerns about PFI stemming from the UK government's experiences with hospital developments. By 2005, for example, a flagship PFI hospital development in west London had been abandoned with researchers describing how 'it was simply too complicated for a health system in which . . . those responsible for purchasing care (along with other interested parties) have become hopelessly fragmented'.[8] Costs had also soared. By 2008, it had been established that under PFIs, 'hospital trusts' annual payments to their private sector partners are higher than expected and are taking 11% of their budget. The additional cost of private over public finance for the first 12 hospitals is about £60M a year, which is 20–25% of the trusts' income.'[9]

In the end, nonetheless, the final decision lay with the leaders of the Stockholm County Assembly, which followed the recommendations of the consultancies whose advice it had sought. One politician for the Assembly's ruling centre-right Moderates party, Torbjörn Rosdahl, stated at the time: 'We know to the single Crown what this will cost. There are no surprises for the taxpayers. We have full control, there are no secrets.'[10]

At first, there had been some ambition to improve on the PFI models that had been employed to build hospitals in other parts of the world. The planners wanted to ensure the future private partners of NKS could integrate technological innovation over the long term. The final contract that was drawn up, however, followed the 'standard' PFI in use across the UK's National Health Service. The change of approach was owed in no small part to the lack of excitement about it from potential private sector partners; many Swedish companies in particular viewed the financial risks of the project as too high. By the end of the procurement process, the tender had just one bidder: Swedish Hospital Partners (SHP), a consortium of the Swedish construction group Skanska and the British investment fund Innisfree. In 2010, the first year of the project's thirty-year contract, the partnership appeared strong. SHP secured financing from the European Investment Bank (EIB) worth €605 million, the Nordic Investment Bank worth €127 million, and several commercial banks. But soon more than a few questions surfaced regarding the project's progress and financing, revealing costs not just in terms of budgets, but the health system's capabilities.

Extortionate costs for likely failures

The financial costs alone were far beyond what anyone in government had anticipated. In 2015, research conducted by two Swedish journalists revealed that spending on building the hospital had skyrocketed. At the time of the inauguration, in May 2018, it had reached kr22.8 billion – twice as much as originally budgeted. By 2040, when the PFI contract underpinning the project ends, the hospital is anticipated to have cost the Swedish public budget as much as kr61.4 billion, or more than five times the original budget.[11] The upfront costs of compensating SHP for 'constantly searching for and delivering innovation, quality, and cost control' alone were €30 million per year, despite little clarity about what this entailed.[12]

Before long, NKS had earned a reputation as the 'most

expensive hospital in the world'.[13] As the true scale of the costs continued to come to light, the media and politicians demanded answers. In March 2018, the new Swedish finance minister called for a government investigation into reports of financial and operational challenges in the PPP, which concluded that key lines in the construction budget had been missed, including for critical equipment and services such as IT cables and lab and medical equipment.[14]

But there were two further, related – and by now familiar – reasons for the soaring costs. For one, although the consortium responsible for the project was formally made up of just two companies, many more had been contracted and subcontracted to deliver various aspects of it. In fact, according to one estimate, only 20 per cent of the total cost of the contract was delivered by SHP.

And on top of construction and vendor costs, spending on the project's management had also spiralled, with the prime beneficiary being US consultancy Boston Consulting Group. BCG was contracted to deliver core elements of the hospital's operations and strategy, including the implementation of a controversial management approach known as 'value-based healthcare'. The strategy had been developed through a collaboration between BCG's Swedish Managing Director and the American management scholar Michael Porter, whose theory of 'value-based competition' argues that healthcare systems should be reimbursed on the basis of patient health outcomes measured against the cost of delivering care. Based on the privatized healthcare model in the United States, this approach is premised on a narrow understanding of value in healthcare as cost-effectiveness,[15] and has been used to justify greater involvement of private sector providers in health services. At NKS, value-based healthcare has been used to structure the hospital around different patient groups rather than the medical specialties of physicians, which entails specialists working across

departments.[16] The use of the approach at NKS has drawn extensive criticism. Researchers and journalists have raised concerns
about the lack of evidence for it, questioning why such a large-
scale hospital development was chosen as a 'pilot project'.[17] The
implementation of the approach has been described in the *British
Medical Journal* (*BMJ*) as 'chaotic, prompting harsh criticism
from medical staff, an IT breakdown, and a patient death during
an emergency stop, as well as [creating] many logistical issues: a
shortage of beds, a lack of changing and waiting rooms in healthcare facilities, and poorly designed wards'.[18]

Despite these issues, BCG was reported in the media as having
billed the hospital kr257 million (£22 million) over six years.[19]
This is the equivalent of more than kr700,000 (£60,000) a month
for each of the nine consultants employed – multiples more than
public sector managers of similar rank and education are paid in
Sweden. These controversial revelations in the spring of 2018 led
to resignations of members of the hospital's board, though the
consultancy has not been found in breach of its contract. Before
long, in September of that year, the hospital's director, Melvin
Samsom, had also stepped down. Although, according to the
BMJ, Samsom stated at the time that 'the time was right to move
on now that the system he introduced was up and running',[20] his
decision followed the hospital's much-criticized choice to contract another consultancy, Nordic Interim AB, for management
services between 2015 and 2018. The total value of those contracts
reached kr133 million (£11.4 million), and even became the subject of an inquiry by the Swedish Competition Authority after it
was revealed they had been awarded on a no-bid basis.[21]

In fact, consultancies have been involved in various aspects of
NKS. They include the Scandinavian consultancy Ramboll, which
states on its website:

> Ramboll was involved in the [NKS] project from an early stage, initially in preliminary studies into the possibility of building a new hospital and subsequently in the preparation of tender documents and in reviewing the documents received. Ramboll was commissioned by Skanska Healthcare, responsible for the design and the building process for the New Karolinska Solna, to carry out project planning of the building structures. Ramboll had the design responsibility for the entire hospital building and the research building, as well as for 8 radiation therapy rooms – just over 75% of the project's total building structures.[22]

This statement epitomizes how much the NKS partnership was relying on private consultants to deliver the project. But this approach had huge financial implications. In 2019, the *BMJ* reported that around 250 doctors and 350 nurses at the hospital had been warned they could lose their jobs because of an unanticipated deficit of kr1.6 billion in the hospital's finances for the year.[23] The bloated cost of outsourcing the hospital's development and parts of its management, which the consulting industry both advocated and benefitted from, ultimately jeopardized the jobs of the medical experts who would actually create value in the hospital. In 2018, Stockholm County Assembly's leader of the opposition, Aida Hadžialić, did not mince her words when she criticized how NKS had been handled: 'This choice was the expression of a political will, based on the idea that privatisation had inevitably positive effects and which led to the construction of one of the most expensive buildings in the world.' A group of Scandinavian management academics was similarly damning, calling the ambition to harness the competition dynamics of the private sector 'magic wishful thinking'. They also emphasized that in leaning on the consulting industry to the extent that the Assembly and consortium had, the 'experience and competence from researchers and independent experts were not utilised'.[24]

This second point hints at a consequence of contracting consultancies far greater than the cost to short-term cash flows alone. Not only is outsourcing at scale and scope to consultancies often far costlier than alternatives, it can also potentially waste the specialized skills and expertise that already exist within the organization and its ecosystem – in the heads of, for example, medical researchers and nurses in the case of NKS. Crucially, doing so can also prevent those people – and their organizations – from learning and improving their skills.

How do organizations learn?

The use of consultants to develop or deliver a core function – as opposed to drawing on the insights of experts – assumes that capabilities can be conjured up at will,[25] and that knowledge can simply be purchased, as though off the shelf. It assumes learning in the contracting organization is not an incremental and collective *process*, but a *transaction*.

This transactional mentality is at odds with extensive research about the importance of the internal dynamics of the (contracting) organization in learning. Research shows that learning in organizations builds on existing knowledge (the collective competences, skills and capabilities of employees) and resources – the sum of which can be understood as the organization's capacity.[26] The knowledge that is built on may be 'explicit' and easily measurable – for example, it could include statistics held on databases and information in internal knowledge management systems. But it is also often 'tacit' – know-how that employees build up over time, which is harder to quantify or capture concretely.[27] This is particularly true in labour-intensive services. In the public sector, owing largely to the long shadow of NPM narratives which did not value experiences derived from long civil service careers, this tacit knowledge is often overlooked as constituting an important resource in learning. The total cumulative knowledge that exists within an organization is often referred to as 'institutional memory'.

Learning, according to these perspectives, involves modifying, reorienting or restructuring existing knowledge and resources for new challenges. Organizations that can evolve can be described as having 'dynamic'[28] or 'learning capabilities'.[29] In this view of learning, other actors in society are also important; interactions with other value-creating individuals and organizations are critical.

In democratic governments, public sector organizations are expected to be able to adapt in response to changing political demands and societal needs. In-house knowledge and resources are therefore not merely a means for achieving current political objectives; they can also be the building blocks of knowledge and resources for use in the future. The COVID-19 pandemic demonstrated this perfectly. A policy report that one of us recently co-authored found that 'public sector capabilities to manage a crisis of this proportion are dependent on the cumulative investments that a state has made in its capacities to govern and manage'.[30] There was no set recipe for preparing for the pandemic; but previous learning and the ability to reorient those capabilities and resources for the COVID-19 response were crucial. The report notes how, for example, in Kerala, India, 'the institutional memory from the successful management of two major floods and an outbreak of a virus in 2018' became the foundation for the pandemic response. Using this prior experience, health officials were able to ensure that 'before its first recorded COVID case, 15 health districts in Kerala had set up control rooms to monitor the situation and coordinate responses, and two hospitals in each district were designated to treat the virus-infected patients'.[31]

Despite operating under a relatively constrained budget compared to countries in the Global North, as well as being a busy tourism hub and home to many of the country's travelling skilled workers, the government's early response succeeded in keeping infection and hospitalization numbers low. Meanwhile, in Rwanda, officials successfully repurposed health infrastructure developed to prevent Ebola from crossing the border from the Democratic Republic of the Congo and combatting HIV.[32] In Vietnam, 'the investments in long-term capacities in the form of public-health infrastructure and services (emergency operations centres and surveillance systems) made in response to SARS epidemics paid off'. The government was able to use the knowledge gleaned from these experiences to launch a successful 'whole-of-society' approach. Among other initiatives, this included leveraging public procurement and R&D funding 'to engage both academia and the private sector in the production of low-cost testing kits', and 'temporarily repurposing garment production to mask production'.[33] In each of these examples, having confronted previous challenges using internal resources and knowledge made governments better prepared for the crisis. The countries described in the report also drew on the expertise and capacity of other actors in society in their COVID-19 responses, from private health providers to intergovernmental bodies, such as the World Health Organization, and also citizen innovations developed at a grassroots level.

Learning from consultants?

The consulting industry does not exist on the scale and scope of today merely because it is an effective broker of knowledge. And where consultants do create knowledge, it may not be effectively shared with clients. One analysis of European governments' uses of management consultancies suggested that the knowledge developed by consultancies when they receive a contract 'is often not built up and kept internally within the public organizations, but rather to a large extent rests with the consulting firm'.[34] In practice, consultancy contracts will stipulate the number and format of 'deliverables' that the client will receive, such as reports on key analytical findings, training workshops or a strategic plan. But the knowledge that is built through the process of developing those deliverables – for example, interview transcripts and statistical data – is not shared. The tacit knowledge that consultants develop remains with them.

Contracting organizations can aim to absorb knowledge from the organizations they contract, but as the research on 'absorptive capacity'[35] suggests, this form of learning is unfeasible without core management and coordination capabilities. The concept of absorptive capacity was first introduced to describe 'the ability of a firm to recognize the value of new, external information, assimilate it, and apply it to commercial ends' that is at the heart of innovation processes.[36] It has since been developed for understanding learning processes in public services and government more widely.[37] Whether in the public or private sector, organizations with absorptive capacity have the managerial and coordination capabilities for understanding in the first place what is a source of valuable external knowledge, and then ensuring it becomes 'appropriated'[38] – and embedded in broader learning processes. Without them, the capacity for building 'institutional memory' is lost and external knowledge is quickly forgotten.[39] Absorptive capacity is an important dimension of an organization's dynamic capabilities, but it is no substitute for the broader foundational management and operational capacity necessary for an organization to grow and evolve. Management consulting firms in particular, which are often dependent on securing future contracts, may have an incentive to prevent clients from learning and becoming independent in such a way that would render the consultancy's services obsolete.

Contracting to consultancies can also directly erode existing in-house knowledge and institutional memory:[40] the less an organization does something, the less it knows how to do it. It is a self-fulfilling process. But the hollowing out of capabilities that occurs as a result does not just reduce the capacity of an organization to do something itself in the short term; it can have cumulative effects over the long term as well. If the Rwandan government had outsourced its Ebola prevention strategy on the Congolese border to a management consultancy, for example, it would not have developed the related knowledge and resources that became foundational to its COVID-19 response.

Beyond budgets: The consequences for future learning

The detrimental consequences for learning of outsourcing often do not become clear for many years. It is only in the 2020s, for example, that policymakers and researchers are identifying the costs of transferring responsibility for public sector IT to management consultants and other private actors, a change that has been taking place since the 1990s.

Many politicians view 'back-office' functions and administrative systems as areas that don't necessarily need to be run by the government, and in fact work better in the hands of business. But IT and data are increasingly valuable, not to mention central to the day-to-day operations of government, and privatizing them has major implications. Public sectors rely on data to deliver services. Think about waste collection – another area of government that is, like IT, often characterized as mundane. Without data about citizens' addresses, details about the logistics of bin collection vans and the ability to communicate times and dates of collections with citizens, waste would pile up in the street. Data is also at the heart of changes that occur in the public sector.[41] Processes of waste collection may not have changed much over the past few decades, but many other public functions have needed to evolve in line with changing political demands, as well as demographic and environmental shifts. I T today is or should be a core activity of government.

The Danish government's approach to public sector digitalization is a useful example. In Denmark, e-government went from playing 'an almost hidden role within the realm of a visionary national Information Society strategy in the early 1990s . . . [to] in the 2000s become a policy field of its own'.[42] Until late in the twentieth century, the private sector only played a very limited role in I T infrastructure and management, and the transfer of responsibility for I T to the private sector occurred relatively quickly. The Danish public sector was an early adopter of e-government reforms, meaning their consequences have emerged sooner than in other countries. The scale of digitalization reforms implemented in the past thirty years also reveals the negative consequences for public sector capacity.

Between 2002 and 2016, the Danish government – under leadership of various ideological hues – adopted several e-government and digitalization strategies that gradually transferred more and more of the public sector I T infrastructure and its management into the hands of consulting companies and other private actors.[43] Privatization was not the primary objective of the strategies, but rather a consequence. The e-government strategies of the early 2000s cited the desire to improve services and make processes more efficient, as had been the goal of wider N P M and Third Way thinking across the

Danish welfare state.[44] Efficiency continued to be a key objective of the reforms throughout the 2000s, though it shifted from being framed as a way of 'freeing up resources'[45] to a means of salvaging the welfare state model in the wake of the financial crisis.[46] Increasingly, during the decade following the financial crisis, the goals of improving processes and services through public sector digitalization were accompanied by a new motive: private sector growth. During this period, Denmark wielded the public sector assets and capabilities developed by its expansive public welfare programmes and regulation as resources for exploitation by the private sector in the pursuit of economic growth. This was true in the digitalization of both administration and service delivery.[47]

In 2017, the Danish government had to face up to the fact that the transfer of responsibility for its public sector IT to external consultants and private suppliers had adversely affected its ability to govern according to political changes. One government report noted that:

> Several state authorities are today unable to build the important bridge between IT and core functions, and to enter into good and value-creating collaborations with the private IT market . . . Several authorities are unable to manage IT systems efficiently and responsibly, and . . . they do not have the necessary control over IT projects.[48]

According to one public manager, some agencies had become dependent on contractors, because 'all the knowledge and know-how and documentation . . . are in the heads of a few employees at certain vendors'. This meant that 'in some instances, we were actually in a situation that it was the IT systems that mandated how soon the changes the politicians wanted could be implemented, and not the other way around'.[49] One such case involved a new EU taxation rule, which Denmark, as a member of the EU, had to implement. The Tax Agency struggled to implement the reform comprehensively, because it required critical changes to the IT infrastructure, which had been outsourced to IT consultancies and companies.[50]

The Danish public sector had lost the ability to keep its IT capabilities up to date. The ability to make changes was under the control of private sector contractors. This loss of knowledge means that public sector managers are often left with no choice but to go to an external contractor for support. Even Scandinavian governments with high fiscal capacity find themselves in this situation. The growing use of the consulting industry across the public sector is thus a fundamentally political issue, because contracting at scale and scope can constrain the options of future democratically elected politicians. Signing a contract with a private provider can take days, but rebuilding the capabilities that may be lost in the process is never so quick – particularly in highly technical fields such as IT. A new government elected with a five-year term may have a democratic mandate to bring historically outsourced services and other contracts back into public hands, but it will be challenging, gradual and expensive to achieve this goal within that time frame, particularly if the previous government outsourced at scale.

Capture by brochuremanship

A loss of knowledge can also undermine the state's capacity to govern relationships with the private sector, whether through regulation, procurement or other forms of partnership.

Throughout the history of capitalism, governments have needed to maintain deep knowledge about developments in markets and specific companies. A skilled government workforce needs to be able to analyse changes both to ensure corporate laws are abided by and to amend or improve those laws where necessary. Engaging with markets has always been important in their regulation for the simple reason that businesses are a key source of information about sector- and economy-wide trends. But with the growth of consulting since the 1980s, many critical areas of regulation have become character- ized not as a learning relationship – in which public sector analysts turn to markets for insights that will help them to make appropriate regulatory decisions – but instead by the outsourcing of the devel- opment of these rules to the market actors who will be affected by them.

The decision to outsource regulation to consultancies and other corporate actors may be a political effort to limit the influence of the state on markets. But it is also often a question of capacity. Regula- tory bodies simply may no longer have the expertise that they need to develop appropriate rules. This is not solely owed to the gradual hollowing out of competence by outsourcing decisions; the chal- lenge of attracting talented economists to work for the public sector when salaries are no match for corporate roles is also frequently cited as an important factor, for example. But the more that respon- sibility for delivering core functions is privatized, the harder it is for the government to ensure in-house regulatory skills are up to date and improving. This 'internal logic of privatization . . . seriously undermines both the constraining power of public rules and the abil- ity of states to exercise their adjudicatory authority through courts'.[51]

That incremental loss of up-to-date knowledge also affects public bodies' ability to negotiate suitable terms for new contracts with consultancies and other providers. Again, this is particularly the case in highly technical areas of public services, such as environmental monitoring, finance and digital technologies. This became apparent in the United Kingdom in the aftermath of the Blair/Brown years, during the period of the new Coalition government's policy to slash spending on consultants. In one instance, a major rail franchise tender was withdrawn because the Department for Transport lacked the in-house contracting skills needed to run the contract competition. The department had grown used to outsourcing the task of tendering to external consultants, and its inability to do so under the moratorium was paralysing: 'Consultants had become essential to the workings of the public sector'.[52]

More recently, in 2018, the Danish public sector was confronted with the consequences of its loss of digital capabilities when a partnership with IBM collapsed entirely. Eighteen months earlier, the regional government body responsible for providing healthcare in the capital, Copenhagen, had entered into a five-year agreement with the IT consultancy to develop a strategy for artificial intelligence and the integration of IBM's AI technology 'Watson' into the region's hospital systems. IBM launched a year-long charm offensive with the region's most senior officials and politicians before the agreement was signed and millions of kroner were handed over to the company. But then, in 2018, the deal folded, and all promises of new welfare technologies died with it, with a former official involved in the contract process subsequently describing how 'it was very oversold what Watson could do. There is something of "the emperor's new clothes" about it.'[53] Had the regional government maintained greater capacity for digital innovation internally, project managers might have spotted shortcomings in IBM's promises much easier and earlier, or at least been able to lean on the expertise of others within the organization for advice.[54] Even in cases of procurement where 'broad functional (e.g. performance) specifications form the basis for assessing success in meeting requirements, in contrast to the use of detailed technical specifications', the public sector still needs to have 'a deep understanding of both technological constraints and the application environment for the technology or product'.[55]

During the Apollo mission of the 1960s and early 1970s, NASA's director of procurement, Ernest Brackett, recognized the import-ance of public sector capabilities in successful contracting and setting favourable terms of reference. He warned that if the agency stopped investing in these capabilities, for example by cutting R&D spend-ing, it would no longer understand its own environment, not know who to collaborate with, or be unable to write the terms of reference for doing so. It would, in his words, be 'captured by brochureman-ship'.[56] The absence of internal digital capabilities and expertise at the Danish regional government body made it susceptible to the Big Con.

'Cronyism' and incapacity

The inability of many governments to contract effectively became all too clear during the early months of the COVID-19 pandemic. In the UK, the extent to which contracting failures were the result of incapacity or evidence of the rise of corruption has been hotly debated in the media, and the subject of academic studies.

As reports that contracts for personal protective equipment (PPE) were being awarded via 'VIP lanes' came to light, ministers were accused of 'cronyism'[57] and the government of creating a 'chu-mocracy'.[58] A report by Transparency International UK found that one in five pandemic response contracts had 'signs of possible cor-ruption', including twenty-four PPE contracts worth £1.6 billion and three testing contracts worth £536 million.[59] In January 2022, the High Court ruled that the government's use of 'VIP lanes' in the awarding of contracts to two firms during the pandemic was unlawful.[60] In May 2020, a healthcare firm that employed the Conservative MP Owen Paterson as a paid consultant won a contract to produce COVID-19 testing kits, facing no competition.[61] An investigation by the parliamentary standards commissioner later found Paterson had 'repeatedly' breached paid lobbying rules, advising that he be served with a thirty-day suspension.[62] The report sparked a national debate, with Prime Minister Boris Johnson facing calls from across the government to ban all outside employment for MPs.[63] The instances of potential 'cronyism' not only involved contracts with companies where an MP was employed, however. In one case that was broadcast on news channels around the world, the Health Secretary Matt Hancock was found to have been involved in the negotiation of a contract between the landlord of his local pub and the Department of Health and Social Care for the manufacture of test tubes. The contract was valued at £30 million – but the landlord's company had no history of manufacturing medical equipment.[64] The UK's cottage industry of COVID-19 contract chancers transcended borders. In another case that wound up in the courts of Miami, a Florida-based jewellery designer with no experience in PPE supply chains established a company to sell hospital gloves and gowns to the NHS. He was awarded two government contracts worth more than £28 million by the Department of Health and Social Care.[65] The Good Law Project, a campaign group led by prominent lawyers, has taken a number of similar cases to courts in England, including one where a PPE contract worth £108 million was awarded to a small pest control company that had net assets of £18,000.[66]

The political scientists Linda Weiss and Elizabeth Thurbon have argued that the UK case demonstrates failures in political agency as much as incapacity. They question the idea that outsourcing and privatization reforms have rendered states 'incapable of preventing or mitigating the viral outbreak'. Through a comparative analysis of British and Australian governments' responses to the pandemic, which have both implemented widespread outsourcing reforms since the 1980s, they argue that the agency of politicians has been critical for 'offsetting' the associated institutional weaknesses. Such differences in the political choices of the countries' governments explain to a large extent why Australia was more successful in containing the pandemic than the UK.[67]

It is indisputable that political agency matters. But contrary to the assumptions of neoliberalism that civil servants use their positions primarily for personal gain – an idea that was reinforced with the adoption of Public Choice Theory-inspired reforms from the 1980s – governments are not inherently corrupt. There have always been individuals who seek to use political office for personal gain – and others whose initially benevolent ambitions become distorted once in power. Perhaps some political parties attract a greater than average share of such people. But the broader architecture of the state, beyond its elected politicians, must have checks and balances to prevent any one individual or self-serving group from capturing the economy. In a healthy democracy, the public sector and its administrative structures are simultaneously what enable elected politicians to realize their mandate, and what prevents these 'cronies' from subverting democracy to their own advantage by enforcing agreed-upon rules and obligations. The public sector's ability to constrain corrupt or anti-democratic choices of politicians must also be understood as a dimension of state capacity. Thus, while there have been many clear instances of egregiously close ties and anti-competitive behaviour in the awarding of COVID-19 contracts, to characterize these processes purely in terms of 'cronyism' and corruption is myopic. The coup of 'cronyism' during the pandemic in the UK could not have happened without the hollowing out of internal contracting capacity. In better days, a minister who sought to provide favours for an old business partner or close friend would be met with administrators whose job it was to ensure procurement was a transparent and fair process. Those civil servants would have the capabilities and resources to ensure the public's interest was upheld. The scale of 'corrupt' contracts in the UK and elsewhere during the pandemic suggests this is not the case today.

The weakness of the public sector also has implications for politics that, while less direct, may well reconfigure our societies. In recent years, political scientists and pundits alike have become acutely interested in the rise of what they term 'populism' and anti-elite sentiment. The election of Donald Trump as US President and the UK's vote to leave the European Union are frequently cited as manifestations of such political trends. According to this view, populations have sought to overturn status quo ruling liberal institutions and reassert popular authority – or 'take back control', as the slogan of the official Vote Leave campaign went during the Brexit referendum. The overriding assumption in such analyses is that voters have been duped by fascistic politicians into voting for political reforms that are fundamentally against the interests of most people, and which make our societies more nativist, isolationist and authoritarian. Right-wing politicians have undeniably capitalized – and, to varying extents, exacerbated – feelings of frustration with existing modes of political decision-making. But the gradual loss of grounded and accountable expertise within many government organizations has also undermined them. In a world where zealots will use a popular sense of political alienation to their own advantage, limiting the demise of public sector capabilities, including through outsourcing to consultancies. Otherwise, governments and public bodies will not only become more reliant on market actors whose interests so often conflict with the public's but also fan the flames of political disillusionment that has gripped societies around the world.

Skeletonizing business

In business organizations – as in the public sector – the collective and cumulative development of knowledge and resources are at the heart of a firm's capacity to innovate products and respond to new customer and social demands.[68]

Outsourcing 'can erode the firm's potential for [existing] organizational learning and development of new technologies'.[69] But the promotion of the consulting industry is also important for understanding the consequences for learning and the development of new capabilities in business. In fact, consultancies' continuous marketing and subsequent introduction of new organization concepts as they ride the wave of a new market niche can itself disrupt learning in business by overturning existing structures.[70] Commodified 'solutions' – a term used in the consulting industry to describe the frameworks, metrics and services on offer – can be influential branding and marketing tools in consulting; but in companies that adopt them, they can have the consequence that managers 'flit from theory to theory',[71] failing to settle on one structure or strategy long enough to foster the development of capabilities before another is introduced. The cycle of adopting and then abandoning the consulting industry's various solutions 'may reinforce a persistent lack of knowledge accumulation within the system of knowledge supply'.[72] Some researchers even view 'forgetfulness' as being at the heart of management consulting, whereby 'the persistent introduction of new ideas . . . permits the repeating of previous mistakes and inhibits organizations from learning'.[73]

Perhaps the most prominent group of approaches associated with the consulting industry are those advocating restructuring, downsizing or delayering in a company. As we saw in Chapter 2, consultancies have long advised companies to cut jobs, and can be brought in precisely because it enables the contracting manager to shift blame for employee losses – and constrain opposition from the wider workforce and trade unions. They can provide 'the confirmation and legitimation of restructuring decisions that have already been made'.[74]

Whether driven by internal management decisions or advocated independently by consultancies, corporate restructuring, downsizing or delayering can result in widespread redundancies. Researchers describe, for example, how the 1997 economic crisis led to greater use of management consultancies and this form of corporate restructuring, which they advocated, in South Korea. In December of that year, the Korean government announced it was seeking financial assistance from the IMF. The conditions of the loan included not just changes in macroeconomic policy and financial regulation, but also increased labour market flexibility and the restructuring of the country's largest conglomerates, 'remoulding the Korean economy in the image of the (idealized) Anglo-American system'.[75] In response, several management consultancies published reports that provided support for the IMF's calls. At the peak of the crisis, in 1998, for example, the McKinsey Global Institute claimed that 'inefficient management and work practices, overstaffing, lack of a performance culture, and poor product and service mixes' were key impediments across industries.[76] On the advice of consultancies, many companies downsized, though there was also frequent trade union and managerial resistance, which sometimes 'resulted in the watering down of previously announced job losses'.[77]

Research has shown that downsizing can 'seriously damage the learning capacity of organizations'.[78] Using data on 4,153 companies based in Australia, for example, one study found a strong link between downsizing and 'deskilling' – the loss of skills and know-ledge key for learning. The findings challenged the hypothesis that downsizing tends to be associated with an increase in the skill pro-file and knowledge base of a firm because it involves an organizational restructure that facilitates multi-skill building and increasing levels of professionalization. In other words, the large-scale redundancies associated with downsizing harmed the firms' capacity for learning, even if new employees were brought in and new strategic goals were defined as part of a broader restructuring process.[79]

In research-intensive firms, the decision to outsource core func-tions can have particularly severe consequences for learning and innovation. This form of corporate governance has nonetheless been widely adopted in many such companies across North America and Europe, and often arrives together with broader reforms aiming to 'maximize shareholder value' (MSV). Although downsizing can harm learning, it is associated with an increase in short-run stock returns, and so shareholders and executives who receive part of their compensation in the form of stock awards are incentivized to intro-duce them. One study found that '[CEOs] of firms announcing layoffs receive 22.8% more total pay in the subsequent year than other CEOs' – resulting almost entirely from increases in stock-based compensation.[80]

Many large consultancies have long advocated shareholder-oriented forms of corporate governance – and, perhaps more importantly, provided the justification for it to internal managers and shareholders, riding a restructuring wave. As early as 2000, economists William Lazonick and Mary O'Sullivan, who identified MSV as an increasingly prominent form of corporate governance, noted that 'management consultants have incessantly promoted the virtues of this approach in Europe and Japan'.[81] The imperative to maximize value for shareholders has in practice undermined innovation in research-intensive sectors in particular. Investment in the necessary capabilities is constrained so that more cash can be distributed via dividends and share buybacks.[82]

In few areas have the consequences of MSV – and the influence of the consulting industry in its entrenchment – been more apparent than in the pharmaceutical industry.[83] The development of new drugs is a highly complex and highly uncertain process, which requires strategic investment in a skilled workforce and technical equipment. Studies have demonstrated that in recent decades, many pharmaceutical companies have reduced investments in R&D as they increase distributions to shareholders, securing greater profits not through creating value from drug innovation, but through cutting operational spending and inflating the prices of existing drugs, often acquired through mergers.

The pharmaceutical industry has historically represented one of the biggest markets for management consultants. Every single one of the world's largest consulting companies today has a pharma and life sciences division that offers advice to pharmaceutical companies large and small on issues including regulatory compliance, supply chain management, mergers and acquisitions, and executive pay. But it is the consulting industry's activities in the realm of corporate governance and financing that have attracted the most unwanted attention over the past decade. One case involving Valeant Pharmaceuticals – dubbed by one critic as 'the pharmaceutical Enron'[84] – stands out for the scale of both investor hubris and the consulting industry's influence. The *Financial Times* even ran with the headline 'McKinsey's fingerprints are all over Valeant', following the company's de facto collapse in 2016.[85]

Apotheosis: Betting on management, stripping out science

Valeant Pharmaceuticals started out like many other small drug makers with roots in the post-war decades, carving out a patent niche and investing heavily in a handful of promising research areas that had benefitted from considerable government funding and development. By the late 2000s, however, the company was struggling to stay afloat, and so its chairman did what had by then become the norm for ailing pharmaceutical companies: he brought in McKinsey.[86] Specifically, he contracted J. Michael Pearson, a veteran of McKinsey's pharmaceuticals division, who immediately set to work slashing spending on R&D, which he viewed as having returns that were too low.

In drug development, the costs of research are often very high because there is so much uncertainty and very few drug candidates make it to market. Since the 1980s, many pharmaceutical companies have slashed spending on internal R&D. In 2017, the industry as a whole was nonetheless spending 25 per cent of net revenues on R&D.[87] Under Pearson's advice, spending on R&D at Valeant quickly fell to just 2 per cent of sales.[88] His new corporate strategy instead involved buying companies that already had a product on the market and raising the prices of those drugs, while slashing spending on operations within those acquisitions, sometimes laying off more than half the workforce in the process.[89] By investing next to nothing in Valeant's core business, Pearson had satisfied shareholders, and in 2008 was brought in permanently as the company's CEO. Under his leadership, Valeant became what is known in business as a 'roll-up' — a company that tries to grow by buying other companies. Valeant acquired more than 100 firms in the space of a few years, and merged with a few others in 'inversion' deals that enabled it to pay very little tax.[90] It acted in many ways like a hedge fund, but with less capital, meaning it had to borrow heavily to keep profit margins growing and became hugely indebted, particularly in the later years of Pearson's tenure.

In public, executives justified their R&D strategy by arguing that it reflected a growing trend in drug development. They argued that 'the majority of innovation [is] coming from outside big industry players', and that 'Big Pharma' was 'primarily sourcing innovation by buying later-stage products driven by biotechs, venture capital, start-ups, foundations, physicians, and academic centers'.[91] While it is true that, since the 1970s, biotech companies had come to play a more prominent role in drug innovation, during this period the efficiency of R&D spending had also declined; the number of new drugs relative to the total amount spent on R&D had plummeted, suggesting those wider industry trends may not be effective. In Valeant's case, the acquired drugs were already developed – according to one university professor, the only scientific research Valeant did was for post-approval trials for the USA's Food and Drug Administration.[92] Pearson viewed the company in terms of its profit margins and its returns to shareholders – of which he was one – rather than as a vehicle for developing new treatments. 'Don't bet on science – bet on management' was reportedly one of his mottos.[93] This approach proved successful in appeasing the company's investors, demonstrating quite damningly how a strategy of maximizing shareholder value is at odds with drug innovation. By 2015, the company's equity market value had soared to around $90 billion.[94]

In the preceding years, McKinsey had been contracted to provide advice on pricing ahead of several of Valeant's portfolio acquisitions, including for the branded drugs Isuprel, which is used to treat arrhythmias, and Nitropress, another life-saving heart medication.

After the acquisitions, Valeant hiked Isuprel's price by 720 per cent, and Nitropress's by 310 per cent.[95] Many other consultancies benefitted from the 'labor-intensive, high-margin' post-merger integration work that came with Pearson's approach.[96]

By then, some dissidents within the consulting industry had voiced concerns about the short-termism of MSV, but Pearson was following a line of thinking that McKinsey had long advocated in its contracts with the pharmaceutical industry. One McKinsey briefing note from 2011 had warned that Big Pharma's level of R&D could become untenable in the eyes of investors, suggesting that companies could shed 'owned commercial, manufacturing, and R&D infrastructure' to remove fixed costs, and instead seek to acquire 'improved capabilities in financial planning, capital allocation, communication, the management of external resources, and market access'.[97] In other words, McKinsey advised pharmaceutical companies to become less like drug developers, and more like financial intermediaries, taking the mantra of maximizing shareholder value to its apotheosis.

As some industry commentators had anticipated, the dearth of in-house R&D capabilities and Pearson's shareholder-oriented price gouging would soon catch up with him. By the time the company's share value started to crash in 2015, Valeant had hiked the prices of sixty-five prescription drugs by a weighted average of 85 per cent – compared to the industry average of 20 per cent.[98] According to *Vanity Fair*, one analyst had concluded that 'in almost every quarter most of its growth in the US had come from price increases', rather than from improvements in treatments.[99]

The demise of the company was triggered in part by the rise to infamy of another pharmaceutical chief executive who was taking Pearson's strategy to its logical extreme. Martin Shkreli was a former hedge fund manager who, in 2015, founded Turing Pharmaceuticals with a view to acquiring drugs that had fallen out of patent, but for which there was no generic version available, and then hiking up the price of that drug. In September of the same year, the *New York Times* reported Turing's decision to increase the price of a sixty-two-year-old anti-parasitic drug overnight from $13.50 to $750 per tablet. In the same article, it mentioned that during the previous month 'two members of Congress investigating generic drug price increases wrote to Valeant Pharmaceuticals' after it increased the prices of Isuprel and Nitropress.[100] Representative Elijah E. Cummings, Ranking Member of the House Committee on Oversight and Government Reform, stated that they 'want to know why Valeant significantly raised the prices of these two vitally important drugs when the only thing that has changed about the drugs is the company that owns them'.[101] The cat was out of the bag: Valeant was forced to admit publicly that it was under investigation by both the House and the Senate for its pricing strategies, and investors started to get spooked.[102] Over the next year, the US Securities and Exchange Commission would also launch an investigation, the share price would plummet by 90 per cent, Pearson would resign, and investors would lose billions.

McKinsey and the other consultancies involved in the Valeant case were not solely responsible for the direction the company took. Valeant and its business model existed within a political and legal infrastructure that facilitated egregious value extraction, part of what the Law Professor Katharina Pistor calls 'the code of capital'.[103] The company's strategy of maximizing shareholder value by price gouging was only possible because the United States does not regulate drug prices. McKinsey's calls to slash R&D spending did not fall on deaf ears and were embraced wholeheartedly by its client – because shareholders are allowed to have short-term interests and suck companies dry without ever creating value through new treatments. But McKinsey nonetheless profited from the extractive direction the company took, and it did not face sanctions or repercussions beyond unfavourable headlines that ultimately have not affected the company's overall growth. In the end, it was patients that paid the price of the strategy it promoted and legitimated.

The influence of the consulting industry, and the role it plays, is inseparable from the broader political economy and ideas about how value is created. The approach taken by former McKinsey consultants epitomizes the offering of consultancies contracting across the economy: that learning, whether organizational or for drug development, can be bought as though off the shelf, rather than developed over time through cumulative resource and knowledge investment. It is an attempt to take shortcuts. It also reveals how in the financialization of many industries, consultancies have served not as passive actors merely mediating between corporate, financial and managerial interests. Rather, they are active agents in the proliferation of ideas and practices of value extraction on a scale never witnessed in history.

8. Colliding Interests: Consultancies and Democracy

In the autumn of 2017, when Hurricane Maria reached the Caribbean, no one anticipated how much devastation would be left in its wake. By the time it retreated from the territory of Puerto Rico, a few days after its arrival on 20 September, entire neighbourhoods had been razed to the ground. When the island's electricity eventually returned, thousands of people would be reported missing. Maria was designated a Category 5 hurricane, and Puerto Rico's official death toll from its destruction would be recorded as 2,975, though other estimates suggest it could be as high as 4,645.[1] The victims included children and healthy adults, but the worst affected groups were those unable to leave their homes or access medical care. Hundreds of thousands more people would be displaced, many of them fleeing to the US mainland. The psychological trauma inflicted on young people who lost homes and family members during the hurricane led one researcher to call them 'The Maria Generation'.[2]

The severity of Hurricane Maria in Puerto Rico was unprecedented. But as other 'increasingly unfamiliar and unpredictable'[3] weather events associated with climate breakdown have demonstrated in recent years, the damage and tragedy of a natural disaster also depends a great deal on the broader infrastructure across the economy and the capabilities of governing bodies. In Puerto Rico, the development of social and economic institutions had been hampered for many decades before Hurricane Maria. And in the final years before the hurricane's arrival, McKinsey had provided external legitimacy for and advice on slashing government spending, retrenching welfare services and privatizing public enterprises. It should not have been surprising that hospitals quickly and tragically reached breaking point, as the hurricane spread across the island.[4]

Puerto Rico became a territory of the United States in 1917, after centuries of colonial domination and war within the Spanish Empire. A local government was established based on the American model. But its economic development has for most of the decades since then not tracked that of the mainland. In the wake of the Second World War, the federal government of the United States in collaboration with local representatives introduced several reforms to the territory with the goal of transforming it from an agriculture-based economy to an industrial powerhouse. The policies introduced at this time, known as 'Operation Bootstrap', were very much in line with reforms being implemented in lower income countries around the world.

Puerto Rico's anticipated transition to a high-income territory of the United States never materialized. And by the 1970s, as a global recession exacerbated the growing economic challenges in the country, the government resorted to a fiscal approach that would cast a long shadow over the island for decades to come. The same law that had made Puerto Rico part of the United States also included the provision that the territory's bonds could be purchased by investors in the other fifty states without them needing to pay tax on the income from interest. This led to soaring demand for the bonds – which the government of Puerto Rico continued to issue, particularly in hard times. By the later decades of the twentieth century, the government was using the money yielded from bond sales to balance its budget.

For many years, although the costs of debt servicing mounted considerably, a federal tax break meant that many technology and service companies moved their operations to the island. But by the mid-2000s, these advantages had all expired – and so had corporate interest in Puerto Rico. Firms fled back to the mainland, leaving citizens with empty office buildings and a dwindling tax base. As jobs dried up, young Puerto Ricans relocated to other states. The population aged, and the proportion needing welfare services swelled. Increasingly, the government was forced to borrow to keep healthcare afloat.

All this came to a head in 2014, when three credit rating agencies downgraded the territory's bonds to 'junk' status – meaning that they became, overnight, close to worthless, as far as investors were concerned. The credit rating agencies believed Puerto Rico no longer had access to the cash needed to meet its debt obligations. In other words, the island's economic crutch had shattered under the weight of its history. Before long, the territory's governors moved to enter what amounted to bankruptcy, defaulting on debt, and effectively transferring responsibility for restructuring future obligations to the federal government. In 2016, President Obama signed into law the Puerto Rico Oversight, Management, and Economic Stability Act – or PROMESA, which means 'promise' in Spanish – that created an Oversight Board to supervise the bankruptcy process. Crucially, it was also tasked with determining a new fiscal blueprint for the territory.

From the outset, Congress's handling of Puerto Rico's latest economic crisis was met with accusations of federal overreach from campaigners and academics. Local activists and journalists, followed later by a dozen members of Congress and the Senate, accused the Oversight Board of treating Puerto Rico like a colony.[5] In its attempts to allay claims of this nature, Congress opted to ensure that the majority of members appointed to the Oversight Board were of Puerto Rican heritage. A report by *New York Magazine* found that the Oversight Board itself also 'decided not to hire a large staff, in part out of a desire, according to several sources, to avoid looking like it was setting up a parallel government'.[6] Instead, it brought in consultants.

Privatizing bankruptcy, avoiding blame

Following a competitive tender, McKinsey was contracted as the Oversight Board's 'Strategic Consultant'.[7] While advisory in principle, in practice this role saw McKinsey consultants at the wheel of various aspects of the economic restructuring process. Journalists on the ground described the interaction between Puerto Ricans and McKinsey consultants as 'a shock – like an emergency airlift from Harvard Business School':

> The senior full-time consultant in Puerto Rico – acting as its 'integrating thought leader' – was a 31-year old graduate of Harvard and the School of Advanced International Studies at Johns Hopkins. A recent graduate of Harvard's Kennedy School of Government was doing 'deep dives' into the education and tourism budgets as well as examining police-department pension projections. A 2016 graduate of Columbia University helmed the 'rightsizing' initiative and assisted with financial calculations to, for example, identify a date when the government 'would run out of funding were it to defer reductions' in personnel costs. The analyst handling hurricane 'damage assessment analysis' was from Yale's class of 2017.[8]

McKinsey's recommendations for Puerto Rico's recovery included a roster of measures to privatize public enterprises, implement 'value-based reforms' across the healthcare system, slash scholarships and employment terms at the University of Puerto Rico, and close down a number of hospitals. It also advised the Oversight Board on 'the proposed repeal of labour laws deemed too protective of workers'.[9] This was an economic reform agenda inspired not by the threat of impending climate disaster or global pandemic, but by notions of productivity that ignore the longer-term consequences of knocking out the public capabilities and infrastructure on which Puerto Ricans rely. The austerity reforms that McKinsey has advocated have been unpopular locally, lending weight to the argument that, often, 'external consultants are used as scapegoats in certain – likely unpopular – reform projects'.[10] In other words, the motivation was not to privatize the process of decision-making. Rather, the use of McKinsey was a means of avoiding blame from the electorate and local politicians critical of the Oversight Board's function. Much as consultancies are wielded by corporate managers for external legitimization in internal conflicts, they can also be used by politicians as a means of sidestepping democratic accountability.

Critics of McKinsey's involvement in Puerto Rico have also identified a potential financial conflict of interest in the company's involvement. In September 2018, a *New York Times* investigation discovered that McKinsey consultants, some of whom had by then been involved in meetings about how much money Puerto Rico's creditors would receive, were set to profit from the very same debt they were helping to restructure. Through a subsidiary, MIO Partners (McKinsey Investment Office Partners), which manages approximately $25 billion of assets for McKinsey employees, alumni and pensioners, McKinsey owned $20 million worth of Puerto Rico's bonds. The bonds were owned through various separately managed accounts and funds attached to MIO Partners, and had been purchased at a low price following the creditors' downgrading of their investment potential in 2014. In buying bonds at a deep discount as the territory was plunged into economic crisis, MIO Partners joined dozens of other intermediaries with assets in what are popularly known as 'vulture funds' – financial actors that 'prey' on distressed debt and then use controversial methods to profit from it. The *New York Times* found that 'if all goes according to plan, McKinsey's hedge fund will more than double its money',[11] arguing the arrangement 'creates a potential conflict of interest between McKinsey's client, which wants to save as much money as possible, and McKinsey itself, which wants to make as much money as possible on the bonds'.[12]

Under normal bankruptcy rules, a potential conflict of interest such as this would need to be declared both in the courts and to the public. But for reasons that are unclear, these disclosure stipulations were left out of PROMESA's legal framework. McKinsey has maintained that its consultants working to restructure Puerto Rico's debt knew nothing about the firm's investments in the country's bonds. But while it may be true that no formal channels of communication exist between these branches of the company, a US Justice Department watchdog stated in 2019 that MIO Partners does not operate as a 'blind trust'.[13] And then, in November 2021, the US Securities and Exchange Commission, which regulates financial markets, fined MIO Partners $18 million, 'alleging that it had inadequate controls to prevent them from misusing inside information they accessed through their consulting work'.[14] It found that the fund was 'investing hundreds of millions of dollars in companies that McKinsey was advising', and that some McKinsey Partners overseeing the investments 'also had access to material nonpublic information as a result of their McKinsey consulting work' about issuers.[15] Puerto Rico was among these clients. Specifically, the SEC found that in January and February 2017, while McKinsey was providing restructuring advice to the Oversight Board, active McKinsey

Partners who had access to material nonpublic information were on the Investment Committee of MIO Partners, overseeing investments including the sale of $1 million worth of Puerto Rican bonds. Until at least June 2017, the fund also invested in the territory's debt via its separately managed accounts and other funds. The SEC concluded that, 'considering the nature of MIO's business, including the Investment Committee's oversight of MIO's investment decisions, the risk of misuse of material nonpublic information was real and significant'.[16] For its part, MIO Partners did not admit or deny these findings, though it accepted a cease-and-desist order, as well as the fine, stating that the two entities are 'operationally separate and follow strict policies to limit information sharing between the two organisations'.[17]

Promises of tight-lipped employees – and the fact that McKinsey's failure to disclose its investments were technically legal under PROMESA – did in any case not allay the concerns of local citizens. In Puerto Rico, the Oversight Board has been nicknamed 'la junta'.[18]

McKinsey is alone in operating an investment fund on behalf of its current Partners and alumni; none of the other Big Four or Big Three have one. In any case, though they are more shocking and headline-grabbing, such potential direct conflicts of interest – where a consultancy stands to profit directly through investments from the choices its clients make – are only the tip of the partiality iceberg. Below the water are various tensions between the interests of consultancies, business clients and governments that are more systemic in nature and raise important questions about the costs for democracy of relying on the consulting industry to deliver core functions in government and business. Conflicts of interest – and the downright undermining of democratically contested standards – can take many forms that are so often overlooked. Tom Peters, the former McKinsey executive who co-authored *In Search of Excellence*, warned against the perils of a consultancy simultaneously providing advice to a company it has investments in. But he did not reflect publicly on why the advice that comes from a consultancy may otherwise be biased – for example, in favour of its other more lucrative clients or markets more generally.

Both sides of the street?

McKinsey has become a go-to in the world of macroeconomic restructuring. In 2021, it was reported that the Italian Ministry of Economy and Finance under the new Prime Minister Mario Draghi had hired McKinsey to help organize Italy's share of the European Union's €730 billion Recovery and Resilience Facility. These funds were launched in February 2021 with the goal of helping member states 'repair the immediate economic and social damage brought about by the coronavirus pandemic'.[19] Italy would be one of the leading recipients, securing around €191.5 billion for investment in transport infrastructure, digitalization, the environment and 'structural reforms to modernize the Italian bureaucracy'.[20] What the economic policies in these areas would entail was left up to the government to develop – though they would need to be signed off by the European Commission. Draghi was given until April 2021 to submit an economic strategy for review in exchange for the funds.

Draghi had been appointed as Prime Minister in February 2021. As President of the European Central Bank from 2011 to 2019, he had overseen the implementation of tough austerity measures in eurozone countries, including Italy and Greece, during the early years of Europe's sovereign debt crisis. He had replaced the left-wing Giuseppe Conte; and the new government argued it was necessary to outsource the development of the recovery plan to

McKinsey because they disagreed with work that had previously been carried out in relation to it during Conte's tenure.[21] A special COVID-19 taskforce established under Conte had also contracted external management consultants.

At just €25,000, the value of McKinsey's contract with Draghi's government was tiny, relative to the scale and scope of the work it would need to carry out. The upfront costs may have been so low because it enabled the government to assign the contract to McKinsey directly, sidestepping normal procurement processes, which would have taken a long time; Italy's procurement code states that for contracts lower than €40,000, there is no need to publish a call for tenders.[22]

From McKinsey's perspective, such contracts might not bring much in terms of upfront money, but taking pro bono or reduced rate contracts 'often turns into further lucrative engagements, either with the institution initially supported or within the field'.[23] In this case, the contracts also endowed McKinsey with unprecedented access to the heart of government.

There are always a variety of approaches a government can adopt during a crisis, with differing distributional implications for the future of its society and economy. The 2008 financial crisis, for example, was met with many different responses by governments, from nationalizing banks to quantitative easing, cuts to public sector spending, and strategies to bolster export-led growth. The combination of policies that a government adopts in its economic agenda creates a particular matrix of 'winners' and 'losers' – those who benefit the most, and those who do not benefit much, or in fact see their living conditions deteriorate. In the United States, for example, research has found that 'the burden of the [2008 financial] crisis fell disproportionately on labour and the poorer segments of society and the power of the labour movement was further eroded, while capital recovered rapidly overall. What is more, some segments of capital were in fact able to gain from the situation.'[24] The economic policy decisions that were taken by the US government and the Federal Reserve had the effect of protecting wealth (capital) above the livelihoods of those that do not derive much or any income from owning wealth. A different set of economic policies that prioritized, for example, job creation over rescuing the investors of failed banks would likely have produced very different distributional effects.

In the case of Puerto Rico, McKinsey's Partners contracted to advise on the economic restructuring were alleged to have benefitted from the advice and information they gleaned via MIO Partners. This was identified as a potential conflict of interest. But across consultancies' work with governments, a systemic conflict of interest also exists. Because most consultancies, including McKinsey, want to secure future contracts from clients in the private sector – which remains a far bigger market than government contracting – there is a disincentive to provide advice that may harm key clients and industries, even if this is the appropriate course of action to achieve the government's goals or for society as a whole. Indeed, having a seat at the table of economic decision-making certainly in government is also likely to be viewed as a potential source of influence – and information – by future clients.

On the one hand, it is ironic that, soon after his appointment, Draghi issued a statement quoting the first Prime Minister of the post-war Italian republic, Alcide De Gasperi: 'The work of renewal will fail . . . if there are not disinterested men ready to toil and sacrifice themselves for the common good.'[25] But in the same way that the managers use consultants to secure external legitimacy, contracting McKinsey has helped to secure support for Draghi's economic recovery plan, both in the European Commission, as well as with the Italian public and national media.

Multilateral organizations are not immune to consultancies' involvement and influence themselves. One researcher has interviewed individuals working both as consultants and in global health policy bodies, where the consulting industry has come to play an increasingly prominent role in recent decades. The advice of consultancies in these organizations ultimately influences how governments collaborate with each other to meet common health challenges, and what strategies are adopted in the public health systems of developing countries. These institutions grew considerably in the wake of the AIDs crisis, as funding from nervous governments in the Global North and Silicon Valley philanthropists, such as Bill and Melinda Gates, increased. Initially, many global health institutions struggled to cope with the influx of cash and the pressure to scale up to deal with new health threats. Like so many other public and private organizations in the mid-2000s, they turned to consultancies – with their offers of pro bono work – for help. Very soon, the consultancies became embedded in the global health organizations.[26]

As far as one of the interviewees was concerned, just choosing for-profit consultancies to advise on health policy decisions constrains the potential outcomes for an organization: 'From the start, you assume that there is a market-based solution.' To exemplify how this might play out in practice, she notes how, following the advice of a consultancy, 'the challenge of medicine pricing is addressed through PPPs or advanced market commitments, rather than by addressing issues related to the patent system, monopoly pricing or other issues'.[27] Much like how shareholder value maximization has been found to shape managerial behaviour within a company, the need to appease existing and potential clientele – in this case, in the extractive pharmaceutical industry – may incentivize consultancies to offer a narrow, market-oriented range of solutions to other clients.

Poachers and gamekeepers

Beyond the potential for political influence when consultancies serve 'both sides of the street' – governments (or international governance organizations) and markets – there is also a risk that consultancies use government knowledge and information in ways that benefit business clients and undermine legislation.

Such cases are usually only revealed later through newspaper investigations or special government inquiries. In the UK, the apparently duplicitous role of the Big Four in developing and then selling insights about new tax rules became the subject of a 2013 inquiry by the parliamentary Public Accounts Committee. The Committee found that Deloitte, Ernst & Young, KPMG and Pricewaterhouse-Coopers had all seconded staff to the Treasury to 'provide tax technical input and commercial experience'. In one complex and contested area of tax law – transfer pricing – there were 'four times as many staff working for the four firms than for HMRC'. Transfer pricing is 'a technique used by multinational corporations to shift profits out of the countries where they operate and into tax havens that involves a multinational selling itself goods and services at an artificially high price'.[28] If the consultancies wanted to shape the rules to a particular end, they were certainly in a good position to do so.[29]

The Public Accounts Committee was however less concerned about the Big Four's ability to influence tax rules through its involvement in drafting legislation than 'by the way that the four firms appear to use their insider knowledge of legislation to sell clients advice on how to use those rules to pay less tax'. Its final report cited the example of KPMG, whose staff had been involved in developing 'controlled foreign company' and 'patent box' rules at the Treasury. Those same employees had then returned to KPMG and produced marketing brochures for potential business clients that highlighted the role they had played in developing the law.[30] Responding to the findings, the Committee's chair, Labour MP Margaret Hodge, declared the actions of the Big Four 'tantamount to a scam', saying they represented a 'ridiculous conflict of interest' and 'poacher turned gamekeeper turned poacher syndrome'. As a former consultant at Price Waterhouse herself, who built a ministerial career under the Blair governments, Hodge was in a better position than most to make this analysis.

Consulting companies do not need to second individuals or even secure contracts with governments to gain knowledge about policy processes and legislative changes that they can then offer to other clients. In some countries, they can simply employ a politician to work for them directly – while that politician is still in office. This can also be an important avenue for influencing future contract decisions.

In many government bodies, including the British House of Commons, the European Parliament and the German Bundestag, there are no rules preventing Members of Parliament from also working for management consulting firms and other companies – and many of them do so.[31] Historically, there have been high-profile instances of alleged conflict of interest resulting from politicians working simultaneously for a consulting company. In 2014, for example, the Conservative MP Stephen Dorrell was accused of conflict of interest for continuing to work as a consultant for KPMG six months before the general election – while the company was preparing a bid for a £1 billion contract from the NHS. His party was in government with the Liberal Democrats. A decade earlier, KPMG was embroiled in another striking case in the UK. The company was involved in government contracts worth more than £12 billion when it transpired that the governing Labour Party was accepting accounting services pro bono from KPMG. To make matters worse, the party's finance director was technically on secondment from the company, which continued to pay his wages. News of this emerged shortly after the Labour leadership refused to review the government's use of PFI, 'despite an overwhelming vote at the party's conference for an investigation into deals which critics argued gave taxpayers poor value for money but made vast sums for private firms'.[32]

It is not inevitable that politicians become captured by private interests – some governments have strict rules to prevent it, and there are many politicians who do not accept income from private sector companies that may create a conflict of interest. Politicians who take on roles with consultancies claim to be able to prevent any interests arising through their consulting work from affecting their political decisions, and vice versa. But the data on this is unambiguous: simultaneously working on behalf of and receiving payment from a third-party company that benefits from information on government policy is very likely to affect the choices a politician makes. One recent analysis using data on MPs in the House of Commons found, for example, that there is a 60 per cent increase in the number of written parliamentary questions that Conservative MPs ask when holding a private sector job. The author concluded:

[T]here is a pattern where MPs who have leading company roles and who work in industries in which information on government policy is more important ask more questions; they ask about details of policies such as plans for and the state of departmental projects; and they do so for ministries that are larger and have greater financial links to the private sector. This targeted pattern in terms of who asks, whom they ask, and what they ask about is more consistent with a scenario in which MPs in private sector positions where information is especially important, consciously or unconsciously, ask more parliamentary questions to elicit information that is potentially useful for their job in the private sector, and thus by extension for the companies they work for.[33]

Why else would consultancies be at such pains to recruit politicians into these jobs in the first place? Indeed, the evidence across countries indicates that, when permitted, 'firms' political connections are associated with improved operation (for example, returns on equity and investment) and stock market performance'.[34] This phenomenon is also present when former consultants move into other areas of the economy. At least, many consultancies believe that people who have previously worked for their company can be a potential source of influence in their new line of work – hence the 'alumni' networks of former employees who go on to become potential clients. In this way, the consulting industry can maintain networks of friendly faces across government, the private sector and NGOs who they can turn to when a contract is out for tender. Beyond these formal networks, the managerial and economic ideas that individuals become accustomed to in their work as management consultants can continue to influence their thinking when they leave the consulting industry.[35] There are many instances of consulting norms and practices spilling into other areas of the economy via former consultants: the CEO of Valeant Pharma, J. Michael Pearson, for example, claimed the company's strategy under his watch was 'basically the education I had through McKinsey'.[36]

It is normal, of course, that people's work experiences influence their future employment behaviour. In the consulting industry, as in many other professional services firms, companies often invest significant money and effort in inculcating a sense of belief in the value of the organization and the identity of the 'consultant' among employees.[37] Indeed, although there are many current and former consultants who are sceptical about the role and practices of their industry, various studies on consultants suggest they perceive their work as overwhelmingly positive, or that when a project fails, the client is to blame.[38] One study found that management consultants in the US public sector believe their ideas are more innovative than those of their civil servant counterparts, for example.[39] The scepticism that consultants encounter from both clients and wider societal narratives may in fact reinforce their sense of identity and value.[40] Relatedly, the intensive and fast-paced nature of consulting work, with sixty-hour weeks sandwiched between drinks with colleagues and hotel stays away to finalize projects, may leave individuals feeling alienated,[41] but it may also paradoxically help to create a feeling of commitment and purpose – even a collective identity – among many consultants that is not common to all types of work.[42] Perhaps because consultants are so often recruited early on in their careers, the norms and practices of the consulting industry are more likely to be formative, shaping workplace behaviour for years to come.

This type of influence is again more challenging to quantify or qualify than the overt conflicts of interest in cases such as McKinsey's investments in Puerto Rico or KPMG's apparent marketing of tax system-undermining information that it gleaned through its work with the UK Treasury. But it nonetheless reveals the considerable and often obscure economic power of the consulting industry.

Hidden capital, minimized taxes

The example of KPMG apparently using its knowledge of tax legislation to assist private sector clients with tax avoidance – or, as it euphemistically put it in its marketing brochure, the 'preparation of defendable expense allocation'[43] – points to how consultancies' work can also undermine democratic rules governing companies. The consulting industry has influenced trends in corporate governance, with consultants securing new contracts with the promise that their novel approaches will best enable shareholders and executives to maximize profits. The consulting industry's means of influencing corporate governance can be at odds with national economic policies, regulatory standards or business norms. Markets do not simply 'exist'; in democracies, they are shaped by governing rules created through political contestation and popular pressure for social protection.[44] Democratic institutions – from electoral systems to trade unions and organized campaigns – have long constrained the extent to which the economy is skewed towards private gain in markets. Nonetheless, market actors throughout the history of capitalism have sought to find ways of subverting standards in the pursuit of profit.

In contemporary advanced economies, taxation is widely viewed not just as a source of government revenue, but as a means of redistributing value in society. In some countries, such as those in Scandinavia, taxation is viewed through the principle of fairness: those who have more, for whatever reason, should share their bounty.

While some large companies recognize the societal importance of paying taxes, many others view them as a cost burden that constrains profits, and seek to minimize the amount they pay, using what is known in business as a 'tax strategy'. Couched in the language of management science, this term in practice refers to activities that enable a company to pay less in taxation than would normally be expected of it through means that may be legal or illegal. Rather confusingly, the correct legal terminology for the former is 'tax avoidance' and the latter is 'tax evasion'. Companies, law firms and accountancies that are found to have committed or assisted with tax evasion are subject to strict penalties.

But there are many ways that companies can minimize the amount of tax they pay that are technically legal – though nonetheless at odds with the principles on which tax rules are based. Often, the lines of legality in tax avoidance are blurred, with even regulators and corporate internal compliance teams finding themselves uncertain about whether a crime has been committed. Tax havens are jurisdictions that levy taxes at a low rate, and usually offer other tax benefits such as credit mechanisms or deductions. They are used by companies to reduce tax liabilities in ways that are both illegal and technically legal. The creation of 'shell companies' registered in these territories is one illegal method; the multinational firm will establish a subsidiary in a tax haven that has no or minimal productive activity, and transfer profits there from a jurisdiction with a higher tax rate. There are, however, various legal ways that companies can use tax havens. As Deloitte itself recognizes in a briefing note on 'Tax Havens and Legitimate Planning', 'one of the most popular ways tax havens is [*sic*] being used by multinationals is for the protection and exploitation of intellectual property'.[45] In these instances, R&D-intensive companies, including many digital technology firms, hold all or some of their intellectual property in subsidiaries registered in tax havens. For these companies, the licensing and sale of intellectual property is an important source of profit, and by 'offshoring' it, the parent company is able to reduce the amount of tax paid on it because licensing fees or foreign sales are only subject to the local tax rate. The Tax Justice Network estimates that between $21 trillion and $32 trillion in financial assets are held in tax havens, and that $427 billion in tax is lost every year to them.[46]

But accounting consultancies in particular have played an even more direct role in the facilitation of 'corporate tax minimization', including in tax havens.[47] Over the past decade, a series of investigations by the International Consortium of Investigative Journalists including the Panama Papers and LuxLeaks have revealed the scale of companies, trusts and foundations connected with tax havens. Probing these revelations further, in 2017 two academics found that the Big Four have offices in forty-three of the fifty-three recognized 'secrecy jurisdictions', with more staff in Luxembourg, the Cayman Islands and Bermuda as a proportion of the total population than any other country.[48] Although the researchers were unable to establish the total revenue that these companies earned through this work, they nonetheless identified that over 80,000 people worked for the four companies across the secrecy jurisdictions where the number of staff employed could be discerned at all. As the researchers pointed out, if the trillions of dollars estimated to be held in tax havens 'is only possible because the apparent depositories for this illicit wealth can secure the local tax and audit services of the Big Four . . . then it follows that [they] are at the heart of the tax haven world'. It follows, in other words, that they are engaged in practices that are not only antithetical to democratic rules governing companies, but also constrain those democracies' access to the resources (taxation) that underpin public sector capacity in services, administration, regulation and innovation.

Arresting development

In their book *On the Trail of Capital Flight from Africa*, the economists Léonce Ndikumana and James K. Boyce unpack the role that global management consulting firms play in capital flight from Africa, which is often done in the attempt to minimize tax payments locally. Drawing on evidence from Angola, South Africa and Côte d'Ivoire, they describe how the 'transnational plunder networks' 'are aided and abetted by enablers', which include consulting firms, along with global banks and financial institutions, auditors and accounting firms, and lawyers for hire. They note how these 'enablers, too, are essential parts of the transnational plunder networks, along with the corporate and government officials they serve, and they share commensurately in the loot'.[49] In the three countries they studied, a total of $487 billion was estimated to have been lost in capital flight over the past four decades – a process in which the role of consultancies and other multinational actors have been systemically critical as enablers and legitimators of their clients' actions.

In few places has the coalescence of corrupt politicians, incapacitated public sectors and consultancies had such dire consequences for economic development, popular disillusionment and democracy as in Angola. Angola is an oil-rich country in southern Africa, facing the Atlantic Ocean to the west and bordering Namibia, Zambia and the Democratic Republic of the Congo. Between 2002 and 2014, following a brutal civil war, the country exported more than half a trillion dollars of oil – a figure that, as the financial journalist Nicholas Shaxson notes in his analysis in the book, could have transformed the lives of the country's population through investments in public infrastructure and services. Instead, much of it ended up in the pockets of the nation's political and business elite via overseas intermediaries and tax havens.[50] Today, Angola remains one of the most unequal countries in the world, with widespread poverty and relatively low literacy.

Capital flight has been disastrous for Angola. It has eroded the tax base that underpins public services and the state bureaucracy, which, in turn, further exacerbates the risks of corruption as the constraining potential of civil servants is undermined. Management consultants from large global firms have served both sides of the street in Angola, enabling capital flight and benefitting from the resultant public sector incapacity and culture of outsourcing, reaping contracts for advice and management that have entrenched the interests of corrupt politicians. They have not driven capital flight, but they have surfed the waves it has created.

Capital flight became particularly egregious in the final years of the dictatorship of José Eduardo dos Santos, with tens of millions of dollars flowing to shell companies of those linked to the regime.[51] Throughout his dictatorship, the state-owned oil and gas company Sonangol had been used as a key vehicle through which to extract wealth. In May 2016, dos Santos appointed his daughter, Isabel, as chairwoman of the company's board in a move that was widely criticized as a last-ditch attempt to maximize revenues and transfer public funds to the dos Santos family network. Once in post, Isabel dos Santos promptly contracted a host of global consulting firms including Boston Consulting Group, McKinsey and PwC to 'restructure' Sonangol.[52] A *New York Times* investigation subsequently revealed that not only had Sonangol also contracted a Maltese company she owned to serve as 'project manager' for the restructuring project, but that the global consulting firms had agreed to be paid by it, rather than by the Angolan government, enabling the obfuscation of value transferred to a shell company linked to dos Santos.[53]

The widespread contracting of consultancies in the Angolan state as a source of legitimation for elite corruption may have 'sapped rather than increased Angola's own technical capacity'. Management consultants have also been contracted as 'extras' in expensive bids to achieve results quickly for genuine tasks: 'the Angolan side of these arrangements seldom seems interested in "concrete, technical learning" or transfer of knowledge . . . For their part, foreigners are in no hurry to [be] making themselves redundant.'[54]

Bargaining against labour

Beyond the laws that constrain how they operate, companies in many countries are also subject to laws to ensure that those working within them are able to do so in safe conditions, are compensated fairly and have the means to organize to improve their terms. In Europe and North America, early labour laws were the result of action by trade unions grappling with dire – and often deadly – conditions in factories during the industrial revolutions of the nineteenth and early twentieth centuries. British trade unions were at the centre of struggles that eventually led to the Factory Act in 1833, which introduced some basic conditions for children working in factories. Today, trade union movements from Bangladesh to Gabon continue to campaign for the abolition of child labour.[55] Later rules, also championed through trade union organizing, sought to go beyond merely providing workers with a basic level of protection from harm, and instead improve their quality of life more generally. Though widely taken as given today in many countries, the two-day weekend via legislation such as the 1938 Fair Labor Standards Act in the United States was in fact only won through extensive campaigning by organized employees. In many countries, a minimum wage was only introduced following widespread strikes demanding it. In 1912, nearly one million miners joined a national strike in the United Kingdom aiming to secure a minimum wage. The strike only ended after thirty-seven days with the passing of the Coal Mines (Minimum Wage) Act, which secured a wage of 6 shillings and 6 pence a day – equal to £25.40 in today's money.

Particularly in their contracts with businesses, consultancies are often enablers and legitimators of executive decisions that undermine the conditions and incomes of workers. We've seen examples of this in the book already – it is an issue that cuts across sectors and the history of consulting. The corporate restructuring processes that consultancies are frequently contracted to advise on often not only deplete capacity, but can also lead to mass job losses, changes in the terms of employment, or wage cuts. During downsizing workers can experience 'emotional exhaustion' as an outcome of the higher levels of job uncertainty and lack of personal control.[56] After downsizing, surviving workers cite adverse changes in working conditions, including higher levels of work demands, lower levels of friendship formation, and supervisor aggression, and it is also adversely associated with an inability to unwind after work and lower job satisfaction.[57]

Labour counsel Damon Silvers has held senior positions within the American trade union movement since the 1990s and also serves as a Visiting Professor of Practice at the UCL Institute for Innovation and Public Purpose, researching labour issues. According to him, the use of management consultants to provide external legitimacy and mitigate potential action by workers for redundancies and job condition changes is far more widespread than is usually recognized in academic literature or the media.[58] Silvers also highlighted how 'cost-cutting' is in many instances achieved by reducing the salaries or wages of those at the lower end of the company hierarchy with the least bargaining power. Even in the absence of collective bargaining agreements, this again can have consequences for the resources underpinning governments, because when employers reduce incomes, there is usually greater demand for publicly provided welfare services.

In 2019, media outlets in the United States reported how, a decade earlier, the United States Postal Service (USPS) had contracted consultants from McKinsey to provide financial advice after posting losses over consecutive years. Included in the raft of proposals drawn up by the team of consultants for slashing operating costs was the suggestion to replace unionized, career employees with non-unionized, non-career employees. Its report described the 'risk' to the USPS of this proposal should the government introduce 'legislation to require provision of full medical benefits to non-career employees' – because, in narrow cost-benefit terms, providing healthcare insurance to non-career employees would increase their cost.[59] The *Huffington Post* reported that 'Another of McKinsey's proposals, to cut costs by establishing public-private partnerships, replaced unionized Postal Service workers with staff at retail stores like Staples.'[60] The National Labor Relations Board subsequently ruled that it had violated the collective bargaining agreement between the American Postal Workers Union and the USPS.[61]

According to a union with 600,000 active and retired members, although proposed changes to contracts and conditions are often developed by consultancies, it can be challenging to pinpoint their involvement, and the assumptions that underpin their proposals can be misleading. In one example involving these union members in the early 2010s, an aerospace manufacturer presented a proposal developed by a large multinational consultancy to freeze the defined benefit pensions for employees at the facility who had been working there for less than 15 years.[62] New hires would also be offered a 401(k) savings plan instead. In recent decades, defined benefit pension schemes, which employers contribute to and guarantee a certain amount of income via annuity at retirement, have been increasingly replaced by 401(k) savings plans in the private sector in the United States, which 'has placed the burden of saving and investing for retirement – and the risk involved – on employees.'[63] At the bargaining table, the aerospace company presented the consultancy's projections suggesting that the 401(k) savings plan would amount to the same value as the existing defined benefits pension scheme over the course of an employee's career. But when the union began to question these estimates, it transpired that the models rested on shaky grounds. For one, it assumed the employee would have a thirty-year career with the company, when in reality new contracts were only for three years. It also did not take into account the high fees associated with 401(k) savings plans. The union 'fought the proposal, but didn't get it off the table. It ended up in a strike. It was pretty long actually, it was rough, and we ended up having to pretty much accept the proposal.'

Company managers have also contracted management consultants directly for advice in collective bargaining agreements and negotiations. Studies from the later decades of the twentieth century 'have suggested that management consultants counsel the use of strategies, including illegal strategies, designed to undermine employees' choice of collective bargaining . . . Anecdotal evidence supports the contention that employer consultants advise strategic implementation even though this would violate the law.'[64] Recently, one legal scholar has made the case for 'more robust regulation to ensure that management consultants are made directly responsible for their actions where the effect of those actions is to cause a violation of employees' rights'. She explores a case where the government of Saskatchewan in Canada contracted an American boutique health consultancy to develop and implement a form of management known as 'Lean' across the province as the public sector looked to reduce spending in the wake of the financial crisis. Although trade union groups were initially supportive of the reform, tensions quickly arose. Consultants were not merely providing 'leadership, strategic alignment, training and the creation of a supportive infrastructure' but were often on the ground 'involved in day-to-day operations'.[65] The New Democratic Party criticized how processes were standardized by the management consultants; a step-by-step guide for making coffee was circulated, for example, and nurses' movements were tracked using a stopwatch. All this suggested that 'consultants had great influence on the [Health] Ministry and were authorized to use systems and methods as they saw fit, and further that they interacted directly with workers, all of which could lead to workplace health and safety and other infringements'.[66] As it stands, however, employment legislation does not recognize this relationship, and so management consultants are not legally responsible for infringements in the way that internal line managers would be.

Democracy dies in the shadow government

Often, when communities find out about the role that consultants have played in the politics of their country, or the restructuring of the company they work for, they are less than pleased. In Puerto Rico, locals have campaigned hard against 'la junta' and the influence of McKinsey in it, which they view as 'just another vulture'[67] among a kettle of extractive multinational companies. In England, the very public involvement of consultancies such as Deloitte in the country's pandemic response has been met with criticism from across civil society, including the British Medical Association, which represents doctors.[68] The American Postal Workers Union successfully fought against the changes McKinsey had proposed to USPS. From Enron to Carillion, and from Valeant Pharma to the Nya Karolinska Solna in Stockholm, former employees have lambasted the role of consulting firms in their organization's undoing. Although very little publicly available data on public opinion about the consulting industry specifically exists, broader polling data on auditing and big business suggests popular views about it are unlikely to be favourable. In 2002, Gallup conducted a poll that found just 3 per cent of American citizens were very confident that the reports provided by an accounting firm following an audit provide an accurate assessment of the corporation's financial situation. For a country famed for its historical aversion to state intervention in the economy, in 2021, only one third of people were satisfied with government regulation of businesses and industries. A 2014 survey found that just 5 per cent of Americans believe that large US companies are doing a 'very good' job of balancing the best interests of the US and its citizens with the best interests of the company.[69]

The consulting industry is very often put to uses that are at odds with the democratic rules that exist to protect the public. But the ubiquity of management consultants in decision-making and operations across the global economy represents a challenge for democracy for an even simpler reason: most people do not know they are there. Today, McKinsey perhaps comes closest among the large consultancies to being a household name. But even then, many whose lives are affected by the company's decisions and actions in government and business haven't heard of it.

The opacity of the consulting industry is nothing new. In 1976, Daniel Guttman and Barry Willner published a book called *The Shadow Government*, which sought to highlight not only the influence of management consultancies and think-tanks in federal government decision-making, but also the fact that this was largely happening without public knowledge. As the scale and scope of contracting to consultancies has increased, it seems transparency has not.

Although there are undoubtedly instances where politicians have employed consultancies with the goal of rolling back the state over time, so often today politicians, civil servants and even managers in business aren't even aware of the consequences of relying on them to deliver core functions. The public's 'visibility of effects'[70] is obfuscated not necessarily because politicians and civil servants try to conceal those effects, but because the individuals overseeing the contract also fail to recognize them. In part, as we saw in the case of

Denmark's gradual loss of IT capabilities through digitalization reforms, this is because of the incremental nature of the 'systemic retrenchment' that results; a loss in state capacity resulting from stunted learning in the public sector occurs slowly when consultancies are contracted over many years.[71]

More generally, this speaks to the wider shortcomings of how consultancies are currently regulated. In the cases explored in this chapter, it has taken expensive government inquiries or newspaper investigations to unearth details of how the companies were influencing and using sensitive legal information. The same level of scrutiny is not mounted against most contracts between public sector bodies and the consulting industry. Indeed, doing so would require an exceptional amount of resources.

As important as they can be for raising awareness among both publics and politicians (it was the *New York Times* that shed light on the scale of MIO Partners' investments in Puerto Rico, for example), post hoc investigations are not a substitute for regulatory bodies. Journalistic investigations will always be necessary, but there is a limit to what newspapers can and are willing to explore – not least because a lot of what happens within government continues to be regarded in the popular imagination as the workings of mundane bureaucracy. The disgrace of Valeant Pharmaceuticals and McKinsey's double dealings in Puerto Rico made for sensational headlines, replete with beguiling baddies and criticism from campaigners. But the backroom contract with an IT consultancy that gradually transfers responsibility for managing a government department's IT networks to a handful of consulting graduates is unlikely to receive the same attention, even if there is a serious conflict of interest.

And in few areas will contracts with the consulting industry have greater consequences for our collective welfare and democratic purposes than in the need to transition to a green economy.

9. Climate Consulting: An Existential Threat?

There are no biographies or history books about Godwin Olu Patrick Obasi. There is no Wikipedia page, no biopic. Just six Tweets mention his name. Beyond a handful of obituaries and commentaries of his professional activities, newspaper archives do not reveal much about his life. But it is in large part thanks to him that people and politicians across the world grasp the ongoing climate breakdown. In 1933, the year that he was born in Ogori, Kogi State, Nigeria, global temperatures were almost two degrees cooler than they are today. The research that Professor Obasi would go on to conduct at universities in North America and Kenya and with the Nigerian Meteorological Service would lead to breakthroughs in our understanding of why the planet is warming and what the role of human activity is in that process.

It was his twenty-year service as Secretary General of the World Meteorological Organization (WMO) that would have the greatest impact. Under his leadership, working with the United Nations Environment Programme, then directed by the Egyptian scientist Mostafa Tolba, the WMO established the Intergovernmental Panel on Climate Change (IPCC) in 1988. Bringing together climate scientists from around the world to review huge quantities of data and existing research, the IPCC published its first report assessing the effects of climate change in 1990. Its authors hoped that with its findings, 'appropriate strategies in response to the issue of climate change can now be firmly based on the scientific foundation that the Report provides'. And that scientific foundation was clear: emissions resulting from human activities were substantially increasing the atmospheric concentrations of greenhouse gases that would 'enhance the greenhouse effect, resulting in additional warming of the earth's surface'. Without a drastic change during the next century, the world would experience a rate of increase in global temperatures that was 'greater than that seen over the past 10,000 years'.[1]

The report did not offer concrete policy recommendations – the objective of the IPCC is not to advise politicians on how to respond to the climate crisis, but to provide governments at all levels with scientific information that they can use to develop climate policies.[2] In various conference proceedings, interviews and articles where he was asked to share his evidence-based expert opinion on the climate crisis, Professor Obasi was nonetheless unequivocal.[3] He knew his role was not to determine the exact actions governments should take, but he did not shy away from emphasizing the scale of systemic efforts that were needed.

In one special issue of the Proceedings of the Indian Academy of Sciences, published in 1993, three years after the first IPCC report, Professor Obasi wrote:

> We have gone beyond the point where sustainable use of the atmosphere as a highly mobile dump for man's waste is possible, without serious consequences . . . Basic changes will be needed if we are to move towards nationally and globally sustainable development. Among others, in the industrially developed countries, there will be a need to evolve economic systems that use resources more sparingly and efficiently, as well as minimizing waste discharge. In developing countries, it will be necessary to ensure socio-economic growth to meet the rising expectations of growing populations and that this takes place in a manner that will minimize resource depletion and environmental stress.[4]

These comments are unsettling not least because they are a reminder of how long we have known about the existential risks of climate breakdown.

In 2018, thirty years after it was founded, the IPCC published its Special Report on Global Warming of 1.5°C. The point at which climate breakdown ceased to be a future likelihood described in numbers and instead became a day-to-day reality for many communities around the world had long passed by the time the report was launched. Rising sea levels, coral death and typhoons have for decades threatened the ability to live on many Pacific islands, for example. In the second half of the twentieth century, entire areas of farmland disappeared under the sea and water salination rendered some staple crops impossible to harvest.[5] In some regions of the world, the frequency and intensity of extreme weather events have increased with growing carbon emissions. Notably, although these consequences are felt disproportionately in the Global South, emissions have been disproportionately produced by countries in the Global North. One recent study using figures dating back to 1850 found that, as of 2015, the USA alone was responsible for 40 per cent of CO_2 emissions in excess of the safe planetary boundary of 350 parts per million of atmospheric CO_2. The most industrialized countries were collectively responsible for 90 per cent of the excess emissions.[6]

Like the organization's first report published in 1990, the 2018 IPCC publication was explicit about the extent of climate breakdown and the role of human activity in that process. Human activity, the report noted, is estimated to have caused approximately 1°C of global warming above pre-industrial levels. Global warming was two to three times higher in the Arctic than the global annual average, and the consequences of anthropogenic emissions to the present will persist for centuries to millennia. The report also described what the likely consequences would be if no action was taken to limit global warming to 1.5°C and temperatures instead rose to 2°C. In the former scenario, extreme heat waves would be experienced by 14 per cent of the world's population at least once every five years; in the latter, that figure would rise to over one third of the planet. Global sea levels would rise higher – and do so faster. With a temperature increase of 1.5°C, many species would become extinct, but three times as many insects (18 per cent), twice as many plants (16 per cent) and twice as many vertebrates (8 per cent) would likely become extinct at 2°C warming. The scientists projected that coral reefs would decline by a further 70–90 per cent at 1.5°C; but at 2°C, they would disappear almost entirely. The reality is that future generations in many parts of the planet will face very uncomfortable and even unliveable conditions if warming is not kept far below 1.5°C. At present, the scientists explained, we are nonetheless a long way from successfully limiting temperature increases even to this level.

But the report also did something unprecedented: it set a deadline for action. And in doing so, it held future politicians and businesses accountable for failing to act now.

The turning point

For the first time in the IPCC's history, the report's authors warned that 'without increased and urgent mitigation ambition in the coming years, leading to a sharp decline in greenhouse gas emissions by 2030, global warming will surpass 1.5°C in the following decades, leading to irreversible loss of the most fragile ecosystems, and crisis after crisis for the most vulnerable people and societies'.[7] In other words, as would be repeated across newspaper headlines and protest placards around the world following the report's publication, 'we have 12 years to limit climate change catastrophe'.[8]

The twelve-year deadline lent weight to the burgeoning global climate movements made up increasingly of Gen Z citizens, anxious not just about the future of an abstract 'humanity', but of the ability of themselves, their children and their grandchildren to live comfortably on the planet. Youth-led campaigns, such as the Rise Up Movement, founded by Vanessa Nakate, and Greta Thunberg's School Strike for Climate, helped others to learn that tinkering around the edges of our planetary boundaries would not be enough. They taught their parents' generation that individual action such as recycling paper and opting for public transport was futile; to limit the excesses of contemporary capitalism's biggest emitters in mining, industrial agriculture and transport, we needed intervention. The next IPCC reports, published in 2021 and 2022, only reinforced their calls, showing that climate change was now 'widespread, rapid, and intensifying'.[9]

Where once environmental issues were confined to the manifestos of green parties, today they are at the forefront of political campaigns across the party spectrum. Opinion polling suggests that more people are becoming increasingly concerned about climate change than ever before. One survey conducted by Pew Research Center in 2020 found that two thirds of US adults think that the federal government should do more on climate, with 60 per cent viewing climate change as 'a major threat to the well-being of the United States'. This was as high a share taking this view as in any Pew Research Center study going back to 2009.[10] A YouGov poll commissioned in October 2021 found that 60 per cent of American adults believe oil and gas companies are 'completely or mostly responsible'.[11] The COVID-19 pandemic has not diverted attention away from the climate crisis. Also in 2021, academics from the

University of Oxford and the United Nations Development Programme conducted the world's largest ever survey on climate
change. It found that 64 per cent of people globally 'believe climate
change is a global emergency, despite the ongoing Covid-19 pandemic'. It also found that those aged under eighteen were 'more
likely to say climate change is an emergency than older people'.[12]

It is safe to say that we are living in unprecedented times – not
just in terms of the extent of climate breakdown, but also popular
concern about it. Demand for radical transformation is high across
populations around the world. A consensus has emerged on the need
to reverse our existential trajectory: the mission is set.[13] No longer
can party leaders and chief executives claim that responsibility for
averting the crisis lies at the feet of those who preceded or came after
them. The 2018 IPCC report made visible not only the effects of
climate change but also the actions of those in power today. It is
precisely because the unprecedented growth in concern for the climate poses a threat to the status quo in our economies that the
consulting industry has become a key actor in the battle for the
future. The consulting industry is riding a new wave – one that rolls
over dying coral reefs and the shores of disappearing islands.

The dawn of climate consulting

Globally, the climate change consulting market is predicted to be
worth more than $8.5 billion by the end of 2028.[14] Consultancies
including KPMG, PwC and McKinsey established environment
advisory arms in the 1990s, but for a long time these remained relatively marginal activities. In the past few years, all the world's largest
consulting firms have established or significantly increased spending
on their sustainability divisions. New service areas such as

adaptation policy, corporate climate risk strategies and the development of metrics for analysing environmental impact have proven to be particularly lucrative: 'Consultancy firms of different hues – management, economic, engineering, and environmental – have all been quick to repurpose existing calculative tools and products to evaluate climate risks and adaptation options.'[15] In the UK, since 2011 more than 10 per cent of UK aid for climate development projects has been channelled through consultancies.[16]

In 2021 alone there were unparalleled investments by consultancies seeking to capture a share of the sustainability boom. In March of that year, BCG expanded its existing Center for Climate Action to become the BCG Center for Climate and Sustainability, with specialist teams joining existing offices around the world. The move came as the company was announced as the official 'Consultancy Partner' of the twenty-sixth 'Conference of Parties' meeting of the United Nations Framework Convention on Climate Change (UNFCCC), also known as COP26, which would be held in Glasgow and hosted by the government of the United Kingdom in November.[17] This was the very first time a UNFCCC meeting had had a formal partnership with a consulting firm, which in itself attests to the deep involvement of consultancies in climate policy today. April 2021 saw the launch of McKinsey Sustainability, an entirely new practice, which aims 'to be the largest private sector catalyst for decarbonization', according to one global managing Partner.[18] One month earlier, McKinsey also acquired the boutique consultancy Vivid Economics, which specializes in economic policy for sustainability topics.[19] PwC recently announced a $12 billion investment in 'recruitment, training, technology and deals designed to capture a booming market for environmental, social and governance advice'.[20] Capgemini launched a 'Sustainable IT' service, offering support to companies looking to reduce their e-waste – outdated hardware and energy lost through digital technologies. (The use of IT in businesses accounts for 4 per cent of the world's total carbon footprint.)[21] In Canada, EY appointed its first ever chief sustainability officer, promoting someone who had previously served as managing Partner of its energy division, serving oil and gas companies.[22] Large consultancies have 'arguably been one of the earliest "winners" from the rapidly emerging and hugely contested domain of climate policy'.[23] Their growth in this area is also giving rise to a new type of consultancy; companies that have historically provided specialist engineering services, such as Arup and AECOM, have reaped huge profits from providing climate adaptation advice.[24]

These figures and developments likely do not even capture the full scale of consultancies' involvement in the climate strategies of both governments and businesses. Beyond the usual reasons for lowballing as a way to secure future contracts, two key features of the climate crisis render it an even safer bet for consultancies in search of future profits. For one, the climate crisis is not going anywhere any time soon. It is not a business fad or a government reform that will be replaced with the next round of restructuring or elections; it is a threat that societies will have to reckon with for as long as humanity exists. It is also not confined to a particular geography or sector; the climate crisis is systemic and affects everything, everywhere. The scale and scope of climate-related challenges that governments and businesses will encounter over coming decades will be unpredictably vast and complex.[25] Because the challenges they face are often shared, organizations within particular sectors or geographies are likely to develop coordinated climate responses. This is true, for example, in development banks, which increasingly provide loans for green infrastructure investments and have sought to ensure that the metrics for evaluating the effectiveness of loans are common across institutions. For consultancies, such approaches create markets with fewer, larger buyers, and are thus a source of fierce competition; a network of banks that adopts a joined-up framework for measuring the environmental impact of its loans is a far more profitable client than a single bank, but securing contracts with these clients before they develop or adopt alternative approaches is key.

Among consultancies large and small, the battle for climate clients has become fierce. Where once environmental considerations were buried within broader 'corporate social responsibility' services, today they are front and centre of consultancies' marketing material. Their websites are replete with beautifully designed free reports on sustainability issues for every sector, from oil and gas to healthcare, and from government to luxury goods. The language that these companies use to describe the climate crisis wouldn't be out of place in a Greenpeace report. Briefing papers have titles such as 'The time for climate action is now'[26] and 'Sustainable finance: it's decision time'.[27] 'We are in the middle of a climate emergency,' says PwC. 'Urgent action is needed to reduce the emissions gap and build resilience to the current and accelerating impacts of climate change.'[28] Every report, every blog post, every pamphlet includes a call to action. BCG urges in one that we 'turn the trajectory of greenhouse gas emissions around to ensure that global warming stays within safe limits'.[29] Elsewhere it calls on companies 'to move aggressively in support of biodiversity'.[30] We are told repeatedly that 'radical transformation'[31] and 'radical bets'[32] are needed – whether to achieve net zero or in the green transition more generally. The implication – and frequently the explicit offering – is that the services of the consulting firm are precisely the 'radical' tool that is needed. Deloitte describes, for example, how 'with our sustainability and climate change consulting services on board, you can be part of a financial revolution that puts the planet first'.[33] There are also 'revolutions' in sustainability,[34] in ESG,[35] in sustainable finance,[36] in 'zero-emission transportation'[37] and in manufacturing.

So, is the consulting industry emerging as a vanguard in our collective mission to save the planet? The marketing narratives would suggest so. A brief look at the history of climate governance, however, suggests something else is at play.

A brief history of (market-driven) climate governance

The publication of the first IPCC report in 1990 was followed by a flurry of other scientific papers attesting to how the carbon-intensive modes of industrialization pursued by rich countries since the nineteenth century had been catastrophic for the planet. But the sectors responsible for the biggest emissions, and the fossil fuel companies that enabled them, showed no intention of slowing down, instead establishing new markets and trading partners around the world, often with the help of public subsidies and other forms of financial support. Consultancies were also ever-present, assisting these clients in their expansion. It was during this period that they began promoting the idea to clients that adopting a sustainability strategy would not only help to stave off the growing pressure from environmental activist groups, but also give clients 'an edge' over competitors. For example, in the wake of campaigns surrounding the disposal of its Brent Spar oil platform that included a consumer boycott, in 1997 Dutch Shell contracted Arthur D. Little along with a boutique environmental consultancy for advice on its sustainable development. In the words of one manager at Shell, the companies were contracted to 'develop tools and performance indicators in order to "identify stakeholders and the risks and opportunities associated with that. How do you report on it and how do you learn from it." '[38] But at the same time that they began to adopt these early sustainability strategies, companies involved in oil and gas exploration, development and production in countries such as the United States became powerful sources of domestic opposition to nationally and internationally binding measures to reduce greenhouse gas emissions.[39] And their emissions grew and grew.

Governments in the Global North did increasingly recognize the need to adopt climate change policies, but the impact of these proved to be wanting. Their policies constituted an approach to climate governance that was fundamentally resistant to systemic change and action by governments, which we define here as 'market-driven climate governance'. Others have described this approach as 'neoliberal', insofar as it 'favors the *least intervention in the decision making of relevant stakeholders*' and 'promotes the development of institutions that provide *a framework for individualized private decision making in responding to climate change* [original italics]'.[40]

Owing to the power of the United States in the global political economy, market-driven climate governance manifested in the response of multilateral institutions. The first IPCC report formed the basis of the UNFCCC in 1995, the first international commitment to combat 'dangerous anthropogenic interferences with the climate system'.[41] From the outset of negotiations on the UNFCCC, the United States under George H.W. Bush successfully challenged the inclusion of legally binding targets and timetables for countries to reduce emissions, advocating instead for countries to develop their own domestic goals and programmes.[42] In the years that followed, countries were free to pursue climate policies that did not harm the profit interests of high-emitting sectors, even if this meant in practice that they also did not reduce emissions significantly – or at all.

During the 1990s and 2000s, the reforms included new financial tools that it was hoped would incentivize good corporate behaviour.

The Kyoto Protocol of 1997 was an international treaty that sought to extend the UNFCCC. In the negotiations, the Clinton administration successfully argued for the inclusion of 'market-based flexibility mechanisms, namely international emissions trading'. In this system, industrialized countries could emit beyond internationally agreed limits by buying 'credits' from other countries that emitted less than their targeted amount of carbon.[43] The resulting birth of global carbon trading created a booming market in carbon credits and related financial instruments across primary and secondary markets that in 2021 were estimated to be worth $277 billion globally,[44] and effectively ensured industrial interests could continue to emit to their shareholders' content. In 2001, the United States ultimately withdrew from the Kyoto Protocol under George W. Bush, citing concerns about its impact on the economy. In his letter to Congress explaining the decision, Bush emphasized his commitment to an approach that limited both international cooperation and government intervention in the United States' response to the climate crisis: 'I am very optimistic that, with the proper focus and working with our friends and allies, we will be able to develop technologies, market incentives, and other creative ways to address global climate change.'[45] In the decade that followed, the only emissions targets adopted by the United States were those developed nationally and determined relative to economic activity, effectively ensuring that actual greenhouse gas intensity would not decrease. One analysis suggested that the target of 18 per cent reduction in emissions relative to economic growth that was adopted through Bush's Climate Change Initiative was in fact 'likely to result in a 32 per cent increase in US greenhouse gas emissions in 2012 compared to the 1990 levels'. The authors also noted that the Climate Change Initiative 'falls considerably short of efforts of the EU, Japan and Canada under the Kyoto Protocol'.[46]

The development of new technologies that reduce demand for fossil fuels and capture emissions will be essential for preventing climate breakdown. But government measures to foster innovation in green technologies during this period were also notably lacking; the dominant assumption was that an eventual demand for reduced emissions would naturally spur private actors to invent climate-friendly technologies – and thus that profit would be the key driver of technological change. Market-driven climate governance instead 'trust[ed] producers to develop new technologies that will incidentally provide a public benefit of a global reduction in greenhouse gas emissions'.[47] Owing to the dominance of this view, governments throughout the 1990s and 2000s for the most part did not introduce economic strategies explicitly to foster the development of green technologies in the private sector. Governments' resistance to shaping green technology markets has resulted in innovation systems in which government is both often the source of demand – the consumer – that procures green technologies, *and* provides the investments necessary for the early-stage development. The failure to recognize this has created huge opportunities for rent extraction, whereby technology companies profit by commercializing knowledge developed through public investments in research; historical data from the past thirty years suggests that key developments in green technological innovation, from renewable energy to transport and the emerging field of carbon sequestration have been driven by public investments and policies.[48] It has also meant that progress in developing carbon-reducing technologies has been far slower than the urgency of the climate crisis demands.

Instead of intervening to constrain the emissions of carbon-intensive industries directly, the United States government adopted – and became a forceful advocate of – self-regulation initiatives. This approach was very much in line with the ideologies shaping government behaviour across industrialized economies at the time. One form of self-regulation that emerged at the turn of the millennium was climate change risk disclosure. Climate change risk disclosure frameworks were developed to encourage companies to report to investors the risks they are facing from both the physical impacts of climate change and the transition to lower emissions. Advocates argue that this is both fairer to existing and potential shareholders, and could also incentivize companies to behave in ways that reduce their exposure to these risks, such as by transitioning their business models to reduce emissions.[49] Publicly traded companies are already mandated by law to provide information about their anticipated material risks. This form of self-regulation emerged 'almost exclusively from within non-elected coalitions of multinationals operating through private, not-for-profit entities'.[50] The Climate Disclosure Standards Board (CDSB), for example, was one of the most prominent advocates and developers of climate change risk disclosure. Established in 2007, the CDSB was a consortium of businesses and environmental NGOs, including some funded by fossil fuel firms, that 'offer[ed] companies a framework for reporting environmental information with the same rigour as financial information'.[51] Board members included a body called the International Emissions Trading Association, which in 2021 was chaired by an executive of global mining giant Rio Tinto.[52] Previous chairs have included a Senior Climate Change Advisor for Shell.[53]

Ultimately, self-regulation, the promise of planet-saving technologies and the creation of new financial incentives have 'held the need for mandatory regulations at bay'.[54] Market-driven climate governance is premised on a belief that the market mechanism can serve as a corrective to climate breakdown. Maintaining this approach has been 'an important part of private sector strategy',[55] insofar as it ensures that companies are not forced to reconfigure operations to reduce emissions in ways that could affect their short-term profits if no other option is viable. In this way, the past thirty years of climate policy have constituted perhaps the greatest experiment in market-driven economics that the world has ever seen.

The 2018, 2021 and 2022 IPCC reports have made abundantly clear that this approach is not working; the planetary impact of human industrial activity has only become worse. The climate battle will only be won when emissions are properly constrained through systemic intervention, including regulation, public investment and market-shaping policies. Despite the huge costs to the planet, many companies whose profits rely on fossil fuel extraction are refusing to curb their emissions. But since 2018, these companies are facing more scrutiny from governments and the public than ever before. This is where the consulting industry comes in.

Manipulating models

Given what we know about the history of the consulting industry – how it benefits from new markets for governance transformations across business and government, in the process also shaping them – and given what we know about the history of climate governance – how certain industries and governments have resisted systemic intervention ever since the first IPCC report in 1990 – it would be naïve to take for granted either demand for genuinely transformative climate advice or the existence of genuinely expert advice as the key drivers of growth across the climate consulting market. There certainly are many companies and governments that want to reduce their climate impact, and there are consultancies that house expertise that is potentially useful for climate action. There are also many, many consultants who would like to use their skills and knowledge in the fight against climate breakdown.

However, governments and businesses may also hire consultancies not to reduce their climate footprint, but to convince others of their *commitment* to mitigating the climate crisis, even if this is not matched with *action*. A number of recent cases and developments lend weight to this hypothesis.

The Australian government's contract with McKinsey to help develop its plan for reaching net zero emissions by 2050 is an important example. Australia is the fourteenth biggest emitter of CO_2 in the world, and has one of the highest total emissions of CO_2 per capita, ahead of the United States, China and Saudi Arabia; key sources of emissions within the country include agriculture, transport and consumer electricity. Although consumption of renewable energy has increased in recent years, 30 per cent of the country's emissions come from coal; a report by the British think-tank Ember launched at COP26 found in fact that Australia has the highest greenhouse gas emissions from coal in the world on a per capita basis.[56] Australia is also one of the world's largest exporters of coal and natural gas; these exports are responsible for roughly three times Australia's annual domestic emissions. In addition, the country produces aluminium for export, which is a significant contributor of carbon dioxide, and is also not included in measures of domestic CO_2 emissions. How Australia responds to the climate crisis will matter for everyone. Australia's actions – or lack thereof – will be consequential for our collective ability to save the planet.

The scale of the country's carbon footprint and the urgency of shrinking it have unfortunately not, however, translated into meaningful action. Political parties and business bodies have long resisted moves to constrain the oil and gas industry, and measures to transition other sectors, such as agriculture, have similarly left much to be desired. In fact, in 2021, there were over 100 oil and gas exploration projects ongoing in the country. In November 2021, the country, under Prime Minister Scott Morrison, was ranked last out of sixty countries and the European Union in the Climate Change Performance Index for its response to the climate crisis.[57] The government has nonetheless been facing some pressure to introduce serious climate mitigation policies from both civil society and scientific groups domestically, as well as multilateral bodies internationally, and in 2021 it contracted McKinsey to help develop the Long-Term Emissions Reduction Plan. The report sets out a strategy for reaching net zero by 2050, using modelling carried out by McKinsey as part of a AUD$6 million contract.

Upon its launch, the report was met with widespread criticism that transcended borders and party lines, as analysts reviewing the models discovered that the government's plan wouldn't achieve the net zero target by 2050 that the government itself has agreed to. The shadow climate change minister described the report as a 'scamphlet on net zero', with the leader of the Greens declaring it 'a recipe for climate collapse in Australia'.[58] According to the modelling, the plan would 'fall 215 metric tons short of reaching only an 85% reduction [in emissions] by 2050'.[59] The remaining 15 per cent reduction in emissions would be achieved through 'further technology breakthroughs' emerging from some unspecified place in the world, at some unspecified point in time before 2050.[60] Although the coal sector would be reduced by 51 per cent, according to the modelling, emissions from the gas industry could be 13 per cent *higher* in 2050 than they are today. A whopping 10–20 per cent of the reduction would come from 'offsets' achieved through a variety of questionable methods, including abatement payments to landowners to incentivize them to manage their soils and plant trees that temporarily store carbon. This is viewed in the report as a cheap form of offsets, because the costs to landowners are far lower than the financial losses that polluting actors would face by directly reducing their emissions, even if doing so would be more effective in the long term.[61] In other words, the economic value that a farmer would lose by not cutting down trees to plant new crops is lower than what a mining company would lose by not producing aluminium. The former is the Australian government's preferred offsetting strategy, even though the latter is far more damaging for the environment. Crucially, the modelling also doesn't account for the physical consequences of climate change,[62] which are likely to be very costly for key industries as well as government-funded infrastructure in Australia. The country has already experienced some of the highest temperature increases linked to climate change in the world.

In January 2022, McKinsey published a report that estimated 'the changes in demand, capital spending, costs, and jobs, to 2050' for high-emitting sectors across sixty-nine countries.[63] Concluding that the transition to net zero by 2050 would cost $275 trillion over thirty years, the report was pessimistic, emphasizing the losses that industries and governments dependent on fossil fuel extraction would experience. But analysts quickly identified problems with the methods consultants had used. For one, the report's most alarming figure – that the countries faced costs of $9.2 trillion per year – did not take the current trajectory as a baseline: 'Business as usual would cost $250 trillion. So based on McKinsey's analysis, the real incremental cost is less than $1 trillion per year in additional investments.'[64] The models that McKinsey used to reach the report's top line figure also assumed no increase in clean energy use, vastly underestimating the growth of solar and wind energy consumption and overestimating the costs of its deployment.

So why did the Australian government recruit McKinsey to help develop its net zero strategy? The company has clearly not been able to do so effectively. Perhaps, then, we have to consider that this was never the government's intention, and that, as others have suggested, McKinsey was instead contracted to create 'the illusion of ambitious climate action',[65] with its models intended 'to lend the plan credibility'.[66] Australia's national science agency CSIRO also applied for the tender to conduct analyses and develop models for the government's net zero strategy. Perhaps it lost out on the tender because it might have been more willing to ruffle feathers among policymakers. One thing is clear: in this case, the consulting industry did not play the role that functional theorists give as the reason for consultancies to exist – unless the function was protecting profits in carbon-intensive industries, and not reducing emissions after all.

Conflicting interests: Running democracy on fumes

Indeed, the writer Ketan Joshi has pointed to another reason why we might doubt whether McKinsey provided advice that was genuinely impartial and aimed first and foremost to help the government achieve net zero by 2050: that many of the consultancy's biggest clients are in the fossil fuel industry.[67] A *New York Times* investigation revealed that in recent years, McKinsey has advised at least forty-three of the hundred biggest polluters, 'including BP, Exxon Mobil, Gazprom and Saudi Aramco, generating hundreds of millions of dollars in fees for the firm'.[68]

In another case that has been the subject of intense scrutiny by both campaigning groups and academics, McKinsey was found to have provided climate advice to the UNFCCC itself that protected the interests of large timber companies and other industrial actors that it had also advised, while promoting measures that harmed the cultural practices of indigenous groups. Globally, 'deforestation and forest degradation account for approximately 11 percent of carbon emissions, more than the entire global transportation sector and second only to the energy sector'.[69] In response to this, during the 2000s, the UNFCCC developed the 'Reducing emissions from deforestation and forest degradation' (REDD) mechanism, which aimed to create a means of offering financial incentives to developing countries to maintain, conserve and manage forests that might otherwise be cut down for profit. Countries that were party to the mechanisms would be able to access funds to compensate groups and businesses for losses incurred by more sustainable uses of forests.

In 2007, the UNFCCC contracted McKinsey to develop a metric for estimating the financial value of maintaining, conserving and managing forests as a source of carbon capture, vis-à-vis other uses of the land, through an extension of REDD known as REDD+. The tool that McKinsey created was based on a Marginal Abatement Curve (MAC), a technique that has long been used by governments to evaluate the cost-effectiveness of different climate strategies.[70] It sought to understand how governments could reduce deforestation for the least cost. Using its MAC tool, McKinsey advocated the reduction of deforestation to be achieved through stopping what is known as 'slash and burn' agriculture by indigenous communities, because this tradition was deemed to create low financial value, and so the communities would require less compensation for the loss of habitats and ways of life.[71] Large timber companies, in contrast, would require higher compensation because the costs of not cutting down forests for them were deemed high. The latter was of course a far greater contributor to deforestation. The approach that McKinsey embedded in the metric it developed for REDD+ and the UNFCCC valued the profits of logging companies far more than the cultural farming practices of indigenous communities, which did not contribute to deforestation on anything like the scale of the logging companies. Crucially, at the time (as environmental groups pointed out), McKinsey's clients included logging companies that operated in the forests of the countries involved in REDD+. The indigenous communities affected most by the mechanism, from Brazil to Bangladesh and Papua New Guinea, were not clients of McKinsey, and did not have direct access to its consultants. In this way, the quantitative tool in which McKinsey embedded its advice once again lent credibility to an approach that protected the interests of lucrative clients. The most effective means of reducing deforestation was not recommended. How impartial was McKinsey's advice?

McKinsey was serving both sides of the street. There was a direct conflict of interest because McKinsey was receiving money from companies that would be affected by the deforestation reduction policies it was helping to develop. In recent years, consultancies large and small have also helped to develop a form of disclosure across powerful industries that have long been significant contributors of CO_2 emissions.

Resisting accountability: The case of ESG

Environmental, social and governance criteria (ESG) are standards that companies can use to demonstrate that their operations do not harm the environment, that they support positive relationships with employees and other communities, and have effective governance structures. Advocates of ESG claim that by encouraging companies to disclose this information, good corporate behaviour is incentivized, because it is rewarded with higher value:[72] 'The pitch that companies should focus on "doing good" is sweetened with the promise that it will also be good for their bottom line and for shareholders.'[73] Depending on the framework the company uses, it will report figures across the three criteria; for example, the number of women employed in senior roles, the amount of electricity its offices use and how many employees cycle to work. Institutional investment funds also increasingly use ESG criteria to make decisions about where to invest.

Demand for corporate ESG frameworks and financial ESG investing metrics has exploded in the past few years. The number of multinational companies that now use ESG when determining executive pay, for example, doubled between 2018 and 2021.[74] The Business Roundtable, a lobbying group made up of the chief executives of large companies in the United States, 'supercharged the ESG movement'[75] following its 2019 meeting, when it endorsed the view that businesses exist to serve stakeholders, and not just shareholders.[76] In February 2021, Bloomberg reported that ESG-designated assets are 'on track to exceed $53 trillion by 2025', representing more than a third of projected total assets under management.[77] Investors with $100 trillion of assets under management have signed on to the United Nations Principles for Responsible Investment, which were 'developed by investors, for investors',[78] and advocate greater use of ESG frameworks in investing.[79]

The consulting industry has been a key supplier of ESG frameworks and related services, advocating their adoption across marketing material. The Big Four, and notably EY, have been particularly vociferous in their efforts to secure ESG clients, owing to the potential for cross-selling ESG services beyond financial reporting advice, such as in executive remuneration.[80] Many smaller sustainability-focused consultancies have also joined the fray, selling frameworks they have developed in-house, or providing advice on how to improve within other frameworks.

Already in 2018, there were over 600 different ESG ratings in play across business.[81] The frameworks on offer 'differ not only in how to measure the various ESG criteria, but also with respect to what criteria are deemed worthy of measurement' in the first place.[82] Despite the proliferation of ESG criteria, however, there is no single definition of 'good' ESG, and the many frameworks in use are not regulated by any single public body. There are different private sector reporting standards for some criteria, including the Sustainability Accounting Standards Board and the Global Reporting Initiative. In 2021, the G7 group of nations and EU central banks endorsed a framework developed by the Task Force on Climate-Related Financial Disclosures (TCFD) to force banks and companies to disclose their exposure to climate-related risks.[83] Members of the Task Force include Partners from Deloitte, EY, PwC and KPMG.[84] In the same year, all of the Big Four, and many other smaller consultancies, launched services offering advice to companies that will be forced to comply with the TCFD framework.

Efforts to standardize corporate ESG metrics have been met with resistance across business. The repudiation of the World Economic Forum's ESG framework among many of its own members is perhaps telling. In January 2020, the Forum launched the 'Stakeholder Capitalism Metrics', a framework using twenty-one ESG metrics that aimed to 'promote alignment among existing ESG frameworks'. Deloitte, EY, KPMG and PwC were all contracted to help 'identify a set of universal, material ESG metrics and recommended disclosures that could be reflected in the mainstream annual reports of companies on a consistent basis across industry sectors and countries'.[85] But by the group's meeting in September 2021, fewer than sixty companies had adopted them.[86] By May 2022, although 150 companies had 'shown their support for the Stakeholder Capitalism Metrics', still only 70 firms had adopted them.[87] The World Economic Forum has a membership of 390 firms, and over 1,000 companies attend the events in-person.

The theory that suggests ESG criteria can incentivize businesses to behave in environmentally and socially responsible ways fundamentally relies on the ability to accurately compare businesses against each other; ESG, according to its advocates, facilitates market competition by providing access to information about accurate estimates of risk that may affect future share value and profitability. If demand for ESG was driven by a widespread commitment to this theory among companies, then there would be much greater support for a universal standard than there has been. Without it, the information that metrics provide is unintelligible, and the whole system flawed. The absence of a universal standard, despite the apparent enthusiasm for ESG, thus suggests other motivations may be at work.

The consequences of this absence are reminiscent of the opinion shopping that client companies were able to do in the years before auditing became standardized. When there are many ESG frameworks to choose from, companies can shop around for the one that best presents the existing practices of the company or at least does not suggest that measures need to be implemented that could undermine other objectives, such as profitability.

But even if universal climate disclosure reporting standards in finance and business were adopted, even if investors and governments could accurately compare information about risks between companies, there remains a critical issue with the information itself – and the ability to accurately quantify it in market terms. Climate risks are 'subject to radical or "Knightian" uncertainty, whereby the probabilities of different outcomes are impossible to calculate. This means sufficient "intellectual capacity" for policy action will potentially never be reached in advance.'[88] In other words, the climate crisis is so complicated that, even if the frameworks are standardized and mandated across business, the methods for assessing criteria are unlikely to provide accurate information about the risks facing companies across different markets. The market conditions necessary for ESG therefore cannot be met, even on its own terms, and are consequently more liable to gaming by participants. Indeed, if the TCFD provides a straightforward and objective measure of climate risk, why do so many consultancies offer related services? Surely there should be no further value to such advice from the perspective of clients.

In August 2021, BlackRock's former sustainable investing chief officer, Tariq Fancy, made headlines after calling ESG frameworks a 'dangerous distraction', stating unequivocally that they do not produce 'any real-world environmental or social impact'. BlackRock is responsible for some of the biggest ESG funds in the world – and has been influential in the TCFD's development – and so Fancy's decision to whistleblow was significant. Crucially, he also highlighted the broader political implications of ESG criteria, arguing that they create 'a giant societal placebo where we think we're making progress even though we're not'. In the end, as he told the *Financial Times*, this 'is going to slow government action'.[89] Viewed from the perspective of business and financial markets, ESG frameworks stave off democratic government intervention by creating the impression that standards are being upheld. By providing these frameworks and advising businesses on how to fulfil their criteria, consultancies large and small play a critical role in stalling meaningful, impactful and accountable responses to the climate crisis – and thus must be recognized as a source of political opposition to our collective interest to transition to a green economy. As one recent study of ESG frameworks concluded, 'when all is said and done, a lot of money will have been spent, a few people (consultants, ESG experts, ESG measurers) will have benefitted, but companies will not be any more socially responsible than they were before ESG was invented'.[90]

Future-proofing: Commitment with action

Since the publication of the first IPCC report in 1990, it has been public knowledge that the climate crisis represents the greatest, most existential challenge of our time. But for thirty years, concerted and collective action to confront it was resisted by governments and businesses who believed that markets driven by profit and share-holder value would provide solutions instead. The IPCC's 2018 Special Report on Global Warming of 1.5°C proved that market-driven climate governance had not worked. In the face of the report's conclusions, and growing popular awareness of them, governments and business actors whose growth depends on the continued extraction and consumption of fossil fuels have doubled down, promising citizens and international observers that they will do better – by enlisting the services of market actors paraded as credible experts: the consulting industry. In championing the consulting industry in this way, scientific evidence and the voices of actual experts who do not have anything like the same backing of resources and power are crowded out. The Professor Obasis of today are ignored. This actively harms the planet – because the longer we wait to develop a system that lives within our planetary means, the worse the impacts of climate breakdown will be.

Climate consulting is a burgeoning source of economic rents. Although it is a relatively new growth area for consultancies, and so research on its impacts and variety is thin, there are many indications that in the era of climate crisis, the consulting industry is playing the same roles it has throughout the history of industrial capitalism. In the climate crisis, big consultancies are riding a new governance wave, and in so doing are providing a veil of *commitment* without the mandate for *action*. Yet today's governments and firms will be the difference between a world where humans are able to live comfortably and equitably, or one where many cannot survive. The next decade will decide the struggles that future generations will face – of extreme temperatures, calamitous weather events, the erosion of land. Many more people will lose the means to farm and provide sustenance. This generation will be the last to experience the historic biodiversity of the planet's land and sea.

The scale of the challenge, and the obfuscating and rent-seeking role the consulting industry has played in it, have even been a source of resistance within one of the biggest consulting companies. Consultants are not known for collective organizing efforts that contradict top company management. But in October 2021, the *New York Times* reported how, in the previous spring, over 1,100 consultants at McKinsey had signed an open letter asking the firm to disclose how much carbon the company's clients emit into the atmosphere.[91]

'The climate crisis is the defining issue of our generation,' they wrote. 'Our positive impact in other realms will mean nothing if we do not act as our clients alter the earth irrevocably.' Responding to the letter, two managing Partners circulated an internal memo, stating that they 'share your view that the climate issue is the defining issue for our planet and all generations', and would host a company-wide 'ask me anything' event on Earth Day. Some signatories were unhappy with this response and resigned, reiterating concerns about clients' emissions.

One of the letter's authors, a consultant who managed contracts related to energy transition and ESG services, published his resignation internally. 'Having looked at the actual hours billed to the world's largest polluters,' he wrote, 'it is very hard to argue today that McKinsey is the "greatest private sector catalyst for decarbonization". It may well be the exact opposite.'[92]

10. Conclusion: A Government That Rows So It Can Steer

Over the past thirty years, market-driven economics has dominated societies around the world. It would be foolish to blame consultancies for all the problems that advanced capitalism has created, from the financialization of our economies and the hollowing out of public organizations, to exacerbating inequality and the climate crisis. The consulting industry has nonetheless simultaneously shaped and benefited from it, surfing the waves of the underlying trends. The huge rents accrued match neither the value of its overall contribution nor the distribution of the risks.

The Big Con is preventing governments and businesses from evolving the capabilities they need to transform our economies for the common good and accelerate the green transition. This is a critical issue for democracy, as well as for innovation – the ability of organizations to respond to the needs and wants of citizens. As we have seen during the pandemic, and as we will see as the climate crisis continues to unfold in the coming years, we need the organizations that make up our economies to do the unprecedented, and take bold steps to mitigate the breakdown of our ways of life.

The Big Con enables decisions to be taken in business that undermine value creation, for example through long-term investments in productive capabilities, and facilitate value extraction. Public sector organizations in particular face challenges in overcoming the Big Con. The financial pressures that result from budget cuts and austerity programmes mean that public sector capacity is often limited. A government official responsible for delivering a new initiative within a short time frame may feel forced to contract an external consultancy that promises value for money and a quick turnaround. Contracting out is rarely the only option, but where it has become a default response to meeting new needs, alternatives are often met with resistance. Visionary calls to invest internally to build up internal capacity over time are viewed as heretical.

Democratically elected governments are the key actors with both the scale of resources and the legitimacy needed to shape economies to solve these large economic and societal problems. Shaping does not mean they must do everything. But they must learn to invest internally, help coordinate other actors and crowd in business investment, taking bold steps at the local, regional and national level to innovate systems and infrastructures, and ultimately achieve democratically mandated programmes.

Innovating from within

Although the UK's National Health Service has in recent decades been subject to increased outsourcing, its early history is a good example of the kind of ambition that must be re-established within governments. The NHS was an organization that evolved and learned in response to changing political and social needs. After the Second World War, millions of young men and women were returning home after a bloody conflict that had torn apart many lives. They wanted security – a safety net – in the new society that they were promised would be built in the ruins. Politicians also realized that economic recovery after the war required a healthy workforce. Healthcare had previously been provided by a patchwork of religious organizations, charities, private physicians and family members. While there had been some improvements in living conditions and life expectancy, progress had been slow. The establishment of the NHS was the cornerstone of the new welfare safety net. But it also made possible the innovation that would lead to key developments in medicine and public health by bringing together a huge workforce with a common mission. With the provision of universal healthcare more people would gain access to and receive medical treatment than ever before.

To achieve this mission, entirely new ways of providing healthcare were needed. Medical professionals had to be trained. Hospitals had to be managed. Administrative systems capable of dealing with population-wide health records had to be established. Radical organizational and public health transformations took place, drawing on the knowledge and experience of public and private actors across society. In the ensuing decades, as most physicians and nurses were now working across the same organization, treatments and techniques could more readily be shared. Important advances in medical research had been made in the UK before the NHS, but the new health system created better ways of monitoring treatments and provided facilities for research on patients being treated. Investigation and diagnostic services improved, leading to key breakthroughs across medicine, from hip replacement surgery to IVF technology and the world's first combined heart, liver and lung transplant.[1]

Today, the role of the NHS in medical breakthroughs is often ignored. The fact that many developments were possible because of the shared learning by medical professionals and administrators working towards a common goal is all but forgotten. Instead, we hear that the welfare states of the twentieth century were sluggish and bureaucratic, that they hindered rather than helped innovation. They were not perfect of course. Communication between parts of the NHS was often slow – and twentieth-century civil servants certainly used a lot of paper (how else could administrators maintain medical records before the proliferation of computers?). But compared to the public sectors of today, where, as one British Conservative politician recently put it, the 'challenging, fulfilling and crunchy issues' are siphoned off for consultants to work on in silos,[2] and where, as a Danish public official noted, digital expertise often 'rests in the minds of a few vendors' and consultants,[3] the organizational thinking that gave us the NHS seems more important than ever.

Meeting today's great challenges of course requires that governments also work in partnership with businesses, but doing so effectively requires that public sector organizations are able to understand their landscape, decide who best to collaborate with, and manage the necessary contracts. None of this is possible without dynamic internal capacity and capabilities. Already in the 1960s, during the Apollo programme, NASA's director of procurement, Ernest Brackett, warned that NASA would lose its intelligence if it kept outsourcing; it would become 'captured by brochuremanship' – to the point that it would not know who to work with or how to write the terms of reference. Public sector organizations around the world have been captured by the Big Con, losing not only capabilities, but also their sense of public purpose and direction, succumbing to the conviction that they can at best fix markets and entering into opaque contracts at scale and scope.

We conclude this book with four proposals for liberating organizations in both the public and private sectors from an over-reliance on the consulting industry and fostering value-creating interactions across the economy. The first two are aimed at governments, addressing the fundamental issue of how public sector organizations can be value creators in the economy, not only fixers, and why this requires rebuilding their internal organizational capabilities. The other proposals are intended to steer the operations of both business and government organizations, addressing how they can ensure that partnerships foster learning and are truly value-creating, and why mandating transparency about consultancies' client interests is critical.

1. A new vision, narrative and remit for the civil service

Rebuilding capabilities in public sector organizations must begin with recognizing government as a value creator in the economy – rather than a wasteful and inefficient value extractor at worst, or a market fixer at best. For this to happen, it must put into place processes and investments that allow it to learn and adapt. This is essential to the development of what one of us has written about and labelled as the 'entrepreneurial state': a network of dynamic public institutions that co-invest along the entire innovation chain, sharing risks in the value-creation process.[4] We would not have the internet or GPS without the risk-taking public institution DARPA (the Defense Advanced Research Projects Agency) in the United States. The same level of public sector investment, creativity and mission-orientation is needed to meet today's social and environmental challenges.[5]

Evidence from the COVID-19 pandemic shows that earlier investments in public organizations often became important sources of capacity and knowledge in the public health response. COVID-19 was not only a health crisis but also a governance crisis, which soon tested the resilience of governing systems and the ability of public sector institutions to adapt, function and innovate in their delivery of public services. In a recent policy paper one of us co-authored with the United Nations Development Programme, we found the pandemic revealed 'core government functions'.[6] These included:

- Adapting and learning in the face of incomplete, at times conflicting, information and radical uncertainty;
- Aligning public services and citizen needs;
- Governing resilient production systems and capabilities to foster symbiotic public-private collaborations and tapping into citizen innovation;
- Capacity to govern data and digital infrastructures, including handling the 'infodemic' while balancing human rights protection; and
- Inter- and intra-governmental learning and coordination (including at different levels of government, e.g. federal and local, inter-ministerial and international).

Even in regions operating under relatively constrained public budgets, from Rwanda to Vietnam and Kerala in India, successful responses to the pandemic at both the local and national level of government so often involved repurposing and reconfiguring systems and knowledge developed through earlier investments in the public sector, whether these were responses to environmental catastrophes or prior health emergencies such as Ebola.[7] In this way, the capacity that is developed when governments don't outsource can 'spill over' as resources for unforeseeable future challenges.

For governments to create value in this way, however, it is also critical that public sector organizations are empowered to take risks. Consultancies are often used by governments (as well as businesses) seeking to avoid blame for failures. Of course, the irony is that even if the reputational damage does land with the consultancy – which it often does not – the financial costs of failure remain the responsibility of the government, as cases from HealthCare.gov to Sweden's Nya Karolinska Solna hospital show. And the greatest cost of outsourcing is that in the end it is much harder to learn from failures when they are the fault of third-party actions – the blame may be outsourced, but so is the learning-by-doing. The broader costs are similarly borne by society; it was UK citizens that ultimately faced the health and economic consequences of the government's decision to outsource to consultancies so much of the early COVID-19 response.

In practical terms, recognizing the state as a value creator – and a risk taker – requires policymakers and the media to evolve the narratives they use when describing the role of the government in the economy. They will be key to creating a new consensus in society that understands the public sector as a critical actor in our economies. Governments *are* producers, too, and to be innovative requires that they take risks – as every successful entrepreneur would also say about innovative companies in the private sector. Public sector managers and organizations should develop tools that enable them to experiment and take risks in ways that foster learning, such as through 'sandboxing' – an approach that supports organizations to test policy programmes within a controlled environment and at a relatively small scale.

A critical reform that follows from recognizing the state as a value creator and risk taker would be to move away from all large-scale prime contracting altogether. Prime contracting is paradoxical because where the costs of failure would be great, risk is transferred to the contracting public sector body in order to incentivize third parties to bid on the tender in the first place. This constitutes an insurmountable contradiction: if the risk of failure remained with the prime contractor, no company would bid for the contract. The only logical response to it, therefore, is to reduce the scale of contracts in order to reduce the potential costs of failure, so that risk is also reduced and can be shared appropriately between the public sector body and its contractor. Mandating that, when a government body does enter into a contract, it is managed internally is also important for helping the public sector to absorb the lessons that invariably emerge from the contracted task.

Eliminating the intermediation by consultancies that prime contracting creates also helps to ensure that governments are able to develop purposeful, direct relationships with businesses, and are able to recognize when that partnership is no longer valuable. The lessons of the Apollo mission are again useful here: public-private contracts were designed with explicit 'no excess profits' clauses and used a fixed-price model with incentives for quality improvement and innovation to prevent the public sector from paying for mediocrity or becoming dependent on a single business (the higher the standards and innovative targets, the more opportunities for innovation from below).[8]

Creating ambitious and strategic visions and building capacity for effective governance cannot be conjured up overnight and is especially a challenge for countries that have ignored investments in long-term capacities. To assist public sector organizations to take up previously outsourced tasks once again, therefore, governments must actively rebuild public sector capabilities.

2. Invest in internal capacity and capability creation

Ensuring that public sector careers attract competent, purpose-oriented and curious individuals is critical. Public sector employees in many countries have neither access to valuable training nor opportunities to develop their skills and knowledge by taking on new challenges. This also has many consequences. If the role of the civil servant is reduced to simply managing contracts with consultants, those keen to add value in the public sector might consider themselves better able to do this in the consulting industry, where salaries are higher. Smart graduates are not only drawn to consulting careers because of the higher salaries, but the fact that consultancies present themselves confidently as value creators; public sector organizations have come to be seen as the opposite. Transforming the role of government to be a successful market shaper, not only a market fixer; a risk taker, not only a de-risker; and a creator of wealth, not only a redistributor, is therefore also important for creating meaningful civil service careers.[9] Providing opportunities for learning through taking on new challenges also helps to retain employees, whether because they see themselves developing a career within the organization, or because they feel valued and empowered to apply new knowledge to new situations in their role. But ultimately, both the development of employees' knowledge and the attractiveness of remaining in an organization are also key for an organization's evolution. Learning is supported – and the capabilities of the government evolve – because existing employees have know-how and longer-term experiences that can be building blocks of innovation.

Digital infrastructure can also be a valuable dimension of public sector capacity. The ability to access data readily and communicate effectively both across departments and with citizens and businesses aids learning because policymakers can more easily respond to changing needs. This was made clear during the COVID-19 pandemic, where reducing infection rates required access to citizen data and trusted channels for communicating with citizens. Around the world, public sector digital infrastructure has been slowly privatized, and its management outsourced through successive e-government and digitalization reforms. This has undermined the value-creating potential of digital infrastructure as a learning resource. To maximize the role that digital infrastructure plays in the evolution of public sector capabilities, therefore, governments can seek to re-establish the in-house IT expertise necessary for managing digital infrastructural and procurement contracts. In 2011, the UK government established a specialist IT unit, Government Digital Service (GDS), that is responsible for both building and maintaining government products and services, and supporting central government departments, devolved administrations and local authorities with specialist digital advice. The success of GDS in building an award-winning public web platform – Gov.uk – inspired similar units around the world, in countries including Canada, the United States and Germany.[10] Notably, it was civil servants involved in the development of the BBC's ground-breaking online streaming platform iPlayer that were able to harness the knowledge they had previously developed within one public organization to meet other needs.

Relatedly, in recent years, several governments have developed public labs, creating safe places to 'sandbox' new instruments and policies and create a more innovative civil service – innovating within government, not only through government. This includes MindLab in Denmark, and Laboratorio de Gobierno in Chile. They have also developed public sector units that provide the functions that management consultancies had come to be used for. In Denmark, for example, the government elected in 2019 recognized that its widespread use of consultancies had undermined capabilities in the public sector. By 2021, it had slashed public sector spending on external management consultants in half, establishing an in-house public sector body responsible for providing data and analysis to government departments that had become reliant on them. Although the empirical evidence on the long-term advantages and challenges of public sector consultancies is limited at the time of writing, there are indications that they may be a useful tool in the protection and rebuilding of core capabilities. Germany's public sector consulting firm, established in 2016, has, for example, been cited as an important factor in the country's relatively low use of the consulting industry in federal, state and local government.

Particularly in public sector organizations operating under a constrained budget, interactions and partnerships with other organizations across the economy may be a key means of evolving public sector capabilities. It may be necessary to contract third parties for services defined clearly in advance to meet capacity demands. In one of its broadest functions, consulting should enable the transfer of knowledge from one organization to another organization as part of a learning process. Across our economies, however, a much narrower definition of consulting reigns, which understands those organizations capable of providing valuable knowledge largely as commercial entities with insights sold as products.

It is critical that we recalibrate the role that the consulting industry plays in our economies, particularly big consultancies, which would invariably result in the scaling down of economic rents that they are able to earn. Those working within these companies can be an important driver of change within them. While large multinational consultancies can create value, in adopting a narrow definition of consulting, we have not only embedded learning processes strictly within market dynamics, but we also don't value or make the most of the knowledge that exists elsewhere across the economy.

Partnerships with research organizations with the explicit goal of sharing knowledge can be important for building public sector capabilities. There are many organizations whose purpose it is to develop knowledge by conducting research in areas that are critical to the functioning of society, whether in health and medicine, the environment or public policy. These include public university departments and the research divisions of charities, trade unions and public sector ministries. While in some countries, public research institutions are key sources of research, such as with DARPA in the United States, their objectives are so often confined to military technology development and commercialization, with no investment in innovation for social uses. Even where public research institutions do exist, they are not widely utilized by government as sources of knowledge. In an economy that values learning and democracy, governments should nonetheless find ways to foster knowledge sharing across all organizations and support a diversity of research institutions that can constitute a source of knowledge for businesses, public sector bodies and other organizations.

Our own academic department, the UCL Institute for Innovation and Public Purpose, for example, hosts a network of 'mission-oriented'[11] public organizations, from public banks to innovation agencies, that learn from each other, sharing the challenges and opportunities that emerge when they move away from market-fixing forms of governance.[12] We are also developing a new curriculum for civil servants, based on the underlying principle of collective value creation and purpose-oriented creative bureaucracies. The skills and tools taught in this programme differ immensely from those underpinned by public choice theory that have long haunted civil servants.[13]

At the level of local and municipal government, where politicians and public managers have in many countries faced increasing budget squeezes since the 1980s, forms of 'progressive procurement' have been developed, such as in Preston in the north of England. Throughout the 2010s, the local authority created a set of rules to ensure that the procurement of goods and services was open, fair and transparent, meaning that citizens could access quality services at a competitive price.[14] Rooted in principles of Community Wealth Building, these approaches recognize that the spending power of local government can be a means to foster dynamic ecosystems of responsible businesses rooted in the community. Proponents of this approach argue that it ensures the wealth that is created through procurement then remains within the community, rather than lining the pockets of shareholders far away. As a result, contracts 'are more likely to support local employment and have a greater tendency to recirculate wealth and surplus locally'.[15] In this kind of partnership, because the contractor is not a rent-seeking multinational consultancy, but a business that depends mutualistically on the prosperity of the community in which it is based, the sharing of knowledge between government and contractor is incentivized, fostering learning and capacity – a much broader definition of 'community wealth'.

Crucially, however, for all types of partnership, whether in business or government, learning cannot be assumed. Rather, to ensure it is achieved, it should be embedded explicitly within contracts and the evaluation of projects, included those delivered in-house.

3. Embed learning – and an end-point – into contract evaluations

In existing contracting processes, value is often viewed in transactional terms: capacity or expertise is provided in exchange for money. But when knowledge-sharing agreements are included in the terms of reference with contractors, procurement and other forms of partnership can also be a source of learning. The self-fulfilling process of weak organizations needing to contract consultants who, in turn, come to rely on those contract relationships must end. That is only possible if learning to become independent is built into capability-building contracts.

Due to the inherently uncertain nature of innovation, it is not always possible to state at the outset what the contractor can learn from procurement, or what new knowledge will emerge from a partnership. How a contract is evaluated can nonetheless both help an organization to identify the lessons learned, and encourage processes of reflection and 'codification' that ensure those lessons become a resource for the future. Rather than evaluating projects using cost-benefit analyses, success can also be understood based on how the organization and ecosystem it exists within benefit *over time* and across multiple parts of the organization and wider economy. The Apollo mission resulted in an enormous amount of 'spillovers' across many technological sectors – from software, to nutrition and camera phones. Evaluation of public programmes should be understood as a dynamic process that requires ongoing and reflexive assessment of whether the system is moving in the right direction via achievement of intermediate milestones and user engagement. A report that one of us co-authored for the BBC proposed that the public value of its television programmes in this way should not only be measured in terms of their direct impact – defined in terms of their immediate scale, audience reach and value for money – but also the indirect impact of contributions that were not immediately visible for individuals, businesses and for society at large.[16] In practical terms this required the BBC to continue reflecting on the impact and lessons learned from various projects at different points in time and across areas.

Governments and businesses could adopt a similar approach for evaluating partnership contracts. Beyond judging simply whether a contract between a municipal government and an environmental consultancy succeeded in developing a strategy for investing in green infrastructure projects locally, the contract evaluation might also assess what employees internally learned from the contracting process. Was that knowledge then applied in subsequent environment-related activities, perhaps even in the implementation of the green infrastructure fund? Did the employees feel more confident or empowered in their roles from the learning process? Key here is whether the consultancy created new local capacity, supporting the public actor to become independent from future consulting needs. For this to happen, the municipal government would, for example, need to recognize gaps in its internal capabilities and bring green infrastructure investment expertise in-house over time. By embedding learning into evaluations, even when it is not clear in the beginning what the 'spillovers' will be, those involved on either side of the contract are forced to consider what the lessons are, and in the process record them in ways that ensure they do become part of the capabilities of the contracting organization.

Big consultancies in particular are nonetheless often influenced by client interests in ways that ultimately inhibit knowledge sharing – or indeed any value creation. Our final proposal therefore redresses the fundamental issue of conflicting interests that undermines not just learning, but also democracy.

4. Mandate transparency and conflicting interests disclosure

Big consultancies are often on both sides of the street – advising, for example, both the leading fossil fuel polluters *and* the government mandated to reduce national emissions, or auditing a large prime contractor while bidding for similar contracts, or writing national tax legislation at the same time as advising clients on how to sidestep it. In democratic societies, it is important for both business and government organizations – and their employees – to know about the conflicting interests another organization has when it enters into a contract with them. This is so that they can be addressed and mitigated – if that is possible. The client may also assess that the risk of a conflicting interest undermining the potential for value creation is so great that it is not worth engaging with a particular organization or group of organizations, even if they appear to be able to provide what is desired. Throughout this book, we have seen many instances where consulting firms are providing advice that is not necessarily in the client's best interest – but happens to benefit other companies they are working for. This is a critical issue in the consulting industry, and any reforms to it will need to confront conflicting interests head on using tools that are appropriate to the specific governance structure or even contract type.

As it stands, there are no rules mandating consulting companies to disclose information about who they work for. Some companies' financial reports describe the amount of revenue that is received within a particular industry, such as pharmaceuticals, or a geographic region, such as North America. But details of particular clients and the nature and value of work that is being carried out are allowed to remain under wraps. Knowledge about conflicting interests is critical for clients seeking to make informed decisions about which company to contract for a service.

Citizens and businesses concerned that politicians and civil servants could abuse public money when contracting have long lobbied for governments to publish information about their contracts with third parties, and many now do this. In the United Kingdom, access to information about contracts during the COVID-19 pandemic has enabled civil society groups and journalists to scrutinize potential relationships between politicians and the company that has been contracted and identify possible 'cronyism'. To fully understand how a consulting firm's clientele might affect the advice it provides, consultancies' contracts should no longer be allowed to operate under a veil of secrecy. In the same way that publicly traded companies are mandated to provide information about their material risks to potential investors via financial reports, companies that provide consulting advice should be mandated to provide clear information about 'conflicting interest' risks to potential clients.

Relatedly, throughout this book we have learned that big consultancies often provide services to governments pro bono or for a fee that is far below market rates because they believe doing so will lead to profitable contracts in the future, whether from the contracting public sector body, or from private sector clients who value the access that working for the government brings. Smaller consultancies are usually unable to lowball in this way, because it essentially entails a huge upfront investment in the salaries of consultants who deliver work the company is not paid for. Fundamentally, this is an issue for democratic accountability, as well as for competition, because when contracts are undervalued to the extent they so often have been in governments like the United Kingdom's over the past decade, it is impossible to assess the influence of consultancies in the public sector. The value of contracts becomes completely disembedded from changes in their scale and scope.

When seeking advice from other organizations, governments should of course try to find the best price for a contract. But rather than turn to the market to determine the lowest bidder, public sector clients should instead calculate an appropriate economic value for the contract in advance, so that it is not possible to factor lowballing into contracting decisions. Ultimately, because there is no such thing as free advice – pro bono contracts usually carry costs for accountability and impartiality in the long term – contracting processes also need to encourage public sector bodies to reject offers of a free lunch.

A government that rows so it can steer

David Osborne and Ted Gaebler's 1992 book *Reinventing Govern-ment*, which influenced the policies of Third Way leaders including Bill Clinton and Tony Blair, offered a vision for how politicians and public sectors could direct the economy to achieve collective needs. It outlined a theory that sought to harness the democratic mecha-nisms of the state and the efficiency-maximizing dynamics of markets. In so doing, it provided a justification for the continued growth in consulting contracts and ultimately the hollowing out of organizations across governments and the wider economy.

But in calling for a government that 'steers more, rows less', it fundamentally failed to recognize how these two functions are related. The less a government rows, the less it learns, the less pro-ductive it becomes: the less it can steer. And when governments cease to deliver a function that still needs to be delivered, they struggle to govern its delivery. This view of government also ignored the shifts in power that emerge when the government stops rowing, and hands over the oars to other actors. In this situation, ultimately, it doesn't matter how much the government yells directions from the cox: if the actors that hold the oars decide they do not want to row, the boat will not go anywhere. If they decide they want to row in a different dir-ection, they can. There are all sorts of reasons why our rowers might decide to stop the boat or change course. Perhaps we are in a race, and they have placed a bet on another team winning. Perhaps they want to join another team, and so are providing them with favours by stalling our own progress. Perhaps they are simply protesting the government's directions and using their rowing power as leverage to change them. Governments, then, need to row so that they can steer the ship as it progresses through inevitably stormy waters.

Around the world, governments, citizens and businesses have begun to recognize the implications of relying on consultancies. From Puerto Rico to Sweden, and the United Kingdom to Australia, politicians and citizens are also organizing to challenge their governments' uses of consultancies where they are contributing to harm. Employees in business and government are becoming frustrated with being reduced to consultancy contract managers and are proposing alternative models of delivery within their organizations. Even within the large, opaque and notoriously hierarchical companies that have for so long dominated the consulting industry, consultants are dissenting, recognizing that the companies they hoped could be a force for good are in fact undermining progress.

But this is only the beginning, and criticizing the current situation alone will achieve little. We must also develop alternatives to the status quo, drawing lessons from successful cases, from Kerala's hospitals to Preston City Council. Learning how to scale up those alternatives is in our interest if we want an economy capable of creating value collectively, with able and purpose-oriented institutions. The challenges we face today demand ambitious responses, from the climate crisis to population health. We can do this if governments, businesses and civil society foster collective intelligence and mutualistic capacity. Only then will our societies begin rowing towards those goals.

Bibliography

Below you can find a list of academic journals, books, journalistic investigations, government reports, policy documents, op-eds and speeches that were referenced in the book. Links to consultancy reports, news articles and website pages are included in the Notes.

Agar, J., *The Government Machine: A Revolutionary History of the Computer*. History of Computing. (Cambridge, MA: MIT Press, 2003).

Agency for Digitisation, 'A Stronger and More Secure Digital Denmark: Digital Strategy 2016–2020' (Copenhagen: Agency for Digitisation, May 2016).

Agency for Digitisation, 'The Digital Path to Future Welfare: EGovernment Strategy 2011–2015' (Copenhagen: Agency for Digitisation, 2011).

Albertson, K. and Stepney, P., '1979 and All That: A 40-Year Reassessment of Margaret Thatcher's Legacy on Her Own Terms', *Cambridge Journal of Economics* 44, no. 2 (19 March 2020), pp. 319–42: https://doi.org/10.1093/cje/bez037

Alderman, L., 'France Hired McKinsey to Help in the Pandemic. Then Came the Questions', *New York Times*, 22 February 2021. Business: https://www.nytimes.com/2021/02/22/business/france-mckinsey-consultants-covid-vaccine.html

Alon-Shenker, P., 'Management Consultants and the Employees of Their Client Organizations: Towards a Model of Employee Protection', *Canadian Labour & Employment Law Journal* 21, no. 1 (4 September 2018), pp. 117–72.

Alvesson, M., 'Managing Consultants: Control and Identity', in T. Clark and M. Kipping (eds), *The Oxford Handbook of Management Consulting* (Oxford, New York: Oxford University Press, 2012).

Alvesson, M. and Sveningsson, S., 'Identity Work in Consultancy Projects: Ambiguity and Distribution of Credit and Blame', in C. N. Candlin and J. Crichton (eds), *Discourses of Deficit*, pp. 159–74. Palgrave Studies in Professional and Organizational Discourse (London: Palgrave Macmillan UK, 2011).

Andrew, J. and Cortese, C., 'Free Market Environmentalism and the Neoliberal Project: The Case of the Climate Disclosure Standards Board', *Critical Perspectives on Accounting*, Thematic issue: Accounting for the Environment, 24, no. 6 (1 September 2013), pp. 397–409: https://doi.org/10.1016/j.cpa.2013.05.010

Assassi, É., 'Un Phénomène Tentaculaire: L'influence Croissante Des Cabinets de Conseil Sur Les Politiques Publiques', Paris: Sénat, 16 March 2022: http://www.senat.fr/rap/r21-578-1/r21-578-11.pdf

Atun, R. A., and McKee, M., 'Is the Private Finance Initiative Dead?', *BMJ* 331, no. 7520 (6 October 2005), pp. 792–93: https://doi.org/10.1136/bmj.331.7520.792

Aucoin, P., 'Administrative Reform in Public Management: Paradigms, Principles, Paradoxes and Pendulums', *Governance* 3, no. 2 (1990), pp. 115–37: https://doi.org/10.1111/j.1468-0491.1990.tb00111.x

Aupperle, K. E., Acar, W. and Booth, D. E., 'An Empirical Critique of *In Search of Excellence*: How Excellent Are the Excellent Companies?', *Journal of Management* 12, no. 4 (1 December 1986), pp. 499–512: https://psycnet.apa.org/record/1987-20512-001

Australian Government, 'Australia's Long-Term Emissions Reduction Plan: Modelling and Analysis', Canberra: Australian Government, November 2021: https://www.industry.gov.au/sites/default/files/November%202021/document/australias-long-term-emissions-reduction-plan-modelling.pdf

Bamforth, N. and Leyland, P., *Accountability in the Contemporary Constitution* (Oxford: Oxford University Press, 2013).

Baraka, C., 'The Failed Promise of Kenya's Smart City', *Rest of World*, 1 June 2021: https://restofworld.org/2021/the-failed-promise-of-kenyas-smart-city/

Becker, M. C. and Zirpoli, F., 'Outsourcing and Competence Hollowing-out: Systems Integrator vs. Knowledge Integrator?', *DRUID Working Papers, Copenhagen Business School* 03–05 (2003): https://ideas.repec.org/p/aal/abbswp/03-05.html

Bergman, S. and Dyfvermark, J., 'Controversial Swedish Hospital Partnership Has Luxembourg Links', *International Consortium of Investigative Journalists* (blog), 30 November 2014: https://www.icij.org/investigations/luxembourg-leaks/controversial-swedish-hospital-partnership-has-luxembourg-links/

Blake, A. M. and Moseley, J. L., 'One Hundred Years after The Principles of Scientific Management: Frederick Taylor's Life and Impact on the Field of Human Performance Technology', *Performance Improvement* 49, no. 4 (2010), pp. 27–34: https://doi.org/10.1002/pfi.20141

Black, E., *IBM and the Holocaust: The Strategic Alliance Between Nazi Germany and America's Most Powerful Corporation* (Washington, DC: Dialog Press, 2012 [2001]).

Bodansky, D., 'The History of the Global Climate Change Regime', *International Relations and Global Climate Change*, 1 January 2001.

Boussebaa, M., Morgan, G. and Sturdy, A., 'Constructing Global Firms? National, Transnational and Neocolonial Effects in International Management Consultancies', *Organization Studies* 33, no. 4 (1 April 2012), pp. 465–86: https://doi.org/10.1177/0170840612443454

Bovaird, T., 'The Ins and Outs of Outsourcing and Insourcing: What Have We Learnt from the Past 30 Years?', *Public Money & Management* 36, no. 1 (2 January 2016), pp. 67–74: https://doi.org/10.1080/09540962.2015.1093298

Bowman, A., Etürk, I., Folkman, P., Froud, J., Haslam, C., Johal, S., Leaver, A., Moran, M., Tsitsianis, N. and Williams, K., *What a Waste: Outsourcing and How It Goes Wrong* (Manchester: Manchester University Press, 2015).

Bowman, J., *Booz, Allen & Hamilton: Seventy Years of Client Service, 1914–1984* (New York: Booz, Allen & Hamilton, 1984).

Boyd, C., 'The Structural Origins of Conflicts of Interest in the Accounting Profession', *Business Ethics Quarterly* 14, no. 3 (July 2004), pp. 377–98: https://doi.org/10.5840/beq200414325

Bradley, J., Gebrekidan, S. and McCann, A., 'Inside the U.K.'s Pandemic Spending: Waste, Negligence and Cronyism', *New York Times*, 17 December 2020: https://www.nytimes.com/interactive/2020/12/17/world/europe/britain-covid-contracts.html

Braun, B., 'From performativity to political economy: index investing, ETFs and asset manager capitalism', *New Political Economy 3*, no. 21 (29 October 2015), pp. 257-273, https://doi.org/10.1080/13563467.2016.1094045

Braun, E. and De Villepin, P., 'How Consultants like McKinsey Took over France', *POLITICO*, 8 February 2021: https://www.politico.eu/article/how-consultants-like-mckinsey-accenture-deloitte-took-over-france-bureaucracy-emmanuel-macron-coronavirus-vaccines/

Brill, S., 'Code Red', *Time*, 10 March 2014.

British Medical Association, 'The Role of Private Outsourcing in the COVID-19 Response', London: British Medical Association, July 2020: https://www.bma.org.uk/media/2885/the-role-of-private-outsourcing-in-the-covid-19-response.pdf

Brookman, J. T., Chang, S. and Rennie, C. G., 'CEO Cash and Stock-Based Compensation Changes, Layoff Decisions, and Shareholder Value', *Financial Review* 42, no. 1 (2007), pp. 99–119: https://doi.org/10.1111/j.1540-6288.2007.00163.x

Brunsson, N. and Olsen, J., *The Reforming Organization* (Bergen: Fagbokforlaget, 1997).

Buissonniere, M., 'D3: Management Consulting Firms in Global Health', in *Global Health Watch: An Alternative World Health Report*, pp. 278–97 (London: Zed Books, 2019).

Buller, A., '"Doing Well by Doing Good"? Examining the Rise of ESG Investing', *Common Wealth*, 20 December 2020: https://www.common-wealth.co.uk/reports/doing-well-by-doing-good-examining-the-rise-of-environmental-social-governance-esg-investing

Burkart, K., 'No McKinsey, It Will Not Cost $9 Trillion per Year to Solve Climate Change', *Climate and Capital Media* (blog), 17 February 2022: https://www.climateandcapitalmedia.com/no-mckinsey-it-will-not-cost-9-trillion-per-year-to-solve-climate-change/

Burkeman, O., 'IBM "dealt directly with Holocaust organisers"', *Guardian*, 29 March 2002. World news: https://www.theguardian.com/world/2002/mar/29/humanities.highereducation

Bush, G. W., 'Text of a Letter From The President to Senators Hagel, Helms, Craig, and Roberts', 13 March 2001: https://georgewbush-whitehouse.archives.gov/news/releases/2001/03/20010314.html

Butler, M. J. R. and Ferlie, E., 'Developing Absorptive Capacity Theory for Public Service Organizations: Emerging UK Empirical Evidence', *British Journal of Management* 31, no. 2 (2020), pp. 344–64: https://doi.org/10.1111/1467-8551.12342

Chenet, H., Ryan-Collins, J. and van Lerven, F., 'Finance, Climate-Change and Radical Uncertainty: Towards a Precautionary Approach to Financial Policy', *Ecological Economics* 183 (1 May 2021): https://doi.org/10.1016/j.ecolecon.2021.106957

Cheng, V., *Case Interview Secrets: A Former McKinsey Interviewer Reveals How to Get Multiple Job Offers in Consulting* (Seattle: Innovation Press, 2012).

Cheung, A. B. L., 'Repositioning the State and the Public Sector Reform Agenda: The Case of Hong Kong', in M. Ramesh, E. Araral and W. Xun (eds), *Reasserting the Public in Public Services: New Public Management Reforms* (New York: Routledge, 2010).

Cheung, A. B. L., 'The Politics of New Public Management: Some Experience from Reforms in East Asia', in K. McLaughlin, S. P. Osborne and E. Ferlie, *New Public Management: Current Trends and Forecasts* (London: Routledge, 2001).

Chong, K., *Best Practice Management Consulting and the Ethics of Financialization in China* (Durham, North Carolina: Duke University Press, 2018)

Christensen, K., Doblhammer, G., Rau, R., and Vaupel, J. W., 'Ageing Populations: The Challenges Ahead', *Lancet* 374, no. 9696 (3 October 2009), pp. 1196–208: https://doi.org/10.1016/S0140-6736(09)61460-4

Christophers, B., *Rentier Capitalism: Who Owns the Economy, and Who Pays for It?* (London: Verso Books, 2020).

Clark, T., *Critical Consulting: New Perspectives on the Management Advice Industry* (Malden, MA: John Wiley & Sons, 2001).

Clark, T. and Salaman, G., 'Telling Tales: Management Gurus' Narratives and the Construction of Managerial Identity', *Journal of Management Studies* 35, no. 2 (1998), pp. 137–61: https://doi.org/10.1111/1467-6486.00088

Cohen, W. M. and Levinthal, D. A., 'Absorptive Capacity: A New Perspective on Learning and Innovation', *Administrative Science Quarterly* 35, no. 1 (1990), pp. 128–52: https://doi.org/10.2307/2393553

Collington, R., 'Disrupting the Welfare State? Digitalisation and the Retrenchment of Public Sector Capacity', *New Political Economy* 27, no. 2 (2022), pp. 312–28: https://doi.org/10.1080/13563467.2021.1952559

Collington, R., 'Digital Public Assets: Rethinking value, access, control and ownership of public sector data', *Common Wealth*, 1 November 2019: https://www.common-wealth.co.uk/reports/digital-public-assets-rethinking-value-access-and-control-of-public-sector-data-in-the-platform-age

Collins, M. and Needell, A., NASM Oral History Project: Glennan #5. Tape recording, 29 May 1987: https://airandspace.si.edu/research/projects/oral-histories/TRANSCPT/GLENNAN5.HTM

Congressional Budget Office, 'Research and Development in the Pharmaceutical Industry', Washington, DC: Congressional Budget Office, April 2021: https://www.cbo.gov/publication/57126

Contracts Finder, 'Support to Health Research Authority: Research Review Programme – Contracts Finder', GOV.UK, 2021: https://www.contractsfinder.service.gov.uk/Notice/d08e4df0-9670-4dab-866f-fd1ce541fe96

Cordelli, C., *The Privatized State* (Princeton, NJ: Princeton University Press, 2020).

Cornell, B. and Damodaran, A., 'Valuing ESG: Doing Good or Sounding Good?', NYU Stern School of Business, 20 March 2020: https://doi.org/10.2139/ssrn.3557432

Costas, J. and Fleming, P., 'Beyond Dis-Identification: Towards a Theory of Self-Alienation in Contemporary Organizations', *Human Relations* 62, no. 3 (2009), pp. 353–78.

Craig, D. and Brooks, R., *Plundering the Public Sector: How New Labour Are Letting Consultants Run off with £70 Billion of Our Money* (London: Constable, 2006).

Crouch, C., '9. The Paradoxes of Privatisation and Public Service Outsourcing', *The Political Quarterly*, Rethinking Capitalism, 86, no. S1 (2015), pp. 156–71: https://doi.org/10.1111/1467-923X.12238

Dannin, E. and Singh, G., 'Collective Bargaining: Theory, Data and a Plan for Future Research', SSRN Scholarly Paper. Rochester, NY: Social Science Research Network, 15 September 2005: https://doi.org/10.2139/ssrn.805144

David, R. J., 'Institutional Change and the Growth of Strategy Consulting in the United States', in M. Kipping and T. Clark (eds), *The Oxford Handbook of Management Consulting* (Oxford, New York: Oxford University Press, 2012): https://doi.org/10.1093/oxfordhb/9780199235049.013.0004

Den Digitale Taskforce, 'På Vej Mod Digital Forvalting: Vision Og Strategi for Den Offentlige Sektor', Copenhagen: Regeringen, January 2002.

Den Digitale Taskforce, 'Strategi for Digital Forvaltning 2004–06', Copenhagen: Den Digitale Taskforce, 2004.

Den Digitale Taskforce, 'Strategi for Digitalisering Af Den Offentlige Sektor 2007–2010', Copenhagen: Den Digitale Taskforce, June 2007.

Denton, H. and Kail, M.-F., 'Nigeria and the World Bank: Learning from the Past, Looking to the Future', Washington, DC: The World Bank, 1995: https://documents1.worldbank.org/curated/en/235001468775775060/pdf/37328.pdf

Dosi, G., Nelson, R. R. and Winter, S. G., 'Introduction', in *The Nature and Dynamics of Organizational Capabilities* (Oxford: Oxford University Press, 2001): https://oxford.universitypressscholarship.com/view/10.1093/0199248540.001.0001/acprof-9780199248544

Drucker, P. F., 'Why Management Consultants', in M. Zimet and R. G. Greenwood (eds), *The Evolving Science of Management*, pp. 475–78 (New York: American Management Associations, 1979).

Drum, B., 'Privatization in Africa', *The Columbia Journal of World Business* 28, no. 1 (1 March 1993), pp. 144–9: https://doi.org/10.1016/0022-5428(93)90060-3

Dufour, M. and Orhangazi, Ö., 'Growth and Distribution after the 2007–2008 US Financial Crisis: Who Shouldered the Burden of the Crisis?', *Review of Keynesian Economics* 4, no. 2 (1 April 2016), pp. 151–74: https://doi.org/10.4337/roke.2016.02.02

Dunleavy, P. and Hood, C., 'From Old Public Administration to New Public Management', *Public Money & Management* 14, no. 3 (1 July 1994), pp. 9–16: https://doi.org/10.1080/09540969409387823

Dunleavy, P., Margetts, H., Bastow, S. and Tinkler, J., *Digital Era Governance: IT Corporations, the State, and E-Government* (Oxford: Oxford University Press,

2006): http://www.oxfordscholarship.com/view/10.1093/acprof:oso/9780199296194.001.0001/acprof-9780199296194

Dunleavy, P. and Margetts, H. Z., 'The Second Wave of Digital Era Governance', SSRN Scholarly Paper. Rochester, NY: Social Science Research Network, 2010: https://papers.ssrn.com/abstract=1643850

Ejersbo, N. and Greve, C., 'Digital Era Governance Reform and Accountability: The Case of Denmark', in T. Christensen and P Lægreid (eds), *The Routledge Handbook to Accountability and Welfare State Reforms* (London: Routledge, 2016).

Eurodad, 'History RePPPeated: How Public Private Partnerships Are Failing', Brussels: Eurodad, September 2018: https://www.eurodad.org/historyrepppeated

Finansministeriet, 'Et Solidt It-Fundament: Strategi for It-Styring i Staten', Copenhagen: Finansministeriet, 2017: https://digst.dk/media/21080/et-solidt-itfundament-strategi-for-itstyring-i-staten-9-12-19.pdf

Fincham, R., 'The Client in the Client–Consultant Relation', in M. Kipping and T. Clark (eds), *The Oxford Handbook of Management Consulting* (Oxford, New York: Oxford University Press, 2012): https://doi.org/10.1093/oxfordhb/9780199235049.013.0004

Finn, D., 'Contracting out Welfare to Work in the USA: Delivery Lessons', Corporate Document Services, Portsmouth: Department for Work and Pensions, 2007: https://pure.port.ac.uk/ws/portalfiles/portal/121182/10.PDF

Fish, A. J. M., Kim, D. H. and Venkatraman, S., 'The ESG Sacrifice', *Cornell University, Working Paper*, 17 November 2019: https://doi.org/10.2139/ssrn.3488475

Fisher, S. Reynolds and White, M. A., 'Downsizing in a Learning Organization: Are There Hidden Costs?', *The Academy of Management Review* 25, no. 1 (2000), pp. 244–51: https://doi.org/10.2307/259273

Foray, D., Mowery, D. C. and Nelson, R. R., 'Public R&D and Social Challenges: What Lessons from Mission R&D Programs?', *Research Policy*, The need for a new generation of policy instruments to respond to the Grand Challenges, 41, no. 10 (1 December 2012), pp. 1697–702: https://doi.org/10.1016/j.respol.2012.07.011

Forsythe, M. and Bogdanich, W., 'At McKinsey, Widespread Furor Over Work With Planet's Biggest Polluters', *New York Times*, 27 October 2021. Business: https://www.nytimes.com/2021/10/27/business/mckinsey-climate-change.html

Forsythe, M., Bogdanich, W. and Hickey, B., 'As McKinsey Sells Advice, Its Hedge Fund May Have a Stake in the Outcome', *New York Times*, 19 February 2019. Business: https://www.nytimes.com/2019/02/19/business/mckinsey-hedge-fund.html

Forsythe, M., Gurney, K., Alecci, S. and Hallman, B., 'How U.S. Firms Helped Africa's Richest Woman Exploit Her Country's Wealth', *New York Times*, 19 January 2020. World: https://www.nytimes.com/2020/01/19/world/africa/isabel-dos-santos-angola.html

Friedman, M., 'The Social Responsibility of Business Is to Increase Its Profits', in W. Ch Zimmerli, M. Holzinger and K. Richter (eds), *Corporate Ethics and Corporate Governance*, pp. 173–8 (Berlin, Heidelberg: Springer Berlin Heidelberg, 2007): https://doi.org/10.1007/978-3-540-70818-6_14

Frone, M. R. and Blais, A.-R., 'Organizational Downsizing, Work Conditions, and Employee Outcomes: Identifying Targets for Workplace Intervention among Survivors', *International Journal of Environmental Research and Public Health* 17, no. 3 (22 January 2020): https://doi.org/10.3390/ijerph17030719

Froud, J., 'The Private Finance Initiative: Risk, Uncertainty and the State', *Accounting, Organizations and Society* 28, no. 6 (1 August 2003), pp. 567–89: https://doi.org/10.1016/S0361-3682(02)00011-9

Fukuyama, F., *The End of History and the Last Man* (London: Penguin, 2020 [1992]).

Gapper, J., 'McKinsey's Fingerprints Are All over Valeant', *Financial Times*, 23 March 2016: https://www.ft.com/content/0bb37fd2-ef63-11e5-aff5-19b4e253664a

Gellman, B. and Poitras, L., 'U.S., British Intelligence Mining Data from Nine U.S. Internet Companies in Broad Secret Program', *Washington Post*, 7 June 2013. Investigations: https://www.washingtonpost.com/investigations/us-intelligence-mining-data-from-nine-us-internet-companies-in-broad-secret-program/2013/06/06/3a0coda8-cebf-11e2-8845-d970ccb04497_story.html

Geys, B. and Mause, K., 'Moonlighting Politicians: A Survey and Research Agenda', *The Journal of Legislative Studies* 19, no. 1 (1 March 2013), pp. 76–97: https://doi.org/10.1080/13572334.2013.737158

Giddens, A., *Beyond Left and Right: The Future of Radical Politics* (Stanford: Stanford University Press, 1994).

Glassman, C. A., 'SEC Speech: SEC Initiatives Under the Sarbanes-Oxley Act of 2002 (C. Glassman)', presented at the College of Business and Economics, California, Fullerton, CA, 28 January 2003: sec.gov/news/speech/spch012803cag.htm

Golshan, T., 'Pete Buttigieg Was Part of McKinsey Team That Pushed Postal Service Privatization', *HuffPost*, 13 December 2019. Politics: https://www.huffpost.com/entry/pete-buttigieg-mckinsey-postal-service_n_5df3dca0e4b0ae01a1e00863

Gore, A., 'From Red Tape to Results: Creating a Government That Works Better and Costs Less – Report of the National Performance Review', 7 September 1993: https://files.eric.ed.gov/fulltext/ED384294.pdf

Government Offices of Sweden, 'Future Challenges for Sweden: Final Report of the Commission on the Future of Sweden', Stockholm, 2013: https://www.regeringen.se/contentassets/389793d478de411fbc83d8f512cb5013/future-challenges-for-sweden--final-report-of-the-commission-on-the-future-of-sweden

Grantham Research Institute on Climate Change and the Environment, 'What Is Climate Change Risk Disclosure?', *Grantham Research Institute on Climate Change and the Environment* (blog), 26 February 2018: https://www.lse.ac.uk/granthaminstitute/explainers/climate-change-risk-disclosure/

Greenwald, G., 'NSA Collecting Phone Records of Millions of Verizon Customers Daily', *Guardian*, 6 June 2013. US news: https://www.theguardian.com/world/2013/jun/06/nsa-phone-records-verizon-court-order

Greenwood, R. and Empson, L., 'The Professional Partnership: Relic or Exemplary Form of Governance?', *Organization Studies* 24, no. 6 (1 July 2003), pp. 909–33: https://doi.org/10.1177/0170840603024006005

Gross, A., Poor, J. and Roberson, M. T., 'Management Consulting in Central Europe', *Consulting to Management* 15, no. 1 (March 2004), pp. 33–8.

Hargadon, A. B., 'Firms as Knowledge Brokers: Lessons in Pursuing Continuous Innovation', *California Management Review* 40, no. 3 (1 April 1998), pp. 209–27: https://doi.org/10.2307/41165951

Harvey, D., *A Brief History of Neoliberalism* (Oxford: Oxford University Press, 2007).

Harvey, G., Walshe, K. and Jas, P., 'Absorptive Capacity: How Organisations Assimilate and Apply Knowledge to Improve Performance', in G. Harvey, K. Walshe and P. Jas (eds), *Connecting Knowledge and Performance in Public Services: From Knowing to Doing*, pp. 226–50 (Cambridge: Cambridge University Press, 2010): https://doi.org/10.1017/CBO9780511762000.012

Heusinkveld, S., *The Management Idea Factory: Innovation and Commodification in Management Consulting* (New York: Routledge, 2013).

Heusinkveld, S. and Benders, J., 'Consultants and Organization Concepts', in M. Kipping and T. Clark (eds), *The Oxford Handbook of Management Consulting* (Oxford, New York: Oxford University Press, 2012): https://doi.org/10.1093/oxfordhb/9780199235049.013.0005

Hickel, J., 'Quantifying National Responsibility for Climate Breakdown: An Equality-Based Attribution Approach for Carbon Dioxide Emissions in Excess of the

Planetary Boundary', *The Lancet Planetary Health* 4, no. 9 (1 September 2020), e399–404: https://doi.org/10.1016/S2542-5196(20)30196-0

Hicks, M., *Programmed Inequality: How Britain Discarded Women Technologists and Lost Its Edge in Computing* (Cambridge, MA: MIT Press, 2017).

Higdon, H., *The Business Healers* (New York: Random House, 1970).

Hodge, G. and Bowman, D., '6. The "Consultocracy": The Business of Reforming Government', in G. Hodge (ed.), *Privatization and Market Development* (Cheltenham: Edward Elgar Publishing, 2006).

Holmstrom, B. and Kaplan, S. N., 'Corporate Governance and Merger Activity in the United States: Making Sense of the 1980s and 1990s', *The Journal of Economic Perspectives* 15, no. 2 (2001), pp. 121–44.

Homburg, C. and Stebel, P., 'Determinants of Contract Terms for Professional Services', *Management Accounting Research* 20, no. 2 (1 June 2009), pp. 129–45: https://doi.org/10.1016/j.mar.2008.10.001

Homburg, V., Pollitt, C. and van Thiel, S., 'Introduction', in C. Pollitt, S. van Thiel and V. Homburg, *New Public Management in Europe: Adaptation and Alternatives*, 1–9 (London: Palgrave Macmillan UK, 2007): https://doi.org/10.1057/9780230625365_1

Hood, C. and Jackson, M., *Administrative Argument* (Dartmouth, NH: Dartmouth Publishing Company, 1991).

Horrocks, I., ' "Experts" and E-Government', *Information, Communication & Society* 12, no. 1 (1 February 2009), pp. 110–27: https://doi.org/10.1080/13691180802109030

Houghton, J. T., Jenkins, G. J. and Ephraums, J. J. (eds), *Climate Change: The IPCC Scientific Assessment* (Cambridge: Cambridge University Press, 1990).

House of Commons Committee of Public Accounts, 'Test and Trace Update: Twenty-Third Report of Session 2021–22', London: House of Commons, 21 October 2021. 12 June 2022: https://publications.parliament.uk/pa/cm5802/cmselect/cmpubacc/182/report.html

Hoxie, R. F., *Scientific Management and Labor* (New York, London: D. Appleton and Company, 1915): http://archive.org/details/scientificmanage00hoxi

Hugh-Jones, D., 'Why Do Crises Go to Waste? Fiscal Austerity and Public Service Reform', *Public Choice* 158 (2014), pp. 209–20: https://doi.org/10.1007/s11127-012-0002-5

Iacobucci, G., 'Covid-19: One in Five Government Contracts Had Signs of Possible Corruption, Report Finds', *BMJ* 373 (23 April 2021), n1072: https://doi.org/10.1136/bmj.n1072

Innes, A., 'The Limits of Institutional Convergence: Why Public Sector Outsourcing Is Less Efficient than Soviet Enterprise Planning', *Review of International Political*

Economy 28, no. 6 (2021), pp. 1705–28: https://doi.org/10.1080/09692290.2020. 1786434

Institute for Government, 'Government Procurement: The Scale and Nature of Contracting in the UK', London: Institute for Government, 2018.

International Labour Office, 'The Effective Abolition of Child Labour', Geneva: ILO, 2022: https://www.ilo.org/public/english/standards/relm/gb/docs/gb280/pdf/gb-3-2-abol.pdf

IPCC, 'AR6 Climate Change 2022: Impacts, Adaptation and Vulnerability', Geneva: IPCC, 4 April 2022: https://www.ipcc.ch/report/sixth-assessment-report-working-group-ii/

IPCC, 'Climate Change Widespread, Rapid, and Intensifying', 9 August 2021: https://www.ipcc.ch/2021/08/09/ar6-wg1-20210809-pr/

IPCC, 'Global Warming of 1.5°C. An IPCC Special Report on the Impacts of Global Warming of 1.5°C above Pre-Industrial Levels and Related Global Greenhouse Gas Emission Pathways, in the Context of Strengthening the Global Response to the Threat of Climate Change, Sustainable Development, and Efforts to Eradicate Poverty', Intergovernmental Panel on Climate Change, 2018: https://www.ipcc.ch/site/assets/uploads/sites/2/2019/06/SR15_Full_Report_High_Res.pdf

Jæger, B. and Löfgren, K., 'The History of the Future: Changes in Danish e-Government Strategies 1994–2010', *Information Polity* 15, no. 4 (1 January 2010), pp. 253–69: https://doi.org/10.3233/IP-2010-0217

Jain, S. H., Powers, B. W. and Sanghavi, D., 'Big Plans, Poor Execution: The Importance of Governmental Managerial Innovation to Health Care Reform', *Journal of General Internal Medicine* 30, no. 4 (April 2015), pp. 395–7: https://doi.org/10.1007/s11606-014-3083-7

Jensen, M. C., 'Agency Costs of Free Cash Flow, Corporate Finance, and Takeovers', *The American Economic Review* 76, no. 2 (1986), pp. 323–9.

Johnston, D. Cay, 'Enron Avoided Income Taxes In 4 of 5 Years', *New York Times, Late Edition (East Coast)*, 17 January 2002: https://www.nytimes.com/2002/01/17/business/enron-s-collapse-the-havens-enron-avoided-income-taxes-in-4-of-5-years.html

Joshi, K., 'Scott Morrison's Net Zero Modelling Reveals a Slow, Lazy and Shockingly Irresponsible Approach to "Climate Action"', *Guardian*, 12 November 2021. Environment: https://www.theguardian.com/environment/2021/nov/13/scott-morrisons-net-zero-modelling-reveals-a-slow-lazy-and-shockingly-irresponsible-approach-to-climate-action

Jupe, R. and Funnell, W., 'Neoliberalism, Consultants and the Privatisation of Public Policy Formulation: The Case of Britain's Rail Industry', *Critical Perspectives on Accounting* 29 (1 June 2015), pp. 65–85: https://doi.org/10.1016/j.cpa.2015.02.001

Kattel, R., Cepilovs, A., Kalvet, T. and Lember, V., *Public Sector Innovation Indicators: Towards a New Evaluative Framework*, 2015: https://doi.org/10.13140/RG.2.1.5150.3120

Kattel, R. and Mazzucato, M., 'Mission-Oriented Innovation Policy and Dynamic Capabilities in the Public Sector', *Industrial and Corporate Change* 27, no. 5 (1 October 2018), pp. 787–801: https://doi.org/10.1093/icc/dty032

Keele, S., 'Outsourcing Adaptation: Examining the Role and Influence of Consultants in Governing Climate Change Adaptation', University of Melbourne, 2017: http://minerva-access.unimelb.edu.au/handle/11343/194276

Keele, S., 'Taming Uncertainty: Climate Policymaking and the Spatial Politics of Privatized Advice', in C. Hurl and A. Vogelpohl (eds), *Professional Service Firms and Politics in a Global Era: Public Policy, Private Expertise*, pp. 53–75 (Cham: Springer International Publishing, 2021).

Kelly, D., *The Red Taylorist: The Life and Times of Walter Nicholas Polakov* (Bingley: Emerald Group Publishing, 2020).

Kersbergen, K. van and Vis, B., *Comparative Welfare State Politics* (Cambridge: Cambridge University Press, 2014).

Kesicki, F., 'Marginal Abatement Cost Curves for Policy Making – Expert-Based vs. Model-Derived Curves', in *33rd IAEE International Conference, 6–9 June 2010* (Rio de Janeiro: UCL Energy Institute, 2011): https://www.homepages.ucl.ac.uk/~ucft347/Kesicki_MACC.pdf

Kipping, M., 'Consultancies, Institutions and the Diffusion of Taylorism in Britain, Germany and France, 1920s to 1950s', *Business History* 39, no. 4 (1 October 1997), pp. 67–83: https://doi.org/10.1080/00076799700000146

Kipping, M., 'Consultants and Internationalization', in T. da Silva Lopes, C. Lubinski and H. J. S. Tworek (eds), *The Routledge Companion to the Makers of Global Business*, pp. 138–55 (Abingdon: Routledge, 2019).

Kipping, M. and Clark, T., 'Researching Management Consulting: An Introduction to the Handbook', in M. Kipping and T. Clark (eds), *The Oxford Handbook of Management Consulting* (Oxford, New York: Oxford University Press, 2012).

Kipping, M. and Engwall, L. (eds), *Management Consulting: Emergence and Dynamics of a Knowledge Industry* (Oxford, New York: Oxford University Press, 2002).

Lammers, C. J., 'Transience and Persistence of Ideal Types in Organizational Theory', in M. Lousbury, S. B. Bacharach and N. Ditomaso (eds), *Research in the Sociology of Organizations*, pp. 203–24 (Greenwich, CT: JAI Press, 1988).

Lapsley, I. and Oldfield, R., 'Transforming the Public Sector: Management Consultants as Agents of Change', *European Accounting Review* 10, no. 3 (1 September 2001), pp. 523–43: https://doi.org/10.1080/713764628

Lazonick, W., 'Innovative Enterprise or Sweatshop Economics?: In Search of Foundations of Economic Analysis', *Challenge* 59, no. 2 (3 March 2016), pp. 65–114: https://doi.org/10.1080/05775132.2016.1147297

Lazonick, W., 'Is the Most Unproductive Firm the Foundation of the Most Efficient Economy? How Penrosian Learning Confronts the Neoclassical Absurdity', *Institute for New Economic Thinking Working Paper Series No. 111*, 2020: https://www.ineteconomics.org/research/research-papers/is-the-most-unproductive-firm-the-foundation-of-the-most-efficient-economy-penrosian-learning-confronts-the-neoclassical-fallacy

Lazonick, W. and Mazzucato, M., 'The Risk-Reward Nexus in the Innovation-Inequality Relationship: Who Takes the Risks? Who Gets the Rewards?', *Industrial and Corporate Change* 22, no. 4 (1 August 2013), pp. 1093–128: https://doi.org/10.1093/icc/dtt019

Lazonick, W. and O'Sullivan, M., 'Maximizing Shareholder Value: A New Ideology for Corporate Governance', *Economy and Society* 29, no. 1 (1 January 2000), pp. 13–35: https://doi.org/10.1080/030851400360541

Lazonick, W. and Sakinç, E., 'Do Financial Markets Support Innovation or Inequity in the Biotech Drug Development Process?', Workshop on Innovation and Inequality: Pharma and Beyond, Scuola Superiore Sant'Anna, Pisa, Italy, 2010.

Lazonick, W, and Shin, J.-S., *Predatory Value Extraction: How the Looting of the Business Enterprise Became the US Norm and How Sustainable Prosperity Can Be Restored* (Oxford: Oxford University Press, 2020).

Lazonick, W., Tulum, Ö., Hopkins, M., Sakinç, M. E. and Jacobsen, K., 'Financialization of the U.S. Pharmaceutical Industry', Institute for New Economic Thinking, 2019: https://www.ineteconomics.org/perspectives/blog/financialization-us-pharma-industry

Leaver, A., 'Outsourcing Firms and the Paradox of Time Travel', *SPERI Blog* (blog), 12 February 2018: http://speri.dept.shef.ac.uk/2018/02/12/outsourcing-firms-and-the-paradox-of-time-travel/

Lee, G. and Brumer, J., 'Managing Mission-Critical Government Software Projects: Lessons Learned from the HealthCare.Gov Project', *IBM Center for The Business of Government*, 2017: http://www.businessofgovernment.org/sites/default/files/Viewpoints%20Dr%20Gwanhoo%20Lee.pdf

Lei, D. and Hitt, M. A., 'Strategic Restructuring and Outsourcing: The Effect of Mergers and Acquisitions and LBOs on Building Firm Skills and Capabilities', *Journal of Management* 21, no. 5 (1 October 1995), pp. 835–59: https://doi.org/10.1177/014920639502100502

Lenin, V. I., 'A "Scientific" System of Sweating', in *Lenin Collected Works*, 18:594–95 (Moscow: Progress Publishers, 1913): https://www.marxists.org/archive/lenin/works/1913/mar/13.htm

Levine, A. S., *Managing NASA in the Apollo Era* (Washington, DC: National Aeronautics and Space Administration, 1982).

Levinson, D. R., 'An Overview of 60 Contracts That Contributed to the Development and Operation of the Federal Marketplace', Washington, DC: Department of Health and Human Services – Office of Inspector General, August 2014.

Levinson, D. R., 'CMS Did Not Always Manage and Oversee Contractor Performance for the Federal Marketplace as Required by Federal Requirements and Contract Terms', Washington, DC: Department of Health and Human Services – Office of Inspector General, September 2015.

Levinson, D. R., 'HealthCare.Gov: CMS Management of the Federal Marketplace – A Case Study', Washington, DC: Department of Health and Human Services – Office of Inspector General, February 2016.

Levitt, A., *Take on the Street: How to Fight for Your Financial Future* (New York: Vintage, 2003).

Leys, C., 'Intellectual Mercenaries and the Public Interest: Management Consultancies and the NHS', *Policy & Politics* 27, no. 4 (1 September 1999), pp. 447–65: https://doi.org/10.1332/030557399782218353

Littler, C. R. and Innes, P., 'Downsizing and Deknowledging the Firm', *Work, Employment and Society* 17, no. 1 (1 March 2003), pp. 73–100: https://doi.org/10.1177/0950017003017001263

Lundvall, B.-Å. and Johnson, B., 'The Learning Economy', *Journal of Industry Studies* 1, no. 2 (1 November 1994), pp. 23–42: https://doi.org/10.1080/13662719400000002

MacDougall, I., 'How McKinsey Is Making $100 Million (and Counting) Advising on the Government's Bumbling Coronavirus Response', *ProPublica*, 15 July 2020: https://www.propublica.org/article/

how-mckinsey-is-making-100-million-and-counting-advising-on-the-governments-bumbling-coronavirus-response?token=SstV5uby4K1aF_907uUoNxUx4Lmau-1g

MacLeod, D., 'Privatization and the Limits of State Autonomy in Mexico: Rethinking the Orthodox Paradox', *Latin American Perspectives* 32, no. 4 (2005), pp. 36–64.

Madell, T., 'The First Public Private Partnership in Health and Medical Care in Sweden', *European Public Private Partnership Law Review* 5, no. 4 (2010), pp. 235–6.

Margetts, H., *Information Technology in Government: Britain and America* (London, New York: Routledge, 1998).

Mazzucato, M., *Mission Economy: A Moonshot Guide to Changing Capitalism* (London: Penguin, 2021).

Mazzucato, M., *The Entrepreneurial State: Debunking Public vs. Private Sector Myths* (London: Penguin, 2018 [2013]).

Mazzucato, M., *The Value of Everything: Making and Taking in the Global Economy* (London: Penguin, 2019 [2017]).

Mazzucato, M., Kattel, R., Quaggiotto, G. and Begovic, M., 'COVID-19 and the Need for Dynamic State Capabilities: An International Comparison', Development Futures Series Working Papers, UNDP Global Policy Network, April 2021.

Mazzucato, M. and Penna, C. C. R., 'Beyond Market Failures: The Market Creating and Shaping Roles of State Investment Banks', *Journal of Economic Policy Reform* 19, no. 4 (1 October 2016), pp. 305–26: https://doi.org/10.1080/17487870.2016.1216416

Mazzucato, M. and Roy, V., 'Rethinking Value in Health Innovation: From Mystifications towards Prescriptions', *Journal of Economic Policy Reform* 22, no. 2 (3 April 2019), pp. 101–19: https://doi.org/10.1080/17487870.2018.1509712

Mazzucato, M., Ryan-Collins, J. and Gouzoulis, G., 'Theorising and Mapping Modern Economic Rents', *UCL IIPP Working Paper Series* WP 2020-13 (June 2020): https://www.ucl.ac.uk/bartlett/public-purpose/sites/public-purpose/files/final_iipp-wp2020-13-theorising-and-mapping-modern-economic-rents_8_oct.pdf

Mazzucato, M., Conway, R., Mazzoli, E. M., Albala, S., 'Creating and Measuring Dynamic Public Value at the BBC: A Scoping Report', London: UCL Institute for Innovation and Public Purpose, 8 December 2020: https://www.ucl.ac.uk/bartlett/public-purpose/publications/2020/dec/creating-and-measuring-dynamic-public-value-bbc

McDonald, D., *The Firm: The Story of McKinsey and Its Secret Influence on American Business* (New York: Simon & Schuster, 2014).

McDougald, M. S. and Greenwood, R., 'Cuckoo in the Nest? The Rise of Management Consulting in Large Accounting Firms', in M. Kipping and T. Clark (eds), *The Oxford Handbook of Management Consulting* (Oxford, New York: Oxford University Press, 2012): https://doi.org/10.1093/oxfordhb/9780199235049.013.0005

McGee, J., 'The Influence of US Neoliberalism on International Climate Change Policy', in N. E. Harrison and J. Mikler (eds), *Climate Innovation: Liberal Capitalism and Climate Change*, pp. 193–214, Energy, Climate and the Environment Series (London: Palgrave Macmillan UK, 2014): https://doi.org/10.1057/9781137319890_8

McGreal, C., 'Revealed: 60% of Americans Say Oil Firms Are to Blame for the Climate Crisis', *Guardian*, 26 October 2021. Environment: https://www.theguardian.com/environment/2021/oct/26/climate-change-poll-oil-gas-companies-environment

McKenna, C. D., 'Agents of Adhocracy: Management Consultants and the Reorganization of the Executive Branch, 1947–1949', *Business and Economic History* 25, no. 1 (1996), pp. 101–11.

McKenna, C. D., 'The Origins of Modern Management Consulting', *Business and Economic History* 24, no. 1 (1995), pp. 51–8.

McKenna, C. D., *The World's Newest Profession: Management Consulting in the Twentieth Century*, (Cambridge: Cambridge University Press, 2010 [2006]).

McLaughlin, K., Osborne. S. P. and Ferlie, E., *New Public Management: Current Trends and Future Prospects* (London: Routledge, 2005).

McLean, B., 'The Valeant Meltdown and Wall Street's Major Drug Problem', *Vanity Fair*, 5 June 2016: https://www.vanityfair.com/news/2016/06/the-valeant-meltdown-and-wall-streets-major-drug-problem

Medina, E., *Cybernetic Revolutionaries: Technology and Politics in Allende's Chile* (London: MIT Press, 2014 [2011]).

Meijling, J., *Nya Karolinska – Ett Pilotprojekt För Marknadsstyrd Vård?* (Stockholm: Arena Idé, 2018): https://arenaide.se/wp-content/uploads/sites/2/2018/03/rapport-nks-meijling-1.pdf

Meriläinen, S., Tienari, J., Thomas, R. and Davies, R., 'Management Consultant Talk: A Cross-Cultural Comparison of Normalizing Discourse and Resistance', *Organization* 11, no. 4 (2004), pp. 539–64.

Mervyn, L. K., *Rethinking Public Private Partnerships* (Cheltenham: Edward Elgar Publishing, 2021).

Micklethwait, J. and Wooldridge, A., *The Witch Doctors: Making Sense of the Management Gurus* (New York: Three Rivers Press, 1998).

Momani, B., 'Management Consultants and the United States' Public Sector', *Business and Politics* 15, no. 3 (October 2013), pp. 381–99: https://doi.org/10.1515/bap-2013-0001

Momani, B., 'Professional Management Consultants in Transnational Governance', in L. Seabrooke and L. Folke Henriksen (eds), *Professional Networks in Transnational Governance*, pp. 245–65 (Cambridge: Cambridge University Press, 2017): https://doi.org/10.1017/9781316855508.016

Morgan, G., Sturdy, A. and Frenkel, M., 'The Role of Large Management Consultancy Firms in Global Public Policy', in D. Stone and K. Moloney (eds), *The Oxford Handbook of Global Policy and Transnational Administration* (Oxford: Oxford University Press, 2019): https://doi.org/10.1093/oxfordhb/9780198758648.013.39

Morozov, E., 'The Planning Machine', *New Yorker*, 6 October 2014: http://www.newyorker.com/magazine/2014/10/13/planning-machine

Morphet, J., *Outsourcing in the UK: Policies, Practices and Outcomes* (Bristol: Bristol University Press, 2021).

Mori, A., 'The impact of public services outsourcing on work and employment conditions in different national regimes', *European Journal of Industrial Relations* 23, no. 4 (1 December 2017), pp. 347–64: https://doi.org/10.1177/0959680117694272

Morrison, A. and Wensley, R., 'Boxing up or Boxed in?: A Short History of the Boston Consulting Group Share/Growth Matrix', *Journal of Marketing Management* 7, no. 2 (1 January 1991), pp. 105–29: https://doi.org/10.1080/0267257X.1991.9964145

Murphy, R. and Stausholm, S., 'The Big Four: A Study of Opacity', Brussels: GUE/NGL – European United Left/Nordic Green Left, 2017: https://openaccess.city.ac.uk/id/eprint/20066/

National Audit Office, 'Departments' Use of Consultants to Support Preparations for EU Exit', London: National Audit Office, 7 June 2019: https://www.nao.org.uk/wp-content/uploads/2019/05/Departments-use-of-consultants-to-support-preparations-for-EU-Exit.pdf

National Audit Office, 'The Choice of Finance for Capital Investment', London: National Audit Office, March 2015: https://www.nao.org.uk/wp-content/uploads/2015/03/The-choice-of-finance-for-capital-investment.pdf

Ndikumana, L. and Boyce, J. K. (eds), *On the Trail of Capital Flight from Africa: The Takers and the Enablers* (Oxford, New York: Oxford University Press, 2022).

Nelson, R. R. and Winter, S. G., *An Evolutionary Theory of Economic Change* (Cambridge, MA: The Belknap Press of Harvard University Press, 1996).

Nikolova, N. and Devinney, T., 'The Nature of Client–Consultant Interaction: A Critical Review', in M. Kipping and T. Clark (eds), *The Oxford Handbook of Management Consulting* (Oxford, New York: Oxford University Press, 2012).

Nippa, M. C. and Petzold, K., 'Economic Functions of Management Consulting Firms – an Integrative Theoretical Framework', *Academy of Management Proceedings* 2002, no. 1 (1 August 2002), B1–6: https://doi.org/10.5465/apbpp.2002.7516887

Obasi, G. O. P., 'Climate and Global Change in Relation to Sustainable Development: The Challenge to Science', *Proceedings of the Indian Academy of Sciences (Earth and Planetary Sciences)* 102, no. 1 (March 1993), pp. 27–34.

O'Leary, M. and Valdmanis, W., 'An ESG Reckoning Is Coming', *Harvard Business Review*, 4 March 2021: https://hbr.org/2021/03/an-esg-reckoning-is-coming

Oliver, D., 'Exclusive: Government Spending on Management Consultants Trebles in Three Years', *BMJ* 366 (5 September 2019), l5404: https://doi.org/10.1136/bmj.l5404

O'Mahoney, J. and Markham, C., *Management Consultancy* (Oxford: Oxford University Press, 2013).

Padgett, J. F. and McLean, P. D., 'Organizational Invention and Elite Transformation: The Birth of Partnership Systems in Renaissance Florence', *American Journal of Sociology* 111, no. 5 (March 2006), pp. 1463–568: https://doi.org/10.1086/498470

Paterlini, M., 'Director of Troubled Karolinska Hospital Resigns', *BMJ* 363 (9 October 2018), k4249: https://doi.org/10.1136/bmj.k4249

Paterlini, M., 'Jobs Come under Threat at Troubled Karolinska Hospital in Sweden', *BMJ* 367 (12 November 2019), l6479: https://doi.org/10.1136/bmj.l6479

Paterlini, M., 'Troubled Rebuild of Stockholm's Landmark Hospital Has Cost Twice as Much as Planned', *BMJ* 361 (25 April 2018), k1816: https://doi.org/10.1136/bmj.k1816

Paulsen, N., Callan, V. J., Grice, T. A., Rooney, D., Gallois, C., Jones, E., Jimmieson, N. L. and Bordia, P., 'Job uncertainty and personal control during downsizing: A comparison of survivors and victims', *Human Relations* 58, no. 4 (1 April 2005), pp. 463–96: https://doi.org/10.1177/0018726705055033

Penrose, E., *The Theory of the Growth of the Firm* (New York: Oxford University Press, 2009 [1959]).

Perl, A. and White, D., 'The Changing Role of Consultants in Canadian Policy Analysis', *Policy and Society* 21 (31 December 2002), pp. 49–73: https://doi.org/10.1016/S1449-4035(02)70003-9

Pistor, K., *The Code of Capital: How the Law Creates Wealth and Inequality* (Princeton, New Jersey: Princeton University Press, 2019).

Pierson, P., *Dismantling the Welfare State?: Reagan, Thatcher and the Politics of Retrenchment* (Cambridge: Cambridge University Press, 1994).

Piggott, J., '2021 Analysis of UK Government Strategic Suppliers', London: Tussell, 2021: https://www.tussell.com/insights/uk-government-strategic-suppliers-2021

Piggott, J., 'Public Sector Consultancy Market: 2021 Retrospective,' London: Tussell, 2022: https://www.tussell.com/insights/public-sector-consultancy-market-2021-retrospective

Polanyi, K., *The Great Transformation: The Political and Economic Origins of Our Time* (Boston: Beacon Press, 2001 [1944]).

Private Finance Panel, 'Public Opportunity, Private Benefit: Progressing the Private Finance Initiative', London: HM Treasury, 1995.

Puyvelde, D. Van, *Outsourcing US Intelligence: Private Contractors and Government Accountability* (Edinburgh: Edinburgh University Press, 2019).

Rice, A. and Valentin Ortiz, L., 'The McKinsey Way to Save an Island: Why Is Bankrupt Puerto Rico Spending More than a Billion Dollars on Expert Advice?', *Intelligencer*, 17 April 2019: https://nymag.com/intelligencer/2019/04/mckinsey-in-puerto-rico.html

Rivett, G., '1948–1957: Establishing the National Health Service', *The Nuffield Trust*, 13 November 2019: https://www.nuffieldtrust.org.uk/chapter/1948-1957-establishing-the-national-health-service

Roper, L. and Pettit, J., 'Development and the Learning Organisation', *Development in Practice Numbers* 12 (1 September 2002): https://doi.org/10.1080/0961450220149654

Rothman, L., 'How American Inequality in the Gilded Age Compares to Today', *Time*, 5 February 2018: https://time.com/5122375/american-inequality-gilded-age/

Rowley, C. and Bae, J., 'Globalisation and Transformation of Human Resource Management in South Korea', *International Journal of Human Resource Management* 13 (1 May 2002), pp. 522–49: https://doi.org/10.1080/09585190110111512

Royal College of General Practitioners, 'Briefing Paper: The Health and Social Care Bill, House of Lords Report Stage Briefing', London, 6 February 2012: https://www.rcgp.org.uk/-/media/Files/Policy/A-Z-policy/12-02-06-RCGP-HoL-Report-Stage-Briefing.ashx?la=en

Sahlin-Andersson, K. and Engwall, L., *The Expansion of Management Knowledge: Carriers, Flows, and Sources* (Stanford: Stanford University Press, 2002).

Saint-Martin, D., *Building the New Managerialist State: Consultants and the Politics of Public Sector Reform in Comparative Perspective* (Oxford: Oxford University Press, 2004).

Saint-Martin, D., 'How the Reinventing Government Movement in Public Administration Was Exported from the U.S. to Other Countries', *International Journal of Public Administration* 24, no. 6 (1 May 2001), pp. 573–604: https://doi.org/10.1081/PAD-100104397

Saint-Martin, D., 'Management Consultancy and the Varieties of Capitalism', in I. Geva-May and M. Howlett (eds), *Routledge Handbook of Comparative Policy Analysis* (London: Taylor & Francis, 2017).

Saint-Martin, D., 'The New Managerialism and the Policy Influence of Consultants in Government: An Historical–Institutionalist Analysis of Britain, Canada and France', *Governance* 11, no. 3 (1998), pp. 319–56: https://doi.org/10.1111/0952-1895.00074

Seabrooke, L. and Sending. O. J., 'Contracting Development: Managerialism and Consultants in Intergovernmental Organizations', *Review of International Political Economy* 27, no. 4 (2 July 2020), pp. 802–27: https://www.tandfonline.com/doi/full/10.1080/09692290.2019.1616601

Securities and Exchange Commission, Investment Advisers Act of 1940, Release No. 5912, Administrative Proceeding File No. 3-20656, In the Matter of MIO Partners, Inc. (2021): https://www.sec.gov/litigation/admin/2021/ia-5912.pdf

Shaoul, J., Stafford, A. and Stapleton, P., 'The Cost of Using Private Finance to Build, Finance and Operate Hospitals', *Public Money & Management* 28, no. 2 (1 April 2008), pp. 101–8: https://doi.org/10.1111/j.1467-9302.2008.00628.x

Shaoul, J., Stafford, A. and Stapleton, P., 'Partnerships and the Role of Financial Advisors: Private Control over Public Policy?', *Policy & Politics* 35, no. 3 (1 July 2007), pp. 479–95: https://doi.org/10.1332/030557307781571678

Shaw, E., 'The British Labour Government and the Private Finance Initiative in the National Health Service: A Case of Pragmatic Policy-Making?', *The Public Sector Innovation Journal* 8, no. 3 (2003).

Shaxson, N., 'Angola: Oil and Capital Flight', in L. Ndikumana and J. K. Boyce, *On the Trail of Capital Flight from Africa: The Takers and the Enablers* (Oxford, New York: Oxford University Press, 2022).

Shin, J.-S. and Chang, H.-J., *Restructuring Korea Inc* (London: RoutledgeCurzon, 2003).

Shleifer, A. and Vishny, R. W., 'The Takeover Wave of the 1980s', *Science* 249, no. 4970 (1990), pp. 745–9.

Skodvin, T. and Andresen. S., 'An Agenda for Change in U.S. Climate Policies? Presidential Ambitions and Congressional Powers', *International Environmental Agreements* 9 (1 August 2009), pp. 263–80: https://doi.org/10.1007/s10784-009-9097-7

Soares de Oliveira, R., *Magnificent and Beggar Land: Angola Since the Civil War* (London: C Hurst & Co Publishers Ltd, 2015).

Steiner, R., Kaiser, C. and Reichmuth, L., 'Consulting for the Public Sector in Europe', in E. Ongaro and S. van Thiel (eds), *The Palgrave Handbook of Public Administration and Management in Europe*, pp. 475–95 (London: Palgrave Macmillan UK, 2018): https://doi.org/10.1057/978-1-137-55269-3_25

Strange, S. (ed.), 'The Big Six Accountants', in *The Retreat of the State: The Diffusion of Power in the World Economy*, pp. 135–46, Cambridge Studies in International Relations (Cambridge: Cambridge University Press, 1996): https://doi.org/10.1017/CBO9780511559143.011

Sturdy, A., 'The Consultancy Process – An Insecure Business?', *Journal of Management Studies* 34, no. 3 (1997), pp. 389–413: https://doi.org/10.1111/1467-6486.00056

Sturdy, A., Handley, K., Clark., T. and Fincham, R., *Management Consultancy: Boundaries and Knowledge in Action* (Oxford: Oxford University Press, 2009): https://doi.org/10.1093/acprof:oso/9780199212644.001.0001

Sturdy, A. and O'Mahoney, J., 'Explaining National Variation in the Use of Management Consulting Knowledge: A Framework', *Management Learning* 49, no. 5 (1 November 2018), pp. 537–58: https://doi.org/10.1177/1350507618788993

Sturdy, A. and Wright, C., 'A Consulting Diaspora? Enterprising Selves as Agents of Enterprise', *Organization* 15, no. 3 (1 May 2008), pp. 427–44: https://doi.org/10.1177/1350508408088538

Sull, D., Sull, C. and Zweig, B., 'Toxic Culture Is Driving the Great Resignation', *MIT Sloan Management Review*, 11 January 2022: https://sloanreview.mit.edu/article/toxic-culture-is-driving-the-great-resignation/

Surowiecki, J., 'Inside the Valeant Scandal', *New Yorker*, 28 March 2016. http://www.newyorker.com/magazine/2016/04/04/inside-the-valeant-scandal

Syal, R., 'Brexit Drives Government Consultancy Fees to £450m in Three Years', *Guardian*, 6 October 2020. https://www.theguardian.com/politics/2020/oct/06/brexit-drives-government-consultancy-fees-to-450m-in-three-years

Syal, R., Bowers, S. and Wintour, P., ' "Big Four" Accountants "Use Knowledge of Treasury to Help Rich Avoid Tax" ', *Guardian*, 26 April 2013. http://www.theguardian.com/business/2013/apr/26/accountancy-firms-knowledge-treasury-avoid-tax

Takala, V. and Kattel, R., 'Dynamic Capabilities in the Public Sector: The Case of the UK's Government Digital Service', *UCL IIPP Working Paper Series*, 2021: https://www.ucl.ac.uk/bartlett/public-purpose/sites/public-purpose/files/final_iipp-2021-01_government-digital-service_kattel_takala.pdf

Tallis, R. and Davis, J. (eds), *NHS SOS: How the NHS Was Betrayed – and How We Can Save It* (London: Oneworld Publications, 2013).

Taylor, F. W., *The Principles of Scientific Management* (Mineola, NY: Dover Publications Inc., 2003 [1911]).

Taylor, M., 'Climate Change in the Caribbean – Learning Lessons from Irma and Maria', *Guardian*, 6 October 2017. Environment: http://www.theguardian.com/environment/2017/oct/06/climate-change-in-the-caribbean-learning-lessons-from-irma-and-maria

Teece, D. J., Pisano, G. and Shuen, A., 'Dynamic Capabilities and Strategic Management', *Strategic Management Journal* 18, no. 7 (1997), pp. 509–33: https://doi.org/10.1002/(SIC,I)1097-0266(199708)18:7<509::AID-SMJ882>3.0.CO;2-Z

The Sutton Trust, 'Elitist Britain', London: The Sutton Trust, 2019: https://www.suttontrust.com/wp-content/uploads/2019/12/Elitist-Britain-2019.pdf

The World Bank, 'Project Completion Report: Guinea-Bissau', Guinea-Bissau: The World Bank, 8 December 1995: https://documents1.worldbank.org/curated/en/423171468250281737/pdf/multiopage.pdf

Thompson, F. and Riccucci, N., 'Reinventing Government', *Annual Review of Political Science* 1 (28 November 2003), pp. 231–57: https://doi.org/10.1146/annurev.polisci.1.1.231

Tingle, M. L., 'Privatization and the Reagan Administration: Ideology and Application', *Yale Law & Policy Review* 6, no. 229 (1988): https://digitalcommons.law.yale.edu/cgi/viewcontent.cgi?article=1126&context=ylpr

Tisdall, P., *Agents of Change: Development and Practice of Management Consultancy* (London: Trafalgar Square Publishing, 1982).

Toffler, B. Ley and Reingold, J., *Final Accounting: Ambition, Greed, and the Fall of Arthur Andersen* (New York: Currency, 2004).

Traub, R., 'Lenin and Taylor: The Fate of "Scientific Management" in the (Early) Soviet Union', *Telos* 1978, no. 37 (21 September 1978), pp. 82–92: https://doi.org/10.3817/0978037082

Trumbo Vila, S. and Peters, M., 'The Bail Out Business: Who Profits from Bank Rescues in the EU?', Amsterdam: Transnational Institute, 2017: https://www.tni.org/files/publication-downloads/tni_bail_out_eng_online0317.pdf

Tulum, Ö., 'Innovation and Financialization in the U.S. Biopharmaceutical Industry', University of Ljubljana, 2018.

Tulum, Ö. and Lazonick, W., 'Financialized Corporations in a National Innovation System: The U.S. Pharmaceutical Industry', *International Journal of Political Economy* 47, no. 3–4 (2 October 2018), pp. 281–316: https://doi.org/10.1080/0 8911916.2018.1549842

Tyson, A. and Kennedy, B., 'Two-Thirds of Americans Think Government Should Do More on Climate', *Pew Research Center Science & Society* (blog), 23 June 2020: https://www.pewresearch.org/science/2020/06/23/two-thirds-of-americans-think-government-should-do-more-on-climate/

UNDP, 'World's Largest Survey of Public Opinion on Climate Change: A Majority of People Call for Wide-Ranging Action', UNDP, 27 January 2021: https://www.undp.org/press-releases/worlds-largest-survey-public-opinion-climate-change-majority-people-call-wide

United Nations, 'United Nations Framework Convention on Climate Change', Geneva: United Nations, 1992: https://unfccc.int/files/essential_background/background_publications_htmlpdf/application/pdf/conveng.pdf

United States General Accounting Office, 'Government Contractors: Are Service Contractors Performing Inherently Governmental Functions?', November 1991: https://www.gao.gov/assets/ggd-92-11.pdf

van de Ven, A. H., review of *In Search of Excellence: Lessons from America's Best-Run Companies* by Thomas J. Peters and Robert H. Waterman, *Administrative Science Quarterly* 28, no. 4 (1983), pp. 621–4: https://doi.org/10.2307/2393015

van den Berg, C., Howlett, M., Migone, A., Howard, M., Pemer, F. and Gunter, H. M., *Policy Consultancy in Comparative Perspective: Patterns, Nuances and Implications of the Contractor State* (Cambridge: Cambridge University Press, 2019).

van Vuuren, D., den Elzen, M., Berk, M. and de Moor, A., 'An Evaluation of the Level of Ambition and Implications of the Bush Climate Change Initiative', *Climate Policy* 2, no. 4 (1 December 2002), pp. 293–301: https://doi.org/10.1016/S1469-3062(02)00067-0

Volberda, H. W., Foss, N. J. and Lyles, M. A., 'Absorbing the Concept of Absorptive Capacity: How to Realize Its Potential in the Organization Field', *Organization Science* 21, no. 4 (1 August 2010), pp. 931–51: https://doi.org/10.1287/orsc.1090.0503

Voldsgaard, A. and Rüdiger, M., 'Innovative Enterprise, Industrial Ecosystems and Sustainable Transition: The Case of Transforming DONG Energy to Ørsted', in M. Lackner, B. Sajjadi and W.-Y. Chin (eds), *Handbook of Climate Change Mitigation and Adaptation*, pp. 1–52 (New York: Springer, 2020): https://doi.org/10.1007/978-1-4614-6431-0_160-1

Waluszewski, A., Hakansson, H. and Snehota, I., 'The Public-Private Partnership (PPP) Disaster of a New Hospital – Expected Political and Existing Business Interaction Patterns', *Journal of Business & Industrial Marketing* 34, no. 5 (1 January 2019), pp. 1119–30: https://doi.org/10.1108/JBIM-12-2018-0377

Wang, Y., 'Global Management Consultancy in China', doctoral thesis, University of New South Wales, Australia, 2009: http://unsworks.unsw.edu.au/fapi/datastream/unsworks:7734/SOURCE01?view=true

Weiss, A. E., *Management Consultancy and the British State: A Historical Analysis Since 1960* (Cham: Palgrave Macmillan, 2019).

Weiss, L. and Thurbon, E., 'Explaining Divergent National Responses to Covid-19: An Enhanced State Capacity Framework', *New Political Economy* 0, no. 0 (30 October 2021), pp. 1–16: https://doi.org/10.1080/13563467.2021.1994545

Werr, A., 'Knowledge Management and Management Consulting', in M. Kipping and T. Clark (eds), *The Oxford Handbook of Management Consulting* (Oxford, New York: Oxford University Press, 2012).

Weschle, S., 'Politicians' Private Sector Jobs and Parliamentary Behaviour', *American Journal of Political Science*, advanced online version, 4 September 2022, https://doi-org/10.1111/ajps.12721

Whitfield, D., 'A Typology of Privatisation and Marketisation', Australian Institute for Social Research, University of Adelaide: European Services Strategy Unit, 2006.

Winter, S. G., 'Understanding Dynamic Capabilities', *Strategic Management Journal* 24, no. 10 (2003), pp. 991–5.

United Nations UN Audiovisual Library, 'World Chronicle 487: G.O.P. Obasi, WMO', accessed 15 September 2021: https://www.unmultimedia.org/avlibrary/asset/2116/2116949

Wright, C. and Kipping, M., 'The Engineering Origins of the Consulting Industry and Its Long Shadow', in M. Kipping and T. Clark (eds), *The Oxford Handbook of Management Consulting* (Oxford, New York: Oxford University Press, 2012).

Wright, C. and Kwon, S.-H., 'Business Crisis and Management Fashion: Korean Companies, Restructuring and Consulting Advice', *Asia Pacific Business Review* 12, no. 3 (1 July 2006), pp. 355–73: https://doi.org/10.1080/13602380600597034

Wu, X., Ramesh, M. and Howlett, M., 'Policy Capacity: A Conceptual Framework for Understanding Policy Competences and Capabilities', *Policy and Society* 34, no. 3–4 (1 September 2015), pp. 165–71: https://doi.org/10.1016/j.polsoc. 2015.09.001

Zahra, S. A. and George, G., 'Absorptive Capacity: A Review, Reconceptualization, and Extension', *The Academy of Management Review* 27, no. 2 (2002), pp. 185–203: https://doi.org/10.2307/4134351

Zollo, M. and Winter, S., 'From Organizational Routines to Dynamic Capabilities', *Working Paper in the INSEAD Series*, 1 January 1999.

Notes

1. Introduction: The Big Con: A Confidence Trick

1 IBIS World, 'Global Management Consultants Industry – Market Research Report', 2021, https://www.ibisworld.com/default.aspx; Research and Markets, 'Management Consulting Services Global Market Report 2022', December 2021, https://www.researchandmarkets.com/reports/5515095/management-consulting-services-global-market#src-pos-2

2 I. MacDougall, 'How McKinsey Is Making $100 Million (and Counting) Advising on the Government's Bumbling Coronavirus Response', *ProPublica*, 15 July 2020, https://www.propublica.org/article/how-mckinsey-is-making-100-million-and-counting-advising-on-the-governments-bumbling-coronavirus-response?token=SstV5uby4K1aF_907uU0NxUx4Lmau-1g

3 J. Armitage, 'List of Companies Handed £30bn of Public Money to Join UK Pandemic Response', 4 May 2021, https://www.standard.co.uk/business/government-covid-private-contracts-30-billion-pwc-deloitte-british-airways-b933081.html

4 J. Piggott, 'Public Sector Consultancy Market: 2021 Retrospective', London: Tussell, 2022, https://www.tussell.com/insights/public-sector-consultancy-market-2021-retrospective

5 M. Johnson, 'Italy's Destiny Hangs on €248bn Recovery Plan, Says Draghi', *Financial Times*, 26 April 2021.

6 M. Mazzucato, J. Ryan-Collins and G. Gouzoulis, 'Theorising and Mapping Modern Economic Rents', *UCL IIPP Working Paper Series* WP 2020-13 (June 2020), https://www.ucl.ac.uk/bartlett/public-purpose/sites/public-purpose/files/final_iipp-wp2020-13-theorising-and-mapping-modern-economic-rents_8_oct.pdf

7 G. Dosi, R. R. Nelson and S. G. Winter, 'Introduction', in *The Nature and Dynamics of Organizational Capabilities* (Oxford: Oxford University Press, 2001), https://oxford.universitypressscholarship.com/view/10.1093/0199248540.00

1.0001/acprof-9780199248544; R. Kattel and M. Mazzucato, 'Mission-Oriented Innovation Policy and Dynamic Capabilities in the Public Sector', *Industrial and Corporate Change* 27, no. 5 (1 October 2018), pp. 787–801, https://doi. org/10.1093/icc/dty032; S. G. Winter, 'Understanding Dynamic Capabilities', *Strategic Management Journal* 24, no. 10 (2003), pp. 991–5.

8   L. Dunhill and R. Syal, 'Whitehall "infantilised" by Reliance on Consultants, Minister Claims', *Guardian*, 29 September 2020. Politics: http://www.theguardian.com/politics/2020/sep/29/whitehall-infantilised-by-reliance-on-consultants-minister-claims

9   A. Innes, 'The Limits of Institutional Convergence: Why Public Sector Outsourcing Is Less Efficient than Soviet Enterprise Planning', *Review of International Political Economy* 28, no. 6 (2021), pp. 1705–28, https://doi.org/10.1080/0969 2290.2020.1786434; B.-Å. Lundvall and B. Johnson, 'The Learning Economy', *Journal of Industry Studies* 1, no. 2 (1 November 1994), pp. 23–42, https://doi. org/10.1080/13662719400000002

10   K. Joshi, 'Scott Morrison's Net Zero Modelling Reveals a Slow, Lazy and Shockingly Irresponsible Approach to "Climate Action"', *Guardian*, 12 November 2021. Environment: https://www.theguardian.com/environment/2021/nov/13/scott-morrisons-net-zero-modelling-reveals-a-slow-lazy-and-shockingly-irresponsible-approach-to-climate-action

11   M. Mazzucato, *Mission Economy: A Moonshot Guide to Changing Capitalism* (London: Penguin, 2021).

2. What is the Consulting Industry?

1   E. Braun and R. Momtaz, 'Use of Consultancies for Vaccine Rollout Sparks Controversy in France', *POLITICO*, 6 January 2021, https://www.politico.eu/article/french-government-defends-mckinsey-coronavirus-vaccine-rollout/

2   E. Braun and P. De Villepin, 'How Consultants like McKinsey Took over France', *POLITICO*, 8 February 2021, https://www.politico.eu/article/how-consultants-like-mckinsey-accenture-deloitte-took-over-france-bureaucracy-emmanuel-macron-coronavirus-vaccines/

3   L. Alderman, 'France Hired McKinsey to Help in the Pandemic. Then Came the Questions', *New York Times*, 22 February 2021. Business: https://www.nytimes.com/2021/02/22/business/france-mckinsey-consultants-covid-vaccine.html

4   Braun and De Villepin, 'How Consultants like McKinsey Took over France'.

5 Alderman, 'France Hired McKinsey to Help in the Pandemic. Then Came the Questions'.

6 É. Assassi, 'Un Phénomène Tentaculaire: L'influence Croissante Des Cabinets de Conseil Sur Les Politiques Publiques' (Paris: Sénat, 16 March 2022), http://www.senat.fr/rap/r21-578-1/r21-578-11.pdf

7 'Prosecutors Open Probe into French Government Use of Consulting Firms', *Financial Times*, 6 April 2022.

8 Assassi, 'Un Phénomène Tentaculaire: L'influence Croissante Des Cabinets de Conseil Sur Les Politiques Publiques', p. 15.

9 Braun and Momtaz, 'Use of Consultancies for Vaccine Rollout Sparks Controversy in France'.

10 D. Saint-Martin, 'The New Managerialism and the Policy Influence of Consultants in Government: An Historical–Institutionalist Analysis of Britain, Canada and France', *Governance* 11, no. 3 (1998), p. 326, https://doi.org/10.1111/0952-1895.00074

11 P. Maurer, 'McKinsey, Citwell, Accenture . . . Ce que l'on sait des commandes passées par le gouvernement à des cabinets privés', Public Senat, 2 March 2021, https://www.publicsenat.fr/article/politique/mckinsey-citwell-accenture-ce-que-l-on-sait-des-commandes-passees-par-le

12 MacDougall, 'How McKinsey Is Making $100 Million (and Counting) Advising on the Government's Bumbling Coronavirus Response'.

13 Dunhill and Syal, 'Whitehall "infantilised" by Reliance on Consultants, Minister Claims'.

14 Consultancy.uk, 'UK Consulting Industry Grows 2.5% in Spite of Pandemic', 20 January 2021, https://www.consultancy.uk/news/26649/uk-consulting-industry-grows-25-in-spite-of-pandemic

15 Consultancy.uk, 'UK Consulting Industry Revenues Hit £14 Billion after Double-Digit Growth', *Consultancy.uk* (blog), 19 January 2022, https://www.consultancy.uk/news/30179/uk-consulting-industry-revenues-hit-14-billion-after-double-digit-growth

16 Armitage, 'List of Companies Handed £30bn of Public Money to Join UK Pandemic Response'.

17 Ibid.

18 Contracts Finder, 'Support to Health Research Authority: Research Review Programme – Contracts Finder', GOV.UK, 2021, https://www.contractsfinder.service.gov.uk/Notice/d08e4df0-9670-4dab-866f-fd1ce541fe96

19 House of Commons Committee of Public Accounts, 'Test and Trace Update: Twenty-Third Report of Session 2021–22' (London, United Kingdom: House of Commons, 21 October 2021), p. 5, 12 June 2022, https://committees.parliament.uk/publications/7651/documents/79945/default/

20 House of Commons Committee of Public Accounts, 'Test and Trace Update: Twenty-Third Report of Session 2021–22'.

21 Date of interview: 13.10.21.

22 Keele, S., 'Outsourcing Adaptation: Examining the Role and Influence of Consultants in Governing Climate Change Adaptation', University of Melbourne, 2017, http://minerva-access.unimelb.edu.au/handle/11343/194276

23 Tett, G., 'Why the US Federal Reserve turned again to BlackRock for help', *Financial Times*, 26 March 2021.

24 BlackRock, 'About Financial Markets Advisory (FMA)', BlackRock, 2021, https://www.blackrock.com/financial-markets-advisory/about-fma

25 A. E. Weiss, *Management Consultancy and the British State: A Historical Analysis Since 1960* (Cham: Palgrave Macmillan, 2019), p. 233.

26 'Business Services,' *Capgemini Worldwide* (blog), 18 July 2017, https://www.capgemini.com/service/business-services/

27 McKinsey & Company, 'McKinsey & Company,' 2021, https://www.mckinsey.com

28 D. Saint-Martin, 'Management Consultancy and the Varieties of Capitalism', in *Routledge Handbook of Comparative Policy Analysis* (London: Taylor & Francis, 2017); Weiss, *Management Consultancy and the British State*.

29 Serco, 'Sector Expertise: Our Key Markets', Serco, 2021, https://www.serco.com/sector-expertise

30 R. Murphy and S. Stausholm, 'The Big Four: A Study of Opacity' (Brussels: GUE/NGL – European United Left/Nordic Green Left, 2017), https://openaccess.city.ac.uk/id/eprint/20066/

31 A. C. Gross and J. Poor, 'The Global Management Consulting Sector', *Business Economics*, October 2008.

32 M. Kipping and T. Clark, 'Researching Management Consulting: An Introduction to the Handbook', in M. Kipping and T. Clark (eds), *The Oxford Handbook of Management Consulting* (Oxford, New York: Oxford University Press, 2012).

33 IBISWorld, 'Global Management Consultants Industry – Market Research Report'; The Business Research Company, 'Management Consulting Services Global Market Report 2020–30'.

34 *Forbes*, 'America's Largest Private Companies', *Forbes*, 2021, https://www.forbes.com/largest-private-companies/list/; 'Global Management Consultants Industry – Market Research Report'; The Business Research Company, 'Management Consulting Services Global Market Report 2020–30'.

35 Statista, 'Biggest Companies in the World by Market Cap 2020', Statista, 2021, https://www.statista.com/statistics/263264/top-companies-in-the-world-by-market-capitalization/

36 Consulting.com, 'The Top 50 Consulting Firms In 2019 By Revenue, Prestige, Growth & Employee Satisfaction', 2021, https://www.consulting.com/top-consulting-firms

37 Saint-Martin, 'Management Consultancy and the Varieties of Capitalism'.

38 A. Sturdy and J. O'Mahoney, 'Explaining National Variation in the Use of Management Consulting Knowledge: A Framework', *Management Learning* 49, no. 5 (1 November 2018), pp. 537–58, https://doi.org/10.1177/1350507618788993

39 J. O'Mahoney and C. Markham, *Management Consultancy* (Oxford: Oxford University Press, 2013).

40 Sturdy and O'Mahoney, 'Explaining National Variation in the Use of Management Consulting Knowledge'.

41 Ibid.

42 Anderlini, 'China Clamps down on US Consulting Groups'.

43 Wright and Kwon, 'Business Crisis and Management Fashion'.

44 Sturdy and O'Mahoney, 'Explaining National Variation in the Use of Management Consulting Knowledge'.

45 A. Bowman et al., *What a Waste: Outsourcing and How It Goes Wrong* (Manchester: Manchester University Press, 2015), p. 3.

46 J. Piggott, '2021 Analysis of UK Government Strategic Suppliers', London: Tussell, 2021, https://www.tussell.com/insights/uk-government-strategic-suppliers-2021

47 Weiss, *Management Consultancy and the British State*, pp. 231–2.

48 P. Curtis, 'Whitehall Supplier Offers Year's Worth of Free Contracts While Times Are Tough', *Guardian*, 2 January 2011.Politics: https://www.theguardian.com/politics/2011/jan/02/kpmg-government-supplier-contracts-consultancy

49 S. Shrikanth, 'Government Use of Consultants Soars in India', *Financial Times*, 26 June 2019.

50 Ibid.

51 C. Baraka, 'The Failed Promise of Kenya's Smart City', *Rest of World*, 1 June 2021, https://restofworld.org/2021/the-failed-promise-of-kenyas-smart-city/

52 C. Yeap, 'Vision 2020: Mission Unrealised', *The Edge Markets*, 12 January 2021, http://www.theedgemarkets.com/article/vision-2020-mission-unrealised; '"Vision Mumbai a Recipe for Disaster"', *Times of India*, 18 December 2003, https://timesofindia.indiatimes.com/city/mumbai/vision-mumbai-a-recipe-for-disaster/articleshow/365817.cms

53 T. Sipahutar, 'Indonesia Picks McKinsey to Revamp Firms with $172b Sales', *Jakarta Post*, 7 February 2020, https://www.thejakartapost.com/news/2020/02/07/indonesia-picks-mckinsey-to-revamp-firms-with-172b-sales.html

54 H. Wootton, 'Senate Scrutinises BCG's $1.32m AusPost Work', *Australian Financial Review*, 4 May 2021, https://www.afr.com/companies/professional-services/senate-scrutinises-bcg-s-1-32m-auspost-work-20210504-p57onz

55 Consultancy.uk, 'Value for Money Questioned in Consulting Firm's Pandemic Charity Role', 27 August 2021, https://www.consultancy.uk/news/28821/value-for-money-questioned-in-consulting-firms-pandemic-charity-role

56 M. Marriage and J. Cotterill, 'McKinsey to Repay Fees from Contract with South Africa Utility', *Financial Times*, 6 July 2018.

57 Cotterill, J., 'Zuma presided over rampant corruption, says South Africa inquiry', *Financial Times*, 5 January 2022.

58 Parker, G. O'Dwyer, M. and Cotterill, J. 'Bain & Co takes legal action to overturn UK state contract ban', *Financial Times*, 2 September 2022.

3. Where Consulting Came From: A Brief History

1 E. Morozov, 'The Planning Machine', *New Yorker*, 6 October 2014, http://www.newyorker.com/magazine/2014/10/13/planning-machine

2 E. Medina, *Cybernetic Revolutionaries: Technology and Politics in Allende's Chile* (London: MIT Press, 2014 [2011]).

3 Weiss, *Management Consultancy and the British State*, p. 3.

4 C. Leys, 'Intellectual Mercenaries and the Public Interest: Management Consultancies and the NHS', *Policy & Politics* 27, no. 4 (1 September 1999), pp. 447–65, https://doi.org/10.1332/030557399782218353

5 N. Bamforth and P. Leyland, *Accountability in the Contemporary Constitution* (Oxford: Oxford University Press, 2013); R. Tallis and J. Davis (eds), *NHS*

SOS: How the NHS Was Betrayed – and How We Can Save It (London: Oneworld Publications, 2013).

6 Royal College of General Practitioners, 'Briefing Paper: The Health and Social Care Bill, House of Lords Report Stage Briefing' (London, 6 February 2012), https://www.rcgp.org.uk/-/media/Files/Policy/A-Z-policy/12-02-06-RCGP-HoL-Report-Stage-Briefing.ashx?la=en

7 J. Moulds, 'NHS Body "Wastes Millions on Flawed Financial Advice"', *Guardian*, 21 July 2018. Society: https://www.theguardian.com/society/2018/jul/21/nhs-trust-wastes-million-on-flawed-financial-advice-london-north-west

8 Weiss, *Management Consultancy and the British State*, p. 231.

9 C. D. McKenna, *The World's Newest Profession: Management Consulting in the Twentieth Century* (Cambridge: Cambridge University Press, 2010); C. D. McKenna, 'The Origins of Modern Management Consulting', *Business and Economic History* 24, no. 1 (1995), pp. 51–8; M. Kipping, 'Consultancies, Institutions and the Diffusion of Taylorism in Britain, Germany and France, 1920s to 1950s', *Business History* 39, no. 4 (1 October 1997), pp. 67–83, https://doi.org/10.1080/00076799700000146

10 McKenna, *The World's Newest Profession*, p. 29.

11 Arthur D. Little, 'History,' Arthur D. Little, 31 May 2017, https://www.adlittle.com/en/about-us/history-0

12 C. Wright and M. Kipping, 'The Engineering Origins of the Consulting Industry and Its Long Shadow', in Tipping and Clark (eds), *The Oxford Handbook of Management Consulting*.

13 R. F. Hoxie, *Scientific Management and Labor* (New York, London: D. Appleton and Company, 1915), http://archive.org/details/scientificmanage00hoxi

14 A. M. Blake and J. L. Moseley, 'One Hundred Years after The Principles of Scientific Management: Frederick Taylor's Life and Impact on the Field of Human Performance Technology', *Performance Improvement* 49, no. 4 (2010), pp. 27–34, https://doi.org/10.1002/pfi.20141

15 F. W. Taylor, *The Principles of Scientific Management* (Mineola, NY: Dover Publications Inc., 2003 [1911]).

16 Ibid.

17 Ibid.

18 V. I. Lenin, 'A "Scientific" System of Sweating', in *Lenin Collected Works*, vol. 18 (Moscow: Progress Publishers, 1913), pp. 594–95, https://www.marxists.org/archive/lenin/works/1913/mar/13.htm; R. Traub, 'Lenin and Taylor: The Fate

of "Scientific Management" in the (Early) Soviet Union', *Telos* 1978, no. 37 (21 September 1978), pp. 82–92, https://doi.org/10.3817/0978037082

19 McKenna, *The World's Newest Profession*, 59; D. Kelly, *The Red Taylorist: The Life and Times of Walter Nicholas Polakov* (Bingley: Emerald Group Publishing, 2020), p. 93.

20 BCG, 'What Is the Growth Share Matrix?', BCG Global, 2021, https://www.bcg.com/about/our-history/growth-share-matrix

21 A. Morrison and R. Wensley, 'Boxing up or Boxed in?: A Short History of the Boston Consulting Group Share/ Growth Matrix', *Journal of Marketing Management* 7, no. 2 (1 January 1991), pp. 105–29, https://www.tandfonline.com/doi/abs/10.1080/0267257X.1991.9964145

22 McKenna, *The World's Newest Profession*.

23 Ibid., pp. 16–17.

24 D. McDonald, *The Firm: The Story of McKinsey and Its Secret Influence on American Business* (New York: Simon & Schuster, 2014), p. 29.

25 Encyclopedia of Chicago, 'Antiunionism', 2021, http://www.encyclopedia.chicagohistory.org/pages/55.html

26 McDonald, *The Firm*, p. 29.

27 McDonald, *The Firm*.

28 R. J. David, 'Institutional Change and the Growth of Strategy Consulting in the United States', in Tipping and Clark (eds), *The Oxford Handbook of Management Consulting*; J. Bowman, *Booz, Allen & Hamilton: Seventy Years of Client Service, 1914–1984* (New York: Booz, Allen & Hamilton, 1984).

29 M. Kipping, 'Consultants and Internationalization', in T. da Silva Lopes, C. Lubinski and H. J. S. Tworek (eds), *The Routledge Companion to the Makers of Global Business* (Abingdon: Routledge, 2019), p. 141.

30 David, 'Institutional Change and the Growth of Strategy Consulting in the United States'.

31 McKenna, *The World's Newest Profession*, p. 102.

32 M. Collins and A. Needell, NASM Oral History Project: Glennan #5, Tape recording, 29 May 1987, https://airandspace.si.edu/research/projects/oral-histories/TRANSCPT/GLENNAN5.HTM

33 Ibid.

34 McKenna, *The World's Newest Profession*, p. 102.

35 Ibid., pp. 81–2.

36 A. S. Levine, *Managing NASA in the Apollo Era* (Washington, DC: National Aeronautics and Space Administration, 1982); Mazzucato, *Mission Economy*, pp. 93–102.

37 David, 'Institutional Change and the Growth of Strategy Consulting in the United States'; C. D. McKenna, 'Agents of Adhocracy: Management Consultants and the Reorganization of the Executive Branch, 1947–1949', *Business and Economic History* 25, no. 1 (1996), pp. 101–11.

38 David, 'Institutional Change and the Growth of Strategy Consulting in the United States'; H. Higdon, *The Business Healers* (New York: Random House, 1970).

39 David, 'Institutional Change and the Growth of Strategy Consulting in the United States'.

40 Saint-Martin, 'Management Consultancy and the Varieties of Capitalism', p. 218.

41 C. Boyd, 'The Structural Origins of Conflicts of Interest in the Accounting Profession', *Business Ethics Quarterly* 14, no. 3 (July 2004), p. 379, https://doi.org/10.5840/beq200414325

42 Ibid., pp. 379–80.

43 S. Strange (ed.), 'The Big Six Accountants', in *The Retreat of the State: The Diffusion of Power in the World Economy*, Cambridge Studies in International Relations (Cambridge: Cambridge University Press, 1996), pp. 135–46, https://doi.org/10.1017/CBO9780511559143.011

44 J. Agar, *The Government Machine: A Revolutionary History of the Computer*, History of Computing (Cambridge, MA: MIT Press, 2003); P. Dunleavy et al., *Digital Era Governance: IT Corporations, the State, and E-Government* (Oxford: Oxford University Press, 2006), http://www.oxfordscholarship.com/view/10.1093/acprof:oso/9780199296194.001.0001/acprof-9780199296194

45 M. Hicks, *Programmed Inequality: How Britain Discarded Women Technologists and Lost Its Edge in Computing* (Cambridge, MA: MIT Press, 2017).

46 Weiss, *Management Consultancy and the British State*.

47 McKenna, *The World's Newest Profession*.

48 Ibid., p. 20.

49 Ibid., p. 237.

50 M. Kipping and L. Engwall (eds), *Management Consulting: Emergence and Dynamics of a Knowledge Industry* (New York, Oxford: Oxford University Press, 2002).

51 D. Harvey, *A Brief History of Neoliberalism* (Oxford: Oxford University Press, 2007).

52 C. Crouch, '9. The Paradoxes of Privatisation and Public Service Outsourcing', *The Political Quarterly*, Rethinking Capitalism, 86, no. S1 (2015), pp. 156–71, https://doi.org/10.1111/1467-923X.12238

53 K. Albertson and P. Stepney, '1979 and All That: A 40-Year Reassessment of Margaret Thatcher's Legacy on Her Own Terms', *Cambridge Journal of Economics* 44, no. 2 (19 March 2020), p. 331, https://doi.org/10.1093/cje/bez037

54 A. Shleifer and R. W. Vishny, 'The Takeover Wave of the 1980s', *Science* 249, no. 4970 (1990), pp. 745–9; B. Holmstrom and S. N. Kaplan, 'Corporate Governance and Merger Activity in the United States: Making Sense of the 1980s and 1990s', *The Journal of Economic Perspectives* 15, no. 2 (2001), pp. 121–44.

55 McKenna, *The World's Newest Profession*, p. 230.

56 G. Hodge and D. Bowman, '6. The "Consultocracy": The Business of Reforming Government', in G. Hodge (ed.), *Privatization and Market Development* (Cheltenham: Edward Elgar Publishing, 2006).

57 Saint-Martin, 'Management Consultancy and the Varieties of Capitalism,' p. 677.

58 Saint-Martin, 'The New Managerialism and the Policy Influence of Consultants in Government', p. 333.

59 A. Perl and D. White, 'The Changing Role of Consultants in Canadian Policy Analysis', *Policy and Society* 21 (31 December 2002), p. 52, https://doi.org/10.1016/S1449-4035(02)70003-9; in: C. van den Berg et al., *Policy Consultancy in Comparative Perspective: Patterns, Nuances and Implications of the Contractor State* (Cambridge: Cambridge University Press, 2019).

60 C. van den Berg et al., *Policy Consultancy in Comparative Perspective: Patterns, Nuances and Implications of the Contractor State* (Cambridge: Cambridge University Press, 2019).

61 Hodge and Bowman, '6. The "Consultocracy": The Business of Reforming Government'.

62 Weiss, *Management Consultancy and the British State.*

63 R. Jupe and W. Funnell, 'Neoliberalism, Consultants and the Privatisation of Public Policy Formulation: The Case of Britain's Rail Industry', *Critical Perspectives on Accounting* 29 (1 June 2015), pp. 65–85, https://doi.org/10.1016/j.cpa.2015.02.001

64 M. L. Tingle, 'Privatization and the Reagan Administration: Ideology and Application', *Yale Law & Policy Review* 6, no. 229 (1988), https://core.ac.uk/download/pdf/72836366.pdf

65 United States General Accounting Office, 'Government Contractors: Are Service Contractors Performing Inherently Governmental Functions?', November 1991, https://www.gao.gov/assets/ggd-92-11.pdf

66 P. Dunleavy and C. Hood, 'From Old Public Administration to New Public Management,' *Public Money & Management* 14, no. 3 (1 July 1994), pp. 9–16, https://doi.org/10.1080/09540969409387823; V. Homburg, C. Pollitt and S. van Thiel, 'Introduction', in C. Pollitt, S. van Thiel and V. Homburg (eds), *New Public Management in Europe: Adaptation and Alternatives* (London: Palgrave Macmillan UK, 2007), pp. 1–9, https://doi.org/10.1057/9780230625365_1; K. McLaughlin, S. P. Osborne and E. Ferlie, *New Public Management: Current Trends and Future Prospects* (London: Routledge, 2005).

67 D. Saint-Martin, *Building the New Managerialist State: Consultants and the Politics of Public Sector Reform in Comparative Perspective* (Oxford: Oxford University Press, 2004).

68 C. Hood and M. Jackson, *Administrative Argument* (Dartmouth, NH: Dartmouth Publishing Company, 1991), p. 19.

69 Hodge and Bowman, '6. The "Consultocracy": The Business of Reforming Government', p. 100.

70 I. Lapsley and R. Oldfield, 'Transforming the Public Sector: Management Consultants as Agents of Change', *European Accounting Review* 10, no. 3 (1 September 2001), p. 530, https://doi.org/10.1080/713764628

71 Hodge and Bowman, '6. The "Consultocracy": The Business of Reforming Government'.

72 Federal Deposit Insurance Corporation, *Volume I: An Examination of the Banking Crises of the 1980s and Early 1990s*, vol. I (Arlington, VA: Federal Deposit Insurance Corporation, 1997), https://www.fdic.gov/bank/historical/history/vol1.html

73 H. Denton and M.-F. Kail, 'Nigeria and the World Bank: Learning from the Past, Looking to the Future' (Washington, DC: The World Bank, 1995), https://documents1.worldbank.org/curated/en/235001468775775060/pdf/37328.pdf

74 B. Drum, 'Privatization in Africa', *The Columbia Journal of World Business* 28, no. 1 (1 March 1993), p. 148, https://doi.org/10.1016/0022-5428(93)90060-3

75 The World Bank, 'Project Completion Report: Guinea-Bissau' (Guinea-Bissau: The World Bank, 8 December 1995), p. 31, https://documents1.worldbank.org/curated/en/423171468250281737/pdf/multiopage.pdf

76 D. MacLeod, 'Privatization and the Limits of State Autonomy in Mexico: Rethinking the Orthodox Paradox', *Latin American Perspectives* 32, no. 4 (2005), pp. 51–2.

77 A. B. L. Cheung, 'Repositioning the State and the Public Sector Reform Agenda: The Case of Hong Kong', in M. Ramesh, E. Araral and W. Xun (eds), *Reasserting the Public in Public Services: New Public Management Reforms* (New York: Routledge, 2010); A. B. L. Cheung, 'The Politics of New Public Management: Some Experience from Reforms in East Asia', in Ramesh et al., *New Public Management*.

78 N. Shaxson, 'Angola: Oil and Capital Flight', in L. Ndikumana and J. K. Boyce (eds), *On the Trail of Capital Flight from Africa: The Takers and the Enablers* (Oxford, New York: Oxford University Press, 2022), p. 46.

79 Francis Fukuyama, *The End of History and the Last Man* (London: Penguin, 2020 [1992]).

80 A. Gross, J. Poor and M. T. Roberson, 'Management Consulting in Central Europe', *Consulting to Management* 15, no. 1 (March 2004), pp. 33–8.

81 Ibid.

82 Wang, 'Global Management Consultancy in China'.

83 J. Wong, 'McKinsey and Chinese Client Spar Over Quality of Services', *Wall Street Journal*, 13 June 2001. Front section: https://www.wsj.com/articles/SB992368049424176605

84 Wang, 'Global Management Consultancy in China'; Wong, 'McKinsey and Chinese Client Spar Over Quality of Services'.

85 Ibid.

86 K. Chong, *Best Practice: Management Consulting and the Ethics of Financialization in China* (Durham, North Carolina: Duke University Press, 2018).

87 Saint-Martin, 'Management Consultancy and the Varieties of Capitalism'; Kipping, 'Consultancies, Institutions and the Diffusion of Taylorism in Britain, Germany and France, 1920s to 1950s'.

88 Sturdy and O'Mahoney, 'Explaining National Variation in the Use of Management Consulting Knowledge'.

89 Saint-Martin, 'Management Consultancy and the Varieties of Capitalism'.

90 Wright and Kwon, 'Business Crisis and Management Fashion'; Wang, 'Global Management Consultancy in China'.

91 Consultancy.asia, 'Oliver Wyman Closes Its Office in Seoul, South Korea,' 11 December 2020, https://www.consultancy.asia/news/3775/oliver-wyman-closes-its-office-in-seoul-south-korea

92 R. Jacob, 'Can You Trust That Audit?', *Fortune Magazine*, 18 November 1991; in Boyd, 'The Structural Origins of Conflicts of Interest in the Accounting Profession', p. 384.

93 Boyd, 'The Structural Origins of Conflicts of Interest in the Accounting Profession', p. 383.

94 A. Levitt, *Take on the Street: How to Fight for Your Financial Future* (New York: Vintage, 2003), p. 116.

95 Boyd, 'The Structural Origins of Conflicts of Interest in the Accounting Profession', p. 385.

96 B. Ley Toffler and J. Reingold, *Final Accounting: Ambition, Greed, and the Fall of Arthur Andersen* (New York: Currency, 2004), p. 387; in Boyd, 'The Structural Origins of Conflicts of Interest in the Accounting Profession'.

97 D. C. Johnston, 'Enron Avoided Income Taxes in 4 of 5 Years', *New York Times, Late Edition (East Coast)*, 17 January 2002.

98 McKenna, *The World's Newest Profession*, p. 216.

99 Boyd, 'The Structural Origins of Conflicts of Interest in the Accounting Profession', p. 380.

100 The Economist, 'Blowing the Whistle on Accountancy', *The Economist*, 22 December 1990; in Boyd, 'The Structural Origins of Conflicts of Interest in the Accounting Profession', p. 386.

101 McKenna, *The World's Newest Profession*, p. 216.

102 C. A. Glassman, 'SEC Speech: SEC Initiatives Under the Sarbanes-Oxley Act of 2002 (C. Glassman)' (College of Business and Economics, California, Fullerton, CA, 28 January 2003), https://www.sec.gov/news/speech/spch012803cag.htm

103 M. S. McDougald and R. Greenwood, 'Cuckoo in the Nest? The Rise of Management Consulting in Large Accounting Firms', in Kipping and Clark (eds), *The Oxford Handbook of Management Consulting*.

4. The Outsourcing Turn: Government by Consultancy and the Third Way

1 Steven Brill, 'Code Red', *Time*, 10 March 2014, p. 36.

2 W. Andrews and A. Werner, 'Healthcare.Gov Plagued by Crashes on 1st Day', *CBS News*, 1 October 2013, https://www.cbsnews.com/news/healthcaregov-plagued-by-crashes-on-1st-day/

3 G. Lee and J. Brumer, 'Managing Mission-Critical Government Software Projects: Lessons Learned from the HealthCare.Gov Project', *IBM Center for The Business of Government*, 2017, http://www.businessofgovernment.org/sites/default/files/Viewpoints%20Dr%20Gwanhoo%20Lee.pdf

4 Brill, 'Code Red'.

5 Lee and Brumer, 'Managing Mission-Critical Government Software Projects: Lessons Learned from the HealthCare.Gov Project'.

6 S. H. Jain, B. W. Powers and D. Sanghavi, 'Big Plans, Poor Execution: The Importance of Governmental Managerial Innovation to Health Care Reform', *Journal of General Internal Medicine* 30, no. 4 (April 2015), pp. 395–7, https://doi.org/10.1007/s11606-014-3083-7

7 D. R. Levinson, 'An Overview of 60 Contracts That Contributed to the Development and Operation of the Federal Marketplace' (Washington, DC: Department of Health and Human Services – Office of Inspector General, August 2014).

8 CGI, 'Company Overview,' 2021, https://www.cgi.com/en/overview

9 CGI Group, '2010 Annual Report' (Montreal: CGI Group, 2010), https://www.cgi.com/sites/default/files/2018-08/cgi-2010-annual-report.pdf

10 L. DePillis, 'Meet CGI Federal, the Company behind the Botched Launch of HealthCare.Gov', *Washington Post*, 17 October 2013.

11 D. R. Levinson, 'CMS Did Not Always Manage and Oversee Contractor Performance for the Federal Marketplace as Required by Federal Requirements and Contract Terms' (Washington, DC: Department of Health and Human Services – Office of Inspector General, September 2015).

12 D. R. Levinson, 'HealthCare.Gov: CMS Management of the Federal Marketplace – A Case Study' (Washington, DC: Department of Health and Human Services – Office of Inspector General, February 2016), p. 20.

13 Ibid., p. 22.

14 Ibid., p. ii.

15 Ibid., p. 10.

16 Ibid., p. ii.

17 W. Lazonick and M. Mazzucato, 'The Risk-Reward Nexus in the Innovation-Inequality Relationship: Who Takes the Risks? Who Gets the Rewards?', *Industrial and Corporate Change* 22, no. 4 (1 August 2013), pp. 1093–128, https://doi.org/10.1093/icc/dtt019

18 Levinson, 'HealthCare.Gov: CMS Management of the Federal Marketplace – A Case Study', p. 14.

19 Levinson, 'HealthCare.Gov: CMS Management of the Federal Marketplace – A Case Study'.

20 D. Saint-Martin, 'How the Reinventing Government Movement in Public Administration Was Exported from the U.S. to Other Countries', *International*

Journal of Public Administration 24, no. 6 (1 May 2001), p. 318, https://doi.org/10.1081/PAD-100104397

21 A. Gore, 'From Red Tape to Results: Creating a Government That Works Better and Costs Less – Report of the National Performance Review', 7 September 1993, https://files.eric.ed.gov/fulltext/ED384294.pdf

22 Ibid., p. 17.

23 F. Thompson and N. Riccucci, 'Reinventing Government', *Annual Review of Political Science* 1 (28 November 2003), p. 237, https://doi.org/10.1146/annurev.polisci.1.1.231

24 Gore, 'From Red Tape to Results: Creating a Government That Works Better and Costs Less – Report of the National Performance Review'.

25 Saint-Martin, 'How the Reinventing Government Movement in Public Administration Was Exported from the U.S. to Other Countries', p. 577.

26 A. Giddens, *Beyond Left and Right: The Future of Radical Politics* (Stanford: Stanford University Press, 1994).

27 Saint-Martin, 'How the Reinventing Government Movement in Public Administration Was Exported from the U.S. to Other Countries', p. 589.

28 Ibid.

29 Ibid.

30 J. Shaoul, A. Stafford and P. Stapleton, 'Partnerships and the Role of Financial Advisors: Private Control over Public Policy?', *Policy & Politics* 35, no. 3 (1 July 2007), p. 483, https://doi.org/10.1332/030557307781571678

31 T. Bovaird, 'The Ins and Outs of Outsourcing and Insourcing: What Have We Learnt from the Past 30 Years?', *Public Money & Management* 36, no. 1 (2 January 2016), pp. 67–74, https://doi.org/10.1080/09540962.2015.1093298

32 Thomson Reuters Practical Law, 'Private Finance Initiative (PFI)', Practical Law, 2021, http://uk.practicallaw.thomsonreuters.com/3-107-7049?transitionType=Default&contextData=(sc.Default)&firstPage=true

33 E. Shaw, 'The British Labour Government and the Private Finance Initiative in the National Health Service: A Case of Pragmatic Policy-Making?', *The Public Sector Innovation Journal* 8, no. 3 (2003), p. 3.

34 B. Christophers, *Rentier Capitalism: Who Owns the Economy, and Who Pays for It?* (London: Verso Books, 2020), p. 260.

35 J. Froud, 'The Private Finance Initiative: Risk, Uncertainty and the State', *Accounting, Organizations and Society* 28, no. 6 (1 August 2003), pp. 567–89, https://doi.org/10.1016/S0361-3682(02)00011-9

36 Gore, 'From Red Tape to Results: Creating a Government That Works Better and Costs Less – Report of the National Performance Review', p. 12.

37 Ibid., p. 70.

38 National Audit Office, 'The Choice of Finance for Capital Investment' (London: National Audit Office, March 2015), https://www.nao.org.uk/wp-content/uploads/2015/03/The-choice-of-finance-for-capital-investment.pdf

39 Shaoul, Stafford and Stapleton, 'Partnerships and the Role of Financial Advisors'.

40 Ibid., p. 485; PricewaterhouseCoopers, 'Richard Abadie,' PwC, 2021, https://www.pwc.co.uk/contacts/r/richard-abadie.html

41 Shaoul, Stafford and Stapleton, 'Partnerships and the Role of Financial Advisors', p. 489.

42 Ibid., p. 490.

43 J. Morphet, *Outsourcing in the UK: Policies, Practices and Outcomes* (Bristol: Bristol University Press, 2021), p. 97.

44 Greater Manchester Health and Social Care Partnership, 'About the Greater Manchester Health & Social Care Partnership', *GMHSC* (blog), 2022, https://www.gmhsc.org.uk/about-devolution/the-partnership/

45 D. Finn, 'Contracting out Welfare to Work in the USA: Delivery Lessons', Corporate Document Services (Portsmouth: Department for Work and Pensions, 2007), p. 15, https://pure.port.ac.uk/ws/portalfiles/portal/121182/10.PDF

46 Cabinet Office, 'Prime Minister's Delivery Unit', 5 August 2005, The National Archives, https://webarchive.nationalarchives.gov.uk/ukgwa/2006 0213212513

47 Weiss, *Management Consultancy and the British State*, p. 13.

48 D. Whitfield, 'A Typology of Privatisation and Marketisation' (Australian Institute for Social Research, University of Adelaide: European Services Strategy Unit, 2006).

49 Hodge and Bowman, '6. The "Consultocracy": The Business of Reforming Government'.

50 Morphet, *Outsourcing in the UK*, p. 97.

51 Dunleavy et al., *Digital Era Governance*.

52 National Partnership for Reinventing Government, 'Access America: Reengineering Through Information Technology' (Washington, DC: National Partnership for Reinventing Government, 1997), https://govinfo.library.unt.edu/npr/library/announc/access/acessrpt.html

53 H. Margetts, *Information Technology in Government: Britain and America* (London; New York: Routledge, 1998), p. 136.

54 Dunleavy et al., *Digital Era Governance*, p. 48.

55 Ibid., p. 133.

56 Dunleavy et al., *Digital Era Governance*.

57 M. Mazzucato, *The Entrepreneurial State: Debunking Public vs. Private Sector Myths* (London: Penguin, 2018 [2013]).

58 McKenna, *The World's Newest Profession*.

59 P. Dunleavy and H. Z. Margetts, 'The Second Wave of Digital Era Governance', SSRN Scholarly Paper (Rochester, NY: Social Science Research Network, 2010), pp. 56–7, https://papers.ssrn.com/abstract=1643850

60 I. Horrocks, ' "Experts" and E-Government', *Information, Communication & Society* 12, no. 1 (1 February 2009), pp. 110–27, https://doi.org/10.1080/13691180802109030; D. Craig and R. Brooks, *Plundering the Public Sector: How New Labour Are Letting Consultants Run off with £70 Billion of Our Money* (London: Constable, 2006).

61 Dunleavy et al., *Digital Era Governance*, p. 54.

62 Weiss, *Management Consultancy and the British State*.

63 G. Greenwald, 'NSA Collecting Phone Records of Millions of Verizon Customers Daily', *Guardian*, 6 June 2013. US news: https://www.theguardian.com/world/2013/jun/06/nsa-phone-records-verizon-court-order

64 B. Gellman and L. Poitras, 'U.S., British Intelligence Mining Data from Nine U.S. Internet Companies in Broad Secret Program', *Washington Post*, 7 June 2013. Investigations: https://www.washingtonpost.com/investigations/us-intelligence-mining-data-from-nine-us-internet-companies-in-broad-secret-program/2013/06/06/3a0c0da8-cebf-11e2-8845-d970ccb04497_story.html

65 D. Van Puyvelde, *Outsourcing US Intelligence: Private Contractors and Government Accountability* (Edinburgh: Edinburgh University Press, 2019).

66 T. Chase Meacham, 'Edward Snowden's Employer: 6 Shocking Facts About Booz Allen Hamilton', *Mic* (blog), 11 June 2013, https://www.mic.com/articles/47783/edward-snowden-s-employer-6-shocking-facts-about-booz-allen-hamilton

67 PricewaterhouseCoopers, 'Infrastructure: Generating Long Term Value from Infrastructure Investments' (London: PwC, May 2010), https://www.pwc.co.uk/assets/pdf/infrastructure-funds-brochure-may2010.pdf

68 N. Mathiason, 'Auditors Face Being Called to Account for Their Role in the Global Financial Crisis', *Guardian*, 24 October 2009. Business: http://www.theguardian.com/business/2009/oct/25/auditors-role-financial-crisis

69 Consultancy.eu, 'Europe's Management Consulting Industry Worth $45 Billion', 23 March 2020, https://www.consultancy.eu/news/3988/europes-management-consulting-industry-worth-45-billion

70 S. Trumbo Vila and M. Peters, 'The Bail Out Business: Who Profits from Bank Rescues in the EU?', Amsterdam: Transnational Institute, 2017, https://www.tni.org/files/publication-downloads/tni_bail_out_eng_online0317.pdf

71 Ibid.

72 D. Hugh-Jones, 'Why Do Crises Go to Waste? Fiscal Austerity and Public Service Reform', *Public Choice* 158 (2014), p. 158, https://doi.org/10.1007/s11127-012-0002-5

73 Boston Consulting Group, 'Adaptive Strategy in Government' (Boston Consulting Group, May 2012), https://image-src.bcg.com/Images/BCG_Adaptive_Strategy_in_Government_May_12_tcm110-105088.pdf

74 McKinsey & Company, 'Growth and Renewal in the Swedish Economy: Development, Current Situation and Priorities for the Future' (McKinsey Global Institute, 2012), https://www.mckinsey.com/~/media/McKinsey/Featured%20Insights/Europe/Growth%20and%20renewal%20in%20the%20Swedish%20economy/MGI_Swedish_economy_Full_report.ashx

75 McKinsey & Company, 'Greece 10 Years Ahead: Defining Greece's New Growth Model and Strategy' (Athens: McKinsey & Company, June 2012), http://sev4enterprise.org.gr/wp-content/uploads/2014/05/EKTHESEIS-5.pdf

76 McKinsey & Company, 'A Window of Opportunity for Europe' (McKinsey Global Institute, June 2015), https://www.mckinsey.com/~/media/McKinsey/Featured%20Insights/Europe/A%20window%20of%20opportunity%20for%20Europe/A_window_of_opportunity_for_Europe%20Full_report.pdf

77 R. Prince, 'Tory Leader David Cameron Attacks Labour's Policy by Power-Point', *Daily Telegraph*, 12 May 2008, http://www.telegraph.co.uk/news/politics/labour/1950578/Labour-Tory-leader-David-Cameron-attacks-Labours-policy-by-PowerPoint.html

78 Guardian Staff, 'Conservative Conference: David Cameron's Speech in Full', *Guardian*, 1 October 2008. Politics: http://www.theguardian.com/politics/2008/oct/01/davidcameron.toryconference1

79 'Obama Budget Official Withdraws over Tax Flap,' *Reuters*, 3 February 2009. World news: https://www.reuters.com/article/uk-obama-killefer-sb-idUKTRE5125BC20090203

80 SBS News, 'Rudd Spends Big on Consultants', *SBS News*, 24 February 2015, https://www.sbs.com.au/news/rudd-spends-big-on-consultants

81 P. Curtis, 'Whitehall Supplier Offers Year's Worth of Free Contracts While Times Are Tough', *Guardian*, 2 January 2011. Politics: https://www.theguardian.com/politics/2011/jan/02/kpmg-government-supplier-contracts-consultancy

82 J. Moulds, 'NHS Body "Wastes Millions on Flawed Financial Advice"', *Guardian*, 21 July 2018. Society: https://www.theguardian.com/society/2018/jul/21/nhs-trust-wastes-million-on-flawed-financial-advice-london-north-west

83 G. Plimmer, 'UK Outsourcing Spend Doubles to £88bn under Coalition', *Financial Times*, 6 July 2014; in Weiss, *Management Consultancy and the British State*.

84 Weiss, *Management Consultancy and the British State*.

85 R. Booth and N. Hopkins, 'London 2012 Olympics: G4S Failures Prompt Further Military Deployment', *Guardian*, 24 July 2012. UK news: http://www.theguardian.com/uk/2012/jul/24/london-2012-olympics-g4s-military

86 'Deaths of People on Benefits Prompt Inquiry Call,' *BBC News*, 10 May 2021. UK, https://www.bbc.com/news/uk-56819727

87 B. Doherty, 'Detention Centre Operator's Contract Extended despite New Owner's Objection', *Guardian*, 8 August 2016. Australia news: http://www.theguardian.com/australia-news/2016/aug/08/detention-centre-operators-contract-extended-despite-owners-objection; C. Alexander, 'Meet the Companies That Run Our Immigration Detention Camps', *Crikey*, 25 February 2014, https://www.crikey.com.au/2014/02/25/meet-the-companies-that-run-our-immigration-detention-camps/

88 N. Perpitch, 'Serco Stripped of Control for Sterilising Hospital's Medical Equipment', *ABC News*, 24 February 2015, https://www.abc.net.au/news/2015-02-24/serco-loses-responsibility-to-sterilise-perth-hospital-equipment/6256756; The Sydney Morning Herald, 'Serco fined $1m for WA hospital failings', 10 June 2015, https://www.smh.com.au/national/western-australia/serco-fined-1m-for-wa-hospital-failings-20150610-ghl3ep.html

89 J. Kollewe, 'Serco to Continue Running Australian Immigration Detention Centres', *Guardian*, 10 December 2014. Business: http://www.theguardian.com/business/2014/dec/10/serco-australian-immigration-detention-centres-contract-christmas-island

90 A. Travis, 'Offender Tagging: Serco to Repay More than £68m in Overcharging', *Guardian*, 19 December 2013. Business: http://www.theguardian.com/business/2013/dec/19/offender-electronic-tagging-serco-repay-68m-overcharging; Press Association, 'Serco fined £22.9m over electronic tagging scandal', *Guardian*, 3 July 2019. Business: https://www.theguardian.com/business/2019/jul/03/serco-fined-229m-over-electronic-tagging-scandal

91 S. Farrell, 'Serco to Lose Out-of-Hours GP Services and Hospital Management Contracts', *Guardian*, 13 December 2013. Business: http://www.theguardian.com/business/2013/dec/13/serco-lose-contract-gp-services-nhs-outsourcing

92 'Shares in Scandal-Hit Serco Dive after Profit Warning', *Reuters*, 14 November 2013. Business news: https://www.reuters.com/article/uk-serco-profit-idUKBRE9AD0GW20131114

93 Guardian, 'FTSE 100's Use of Tax Havens – Get the Full List', *Guardian*, 12 May 2013, https://www.theguardian.com/news/datablog/2013/may/12/ftse-100-use-tax-havens-full-list

94 C. Knaus, 'Serco a High-Risk Client with History of Failures, Offshore Law Firm Found', *Guardian*, 6 November 2017. Business: http://www.theguardian.com/business/2017/nov/06/serco-a-high-risk-client-with-history-of-failures-offshore-law-firm-found

95 D. Oliver, 'Exclusive: Government Spending on Management Consultants Trebles in Three Years', *BMJ* 366 (5 September 2019), p. l5404, https://doi.org/10.1136/bmj.l5404

96 G. Plimmer and D. Oakley, 'Falling Serco Share Price Unsettles Investors', *Financial Times*, 30 November 2014.

97 A. Mori, 'The impact of public services outsourcing on work and employment conditions in different national regimes', *European Journal of Industrial Relations* 23, no. 4 (1 December 2017), pp. 347–64, https://doi.org/10.1177/0959680117694272

98 R. Davies and D. Sabbagh, 'Carillion Crisis Deepens amid Scramble to Save Jobs after Firm Collapses', *Guardian*, 15 January 2018. Business: http://www.theguardian.com/business/2018/jan/15/carillion-fallout-deepens-as-workers-face-pay-being-stopped-in-48-hours

99 R. Wearmouth, 'Just 2 of 1,200 Carillion Apprentices Offered Placements by Government', *HuffPost UK*, 3 April 2018, https://www.huffingtonpost.co.uk/entry/carillion-government-department_uk_5ac3451be4b09712fec3fc06

100 A. Leaver, 'Outsourcing Firms and the Paradox of Time Travel', *SPERI Blog* (blog), 12 February 2018, http://speri.dept.shef.ac.uk/2018/02/12/outsourcing-firms-and-the-paradox-of-time-travel/

101 M. Vincent, 'Why Carillion Has Gone into Liquidation Rather than Administration', *Financial Times*, 15 January 2018, https://www.ft.com/content/a4dd80be-f9f1-11e7-a492-2c9be7f3120a

102 Leaver, 'Outsourcing Firms and the Paradox of Time Travel'.

103 M. O'Dwyer and G. Plimmer, 'KPMG sued for £1.3bn over Carillion audit', *Financial Times*, 3 February 2022.

104 Ibid.

105 Financial Reporting Council, 'Sanctions against KPMG and others in connection with Regenersis & Carillion audits', 25 July 2022, https://www.frc.org.uk/news/july-2022/sanctions-against-kpmg-and-others-in-connection-wi

106 T. Howard and L. Clarence-Smith, 'KPMG Facing £1.3bn Claim for Carillion "Failures"', *The Times*, 4 February 2022. Business: https://www.thetimes.co.uk/article/kpmg-facing-1-3bn-claim-for-carillion-failures-xfm7g5pfj

107 M. O'Dwyer and G. Plimmer, 'KPMG sued for £1.3bn over Carillion audit', *Financial Times*, 3 February 2022.

108 Ibid.

109 Davies and Sabbagh, 'Carillion Crisis Deepens amid Scramble to Save Jobs after Firm Collapses'.

110 G. Smith, J. Creery and E. Goldberg, 'FirstFT: EY boss targets $10bn boost from Silicon Valley tie-ups', *Financial Times*, 20 July 2022.

111 J. Kollewe, 'EY Plans to Spin off Audit Business in Shake-up for Industry', *Guardian*, 27 May 2022. Business: https://www.theguardian.com/business/2022/may/27/ey-plans-to-spin-off-audit-business-in-shake-up-for-industry

112 M. O'Dwyer, 'PwC set for record revenues as it rejects audit and consulting split', *Financial Times*, 17 July 2022.

113 M. O'Dwyer, 'KPMG hit with half of UK accounting fines as penalties reach new record', *Financial Times*, 28 July 2022.

114 G. Plimmer and M. O'Dwyer, 'KPMG Wins UK Government Contracts despite Withdrawing from Bidding after Scandals', *Financial Times*, 24 April 2022.

5. The Big Confidence Trick: Consultology and Economic Rents

1 Name changed to protect anonymity. Date of interview: 16.10.21.

2 K. Sahlin-Andersson and L. Engwall, *The Expansion of Management Knowledge: Carriers, Flows, and Sources* (Stanford: Stanford University Press, 2002).

3 N. Nikolova and T. Devinney, 'The Nature of Client–Consultant Interaction: A Critical Review', in Kipping and Clark (eds), *The Oxford Handbook of Management Consulting*.

4 P. Tisdall, *Agents of Change: Development and Practice of Management Consultancy* (London: Trafalgar Square Publishing, 1982); A. Sturdy, 'The Consultancy Process – An Insecure Business?', *Journal of Management Studies* 34, no. 3 (1997), pp. 389–413, https://doi.org/10.1111/1467-6486.00056

5 A. B. Hargadon, 'Firms as Knowledge Brokers: Lessons in Pursuing Continuous Innovation', *California Management Review* 40, no. 3 (1 April 1998), pp. 209–27, https://doi.org/10.2307/41165951; P. F. Drucker, 'Why Management Consultants', in M. Zimet and R. G. Greenwood (eds), *The Evolving Science of Management* (New York: American Management Associations, 1979), pp. 475–8.

6 McKenna, *The World's Newest Profession*.

7 Nikolova and Devinney, 'The Nature of Client–Consultant Interaction: A Critical Review'.

8 Ibid.

9 T. Clark and G. Salaman, 'Telling Tales: Management Gurus' Narratives and the Construction of Managerial Identity', *Journal of Management Studies* 35, no. 2 (1998), pp. 137–61, https://doi.org/10.1111/1467-6486.00088

10 L. Rothman, 'How American Inequality in the Gilded Age Compares to Today', *Time*, 5 February 2018, https://time.com/5122375/american-inequality-gilded-age/

11 New York Herald, 'Arrest of the Confidence Man', 1849, https://lostmuseum.cuny.edu/archive/arrest-of-the-confidence-man-newyork-herald

12 R. Fincham, 'The Client in the Client–Consultant Relationship', in Kipping and Clark (eds), *The Oxford Handbook of Management Consulting*.

13 A. Sturdy et al., *Management Consultancy: Boundaries and Knowledge in Action* (Oxford: Oxford University Press, 2009), https://doi.org/10.1093/acprof:oso/9780199212644.001.0001

14 J. Micklethwait and A. Wooldridge, *The Witch Doctors: Making Sense of the Management Gurus* (New York: Three Rivers Press, 1998), p. 58.

15 Mazzucato, *The Entrepreneurial State*.

16 M. Mazzucato, J. Ryan-Collins and G. Gouzoulis, 'Theorising and Mapping Modern Economic Rents', *UCL IIPP Working Paper Series* WP 2020-13 (June 2020), https://www.ucl.ac.uk/bartlett/public-purpose/sites/public-purpose/files/final_iipp-wp2020-13-theorising-and-mapping-modern-economic-rents_8_oct.pdf

17 McKenna, *The World's Newest Profession*, p. 3.

18 Ibid., pp. 157–8.

19 Management Consultant Association, 'MCA Member Survey 2021' (London: MCA, 2021), https://www.mca.org.uk/wp-content/uploads/sites/60/2021/01/MCA-Member-Survey-Report-2021.pdf

20 McKenna, *The World's Newest Profession*.

21 The Sutton Trust, 'Elitist Britain' (London: The Sutton Trust, 2019), https://www.suttontrust.com/wp-content/uploads/2019/12/Elitist-Britain-2019.pdf

22 M. Alvesson, 'Managing Consultants: Control and Identity', in Kipping and Clark (eds), *The Oxford Handbook of Management Consulting*, p. 311.

23 A. Sturdy and C. Wright, 'A Consulting Diaspora? Enterprising Selves as Agents of Enterprise', *Organization* 15, no. 3 (1 May 2008), pp. 427–44, https://doi.org/10.1177/1350508408088538

24 McDonald, *The Firm*.

25 McKinsey & Company, 'McKinsey Alumni Center', 2021, https://www.mckinsey.com/alumni/

26 McKenna, *The World's Newest Profession*.

27 PricewaterhouseCoopers, 'Millennials at Work: Reshaping the Workplace' (London: Pricewaterhouse Coopers, 2011), https://www.pwc.com/co/es/publicaciones/assets/millennials-at-work.pdf

28 PricewaterhouseCoopers, 'Graduate Jobs', PwC, accessed 4 March 2022, https://www.pwc.co.uk/careers/student-careers/undergraduate-graduate-careers/our-programmes/graduate-opportunities.html

29 A. Gross, 'Millennial Management Consultants Yearn for Meaning at Work,' *Financial Times*, 29 January 2020, https://www.ft.com/content/e12e305c-2363-11ea-b8a1-584213ee7b2b

30 D. Sull, C. Sull and B. Zweig, 'Toxic Culture Is Driving the Great Resignation', *MIT Sloan Management Review*, 11 January 2022, https://sloanreview.mit.edu/article/toxic-culture-is-driving-the-great-resignation/

31 BCG, 'Students & Graduates', 2021, https://careers.bcg.com/students

32 McKinsey, 'Students', 2021, https://www.mckinsey.com/careers/students

33 KPMG, 'Graduate', 2021, https://www.kpmgcareers.co.uk/graduate/

34 Date of interview: 13.10.21.

35 Fincham, 'The Client in the Client–Consultant Relationship'.

36 B. Momani, 'Professional Management Consultants in Transnational Governance', in L. Seabrooke and L. Folke Henriksen (eds), *Professional Networks in Transnational Governance* (Cambridge: Cambridge University Press, 2017), p. 249, https://doi.org/10.1017/9781316855508.016

37 Alvesson, 'Managing Consultants: Control and Identity', p. 319.

38 Fincham, 'The Client in the Client–Consultant Relationship'; A. Werr, 'Knowledge Management and Management Consulting,' in Kipping and Clark (eds), *The Oxford Handbook of Management Consulting*.

39 Date of interview: 13.10.21.

40 V. Cheng, *Case Interview Secrets: A Former McKinsey Interviewer Reveals How to Get Multiple Job Offers in Consulting* (Seattle: Innovation Press, 2012).

41 Nikolova and Devinney, 'The Nature of Client–Consultant Interaction: A Critical Review'.

42 Micklethwait and Wooldridge, *The Witch Doctors*, p. 54.

43 Deloitte, 'Deloitte University: The Leadership Center', Deloitte United States, 2021, https://www2.deloitte.com/us/en/pages/about-deloitte/articles/deloitteuniversity-leadership-center.html

44 'Capgemini University', *Capgemini US* (blog), 24 July 2017, https://www.capgemini.com/us-en/careers/learning-development/capgemini-university/

45 McKinsey Global Institute, 'About MGI', 2021, https://www.mckinsey.com/mgi/overview/about-us

46 Deloitte, 'Center for the Edge', Deloitte United States, 2021, https://www2.deloitte.com/us/en/pages/center-for-the-edge/topics/center-for-the-edge.html

47 Micklethwait and Wooldridge, *The Witch Doctors*, p. 55.

48 P. Aucoin, 'Administrative Reform in Public Management: Paradigms, Principles, Paradoxes and Pendulums', *Governance* 3, no. 2 (1990), pp. 115–37, https://doi.org/10.1111/j.1468-0491.1990.tb00111.x; Saint-Martin, 'Management Consultancy and the Varieties of Capitalism'.

49 Weiss, *Management Consultancy and the British State*.

50 K. E. Aupperle, W. Acar and D. E. Booth, 'An Empirical Critique of *In Search of Excellence*: How Excellent Are the Excellent Companies?', *Journal of Management* 12, no. 4 (1 December 1986), pp. 499–512, https://doi.org/10.1177/014920638601200405

51 A. H. Van de Ven, review of *In Search of Excellence: Lessons from America's Best-Run Companies* by Thomas J. Peters and Robert H. Waterman, *Administrative Science Quarterly* 28, no. 4 (1983), pp. 621–4, https://doi.org/10.2307/2393015

52 Micklethwait and Wooldridge, *The Witch Doctors*.

53 Saint-Martin, 'Management Consultancy and the Varieties of Capitalism'.

54 G. Morgan, A. Sturdy and M. Frenkel, 'The Role of Large Management Consultancy Firms in Global Public Policy', in D. Stone and K. Moloney (eds), *The Oxford Handbook of Global Policy and Transnational Administration* (Oxford: Oxford University Press, 2019), https://doi.org/10.1093/oxfordhb/9780198758648.013.39

55 Nikolova and Devinney, 'The Nature of Client–Consultant Interaction: A Critical Review'.

56 Date of interview: 13.10.21.

57 Ibid.

58 McKenna, *The World's Newest Profession*, pp. 230–31.

6. Evading the Risks, Reaping the Rewards: The Business Model

1 Date of interview: 13.10.21.

2 'David Cameron promises in/out referendum on EU', *BBC News*, 23 January 2013. Politics: https://www.bbc.com/news/uk-politics-21148282

3 McKinsey & Company, 'Rethinking Supply Chain Strategies after Brexit', 7 May 2019, https://www.mckinsey.com/featured-insights/europe/brexit-the-bigger-picture-rethinking-supply-chains-in-a-time-of-uncertainty; McKinsey & Company, 'Brexit: The Bigger Picture – Revitalising UK Exports in the New World of Trade' (London: McKinsey & Company, March 2019), https://www.mckinsey.com/~/media/McKinsey/Featured%20Insights/Europe/Brexit%20The%20bigger%20picture%20Revitalizing%20UK%20exports%20in%20the%20new%20world%20of%20trade/Brexit-the-bigger-picture.pdf; McKinsey & Company, 'Brexit: The Bigger Picture – Rethinking Talent for the Long Term' (London: McKinsey & Company, November 2019), https://www.mckinsey.com/~/media/McKinsey/Featured%20Insights/Europe/Brexit%20The%20bigger%20picture%20Rethinking%20talent%20for%20the%20long%20term/Brexit-The-bigger-picture-Rethinking-talent-for-the-long-term.pdf

4 'Brexit and Beyond – What's Ahead for Aerospace & Defense', BCG Global, 2021, https://www.bcg.com/industries/Aerospace-defense/

brexit-and-beyond; 'Biopharma's Countdown to Brexit', BCG Global, 8 January 2021, https://www.bcg.com/publications/2018/biopharma-countdown-to-brexit; 'What Brexit Means for Financial Institutions', BCG Global, 19 August 2020,https://www.bcg.com/publications/2016/strategy-what-brexit-means-for-financial-institutions

5 'Brexit Global Contacts | Deloitte | Insights, Perspectives', Deloitte Bangladesh, accessed 10 November 2021, https://www2.deloitte.com/bd/en/pages/about-deloitte/articles/gx-brexit-global-contacts.html

6 PwC, 'Brexit Impact Assessment Tool', PwC Suite, 2021, https://thesuite.pwc.com/resources/brexit-impact-assessment-tool

7 PricewaterhouseCoopers, 'Beyond Brexit', PwC, 2021, https://www.pwc.co.uk/the-eu-referendum.html

8 C. Cornish, 'Management Consultants Make Hay out of Brexit Uncertainty', *Financial Times*, 13 March 2017.

9 Ibid.

10 A. Gross, 'Management Consulting Sector Boosted by Brexit Planning', *Financial Times*, 16 July 2019.

11 R. Syal, 'Brexit Drives Government Consultancy Fees to £450m in Three Years', *Guardian*, 6 October 2020. Politics: https://www.theguardian.com/politics/2020/oct/06/brexit-drives-government-consultancy-fees-to-450m-in-three-years

12 National Audit Office, 'Departments' Use of Consultants to Support Preparations for EU Exit' (London: National Audit Office, 7 June 2019), https://www.nao.org.uk/wp-content/uploads/2019/05/Departments-use-of-consultants-to-support-preparations-for-EU-Exit.pdf

13 Ibid., p. 22.

14 Private Finance Panel, 'Public Opportunity, Private Benefit: Progressing the Private Finance Initiative' (London: HM Treasury, 1995), p. 12; in Froud, 'The Private Finance Initiative'.

15 P. S. Eyres, 'The Top Seven Legal Risks for Consultants', *Consulting to Management* 17, no. 1 (March 2006), pp. 9–10, 20; C. Homburg and P. Stebel, 'Determinants of Contract Terms for Professional Services', *Management Accounting Research* 20, no. 2 (1 June 2009), pp. 129–45, https://doi.org/10.1016/j.mar.2008.10.001

16 Froud, 'The Private Finance Initiative', pp. 580–81.

17 Froud, 'The Private Finance Initiative'.

18 Homburg and Stebel, 'Determinants of Contract Terms for Professional Services'.

19 J. F. Padgett and P. D. McLean, 'Organizational Invention and Elite Transformation: The Birth of Partnership Systems in Renaissance Florence', *American Journal of Sociology* 111, no. 5 (March 2006), pp. 1463–568, https://doi.org/10.1086/498470

20 R. Greenwood and L. Empson, 'The Professional Partnership: Relic or Exemplary Form of Governance?', *Organization Studies* 24, no. 6 (1 July 2003), pp. 909–33, https://doi.org/10.1177/0170840603024006005

21 We use data from: Consulting.com, 'The Top 50 Consulting Firms In 2019 By Revenue, Prestige, Growth & Employee Satisfaction'.

22 B. Braun, 'From performativity to political economy: index investing, ETFs and asset manager capitalism', *New Political Economy* 3, no. 21 (29 October 2015), pp. 257-273, https://doi.org/10.1080/13563467.2016.1094045.

23 M. C. Jensen, 'Agency Costs of Free Cash Flow, Corporate Finance, and Takeovers', *The American Economic Review* 76, no. 2 (1986), pp. 323–9; M. Friedman, 'The Social Responsibility of Business Is to Increase Its Profits', in W. Ch Zimmerli, M. Holzinger and K. Richter (eds), *Corporate Ethics and Corporate Governance* (Berlin, Heidelberg: Springer Berlin Heidelberg, 2007), pp. 173–8, https://doi.org/10.1007/978-3-540-70818-6_14

24 W. Lazonick, 'Innovative Enterprise or Sweatshop Economics?: In Search of Foundations of Economic Analysis', *Challenge* 59, no. 2 (3 March 2016), pp. 65–114, https://doi.org/10.1080/05775132.2016.1147297

25 Lazonick and Mazzucato, 'The Risk-Reward Nexus in the Innovation-Inequality Relationship', p. 1098; W. Lazonick and M. O'Sullivan, 'Maximizing Shareholder Value: A New Ideology for Corporate Governance', *Economy and Society* 29, no. 1 (1 January 2000), pp. 13–35, https://doi.org/10.1080/030851400360541

26 Jensen, 'Agency Costs of Free Cash Flow, Corporate Finance, and Takeovers', p. 323.

27 Lazonick and Mazzucato, 'The Risk-Reward Nexus in the Innovation-Inequality Relationship'.

28 R. Steiner, C. Kaiser and L. Reichmuth, 'Consulting for the Public Sector in Europe', in E. Ongaro and S. van Thiel (eds), *The Palgrave Handbook of Public Administration and Management in Europe* (London: Palgrave Macmillan UK, 2018), pp. 475–95, https://doi.org/10.1057/978-1-137-55269-3_25

29 'BCG Platinion | AllofUs', accessed 11 November 2021, https://allofus.com/; 'Bain & Company and QVARTZ Have Joined Forces to Provide Unparalleled Consulting Services in the Nordics', Bain, accessed 11 November 2021, https://www.bain.com/about/media-center/press-releases/2020/bain-company-and-qvartz-have-joined-forces-to-provide-unparalleled-consulting-services-in-the-nordics/; K. Kivestu, 'Acquisitions by Consulting Companies', RocketBlocks, 2021, https://www.rocketblocks.me/blog/mckinsey-analytics-overview.php

7. Infantilizing Organizations: When Learning Is Undermined Across Government and Business

1 Government Offices of Sweden, 'Future Challenges for Sweden: Final Report of the Commission on the Future of Sweden' (Stockholm, 2013), https://www.regeringen.se/contentassets/389793d478de411fbc83d8f512cb5013/future-challenges-for-sweden--final-report-of-the-commission-on-the-future-of-sweden

2 K. Christensen et al., 'Ageing Populations: The Challenges Ahead', *Lancet* 374, no. 9696 (3 October 2009), pp. 1196–208, https://doi.org/10.1016/S0140-6736(09)61460-4

3 K. van Kersbergen and B. Vis, *Comparative Welfare State Politics* (Cambridge: Cambridge University Press, 2014).

4 Government Offices of Sweden, 'Future Challenges for Sweden: Final Report of the Commission on the Future of Sweden'.

5 T. Madell, 'The First Public Private Partnership in Health and Medical Care in Sweden', *European Public Private Partnership Law Review* 5, no. 4 (2010), pp. 235–6.

6 Öhrlings PricewaterhouseCooper, 'Supplement to the "Evaluation of Alternative Solutions for Financing and Maintenance of New Karolinska Hospital"' (Stockholm: Öhrlings PricewaterhouseCooper, 2007); in A. Waluszewski, H. Hakansson and I. Snehota, 'The Public-Private Partnership (PPP) Disaster of a New Hospital – Expected Political and Existing Business Interaction Patterns', *Journal of Business & Industrial Marketing* 34, no. 5 (1 January 2019), pp. 1119–30, https://doi.org/10.1108/JBIM-12-2018-0377

7 Eurodad, 'History RePPPeated: How Public Private Partnerships Are Failing' (Brussels: Eurodad, September 2018), https://d3n8a8pro7vhmx.cloudfront.

net/eurodad/pages/508/attachments/original/1590679608/How_Public_
Private_Partnerships_are_failing.pdf?1590679608

8 R. A. Atun and M. McKee, 'Is the Private Finance Initiative Dead?', *BMJ*
331, no. 7520 (6 October 2005), pp. 792–3, https://doi.org/10.1136/
bmj.331.7520.792

9 J. Shaoul, A. Stafford and P. Stapleton, 'The Cost of Using Private Finance to
Build, Finance and Operate Hospitals', *Public Money & Management* 28, no. 2
(1 April 2008), p. 101, https://doi.org/10.1111/j.1467-9302.2008.00628.x

10 S. Bergman and J. Dyfvermark, 'Controversial Swedish Hospital Partnership
Has Luxembourg Links', *International Consortium of Investigative Journalists*
(blog), 30 November 2014, https://www.icij.org/investigations/luxembourg-
leaks/controversial-swedish-hospital-partnership-has-luxembourg-links/

11 M. Paterlini, 'Troubled Rebuild of Stockholm's Landmark Hospital Has Cost
Twice as Much as Planned', *BMJ* 361 (25 April 2018), k1816, https://doi.
org/10.1136/bmj.k1816

12 Waluszewski, Hakansson and Snehota, 'The Public-Private Partnership (PPP)
Disaster of a New Hospital – Expected Political and Existing Business Interaction
Patterns'.

13 L. K. Mervyn, *Rethinking Public Private Partnerships* (Cheltenham: Edward Elgar
Publishing, 2021); Eurodad, 'History RePPPeated: How Public Private Partnerships Are Failing'.

14 Eurodad, 'History RePPPeated: How Public Private Partnerships Are Failing',
p. 17.

15 M. Mazzucato and V. Roy, 'Rethinking Value in Health Innovation: From Mystifications towards Prescriptions', *Journal of Economic Policy Reform* 22, no. 2
(3 April 2019), pp. 101–19, https://doi.org/10.1080/17487870.2018.1509712

16 Paterlini, 'Troubled Rebuild of Stockholm's Landmark Hospital Has Cost Twice
as Much as Planned'.

17 J. Meijling, *Nya Karolinska – Ett Pilotprojekt För Marknadsstyrd Vård?* (Stockholm: Arena Idé, 2018), https://arenaide.se/wp-content/uploads/
sites/2/2018/03/rapport-nks-meijling-1.pdf

18 Paterlini, 'Troubled Rebuild of Stockholm's Landmark Hospital Has Cost Twice
as Much as Planned'.

19 Ibid.

20 M. Paterlini, 'Director of Troubled Karolinska Hospital Resigns', *BMJ* 363
(9 October 2018), k4249, https://doi.org/10.1136/bmj.k4249

21 Eurodad, 'History RePPPeated: How Public Private Partnerships Are Failing', p. 18.

22 Ramboll Group, 'New Karolinska Solna – a World-Class Hospital,' Ramboll Group, 2021, https://ramboll.com/projects/group/new-karolinska-solna

23 M. Paterlini, 'Jobs Come under Threat at Troubled Karolinska Hospital in Sweden', *BMJ* 367 (12 November 2019), p. l6479, https://doi.org/10.1136/bmj.l6479

24 Waluszewski, Hakansson and Snehota, 'The Public-Private Partnership (PPP) Disaster of a New Hospital – Expected Political and Existing Business Interaction Patterns'.

25 M. Mazzucato et al., 'COVID-19 and the Need for Dynamic State Capabilities: An International Comparison', Development Futures Series Working Papers (UNDP Global Policy Network, April 2021).

26 X. Wu, M. Ramesh and M. Howlett, 'Policy Capacity: A Conceptual Framework for Understanding Policy Competences and Capabilities', *Policy and Society* 34, no. 3–4 (1 September 2015), pp. 165–71, https://doi.org/10.1016/j.polsoc.2015.09.001

27 M. Zollo and S. Winter, 'From Organizational Routines to Dynamic Capabilities', *Working Paper in the INSEAD Series*, 1 January 1999; R. R. Nelson and S. G. Winter, *An Evolutionary Theory of Economic Change* (Cambridge, MA: The Belknap Press of Harvard University Press, 1996).

28 V. Takala and R. Kattel, 'Dynamic Capabilities in the Public Sector: The Case of the UK's Government Digital Service', *UCL IIPP Working Paper Series*, 2021, https://www.ucl.ac.uk/bartlett/public-purpose/sites/public-purpose/files/final_iipp-2021-01_government-digital-service_kattel_takala.pdf; D. J. Teece, G. Pisano and A. Shuen, 'Dynamic Capabilities and Strategic Management', *Strategic Management Journal* 18, no. 7 (1997), pp. 509–33, https://doi.org/10.1002/(SICI)1097-0266(199708)18:7<509::AID-SMJ882>3.0.CO;2-Z

29 L. Roper and J. Pettit, 'Development and the Learning Organisation', *Development in Practice Numbers* 12 (1 September 2002), https://doi.org/10.1080/0961450220149654

30 Mazzucato et al., 'COVID-19 and the Need for Dynamic State Capabilities: An International Comparison', p. 3.

31 Ibid., p. 11.

32 Ibid., p. 12.

33 Ibid., p. 15.

34 Steiner, Kaiser and Reichmuth, 'Consulting for the Public Sector in Europe'.

35 W. M. Cohen and D. A. Levinthal, 'Absorptive Capacity: A New Perspective on Learning and Innovation', *Administrative Science Quarterly* 35, no. 1 (1990), pp. 128–52, https://doi.org/10.2307/2393553; H. W. Volberda, N. J. Foss and M. A. Lyles, 'Absorbing the Concept of Absorptive Capacity: How to Realize Its Potential in the Organization Field', *Organization Science* 21, no. 4 (1 August 2010), pp. 931–51, https://doi.org/10.1287/orsc.1090.0503

36 Cohen and Levinthal, 'Absorptive Capacity', p. 128.

37 R. Kattel et al., *Public Sector Innovation Indicators: Towards a New Evaluative Framework*, 2015, https://doi.org/10.13140/RG.2.1.5150.3120; M. J. R. Butler and E. Ferlie, 'Developing Absorptive Capacity Theory for Public Service Organizations: Emerging UK Empirical Evidence', *British Journal of Management* 31, no. 2 (2020), pp. 344–64, https://doi.org/10.1111/1467-8551.12342; G. Harvey et al., 'Absorptive Capacity: How Organisations Assimilate and Apply Knowledge to Improve Performance', in G. Harvey, K. Walshe and P. Jas (eds), *Connecting Knowledge and Performance in Public Services: From Knowing to Doing* (Cambridge: Cambridge University Press, 2010), pp. 226–50, https://doi.org/10.1017/CBO9780511762000.012; Kattel and Mazzucato, 'Mission-Oriented Innovation Policy and Dynamic Capabilities in the Public Sector'.

38 S. A. Zahra and G. George, 'Absorptive Capacity: A Review, Reconceptualization, and Extension', *The Academy of Management Review* 27, no. 2 (2002), pp. 185–203, https://doi.org/10.2307/4134351

39 M. C. Becker and F. Zirpoli, 'Outsourcing and Competence Hollowing-out: Systems Integrator vs. Knowledge Integrator?', *DRUID Working Papers, Copenhagen Business School* 03–05 (2003), https://ideas.repec.org/p/aal/abbswp/03-05.html

40 C. van den Berg et al., 'Policy Consultancy in Comparative Perspective', in *Policy Consultancy in Comparative Perspective* (Cambridge: Cambridge University Press, 2019), pp. 1–19; L. Seabrooke and O. J. Sending, 'Contracting Development: Managerialism and Consultants in Intergovernmental Organizations', *Review of International Political Economy* 27, no. 4 (2 July 2020), pp. 802–27, https://doi.org/10.1080/09692290.2019.1616601

41 R. Collington, 'Digital Public Assets: Rethinking Value, Access, Control and Ownership of Public Sector Data', *Common Wealth*, 1 November 2019, https://www.common-wealth.co.uk/reports/digital-public-assets-rethinking-value-access-and-control-of-public-sector-data-in-the-platform-age

42 B. Jæger and K. Löfgren, 'The History of the Future: Changes in Danish e-Government Strategies 1994–2010', *Information Polity* 15, no. 4 (1 January 2010), p. 253, https://doi.org/10.3233/IP-2010-0217

43 Agency for Digitisation, 'The Digital Path to Future Welfare: EGovernment Strategy 2011–2015' (Copenhagen: Agency for Digitisation, 2011); Agency for Digitisation, 'A Stronger and More Secure Digital Denmark: Digital Strategy 2016–2020' (Copenhagen: Agency for Digitisation, May 2016); Den Digitale Taskforce, 'Strategi for Digitalisering Af Den Offentlige Sektor 2007–2010' (Copenhagen: Den Digitale Taskforce, June 2007); Den Digitale Taskforce, 'Strategi for Digital Forvaltning 2004–06' (Copenhagen: Den Digitale Taskforce, 2004); Den Digitale Taskforce, 'På Vej Mod Digital Forvalting: Vision Og Strategi for Den Offentlige Sektor' (Copenhagen: Regeringen, January 2002).

44 N. Ejersbo and C. Greve, 'Digital Era Governance Reform and Accountability: The Case of Denmark', in T. Christensen and P Lægreid (eds), *The Routledge Handbook to Accountability and Welfare State Reforms* (London: Routledge, 2016).

45 Den Digitale Taskforce, 'Strategi for Digitalisering Af Den Offentlige Sektor 2007–2010'.

46 Agency for Digitisation, 'The Digital Path to Future Welfare: EGovernment Strategy 2011–2015'.

47 R. Collington, 'Disrupting the Welfare State? Digitalisation and the Retrenchment of Public Sector Capacity', *New Political Economy* 27, no. 2 (2022), pp. 312–28, https://doi.org/10.1080/13563467.2021.1952559

48 Finansministeriet, 'Et Solidt It-Fundament: Strategi for It-Styring i Staten' (Copenhagen: Finansministeriet, 2017), p. 5, https://digst.dk/media/21080/et-solidt-itfundament-strategi-for-itstyring-i-staten-9-12-19.pdf

49 Collington, 'Disrupting the Welfare State?'

50 Ibid.

51 C. Cordelli, *The Privatiẓed State* (Princeton, NJ: Princeton University Press, 2020), p. 10.

52 Weiss, *Management Consultancy and the British State*, p. 201.

53 S. Villadsen, 'Tidligere topembedsmand langer ud efter IBM efter kollapset samarbejde med Region H: "Det blev meget kraftigt oversolgt, hvad Watson kunne"', *Computerworld*, 19 November 2018, https://www.computerworld.dk/art/245441/tidligere-topembedsmand-langer-ud-efter-ibm-efter-kollapset-samarbejde-med-region-h-det-blev-meget-kraftigt-oversolgt-hvad-watson-kunne

54 R. Collington and R. Møller Stahl, 'Ligner en naturlov, er det ikke: Medmindre vi ændrer kurs, vil kontrollen over teknologien ligge hos nogle få tech-oligarker', *Politiken*, 3 October 2021, https://politiken.dk/debat/debatindlaeg/art8399475/Medmindre-vi-%C3%A6ndrer-kurs-vil-kontrollen-over-teknologien-ligge-hos-nogle-f%C3%A5-tech-oligarker

55 D. Foray, D. C. Mowery and R. R. Nelson, 'Public R&D and Social Challenges: What Lessons from Mission R&D Programs?', *Research Policy*, The need for a new generation of policy instruments to respond to the Grand Challenges, 41, no. 10 (1 December 2012), p. 1699, https://doi.org/10.1016/j.respol.2012.07.011

56 Levine, *Managing NASA in the Apollo Era*; Mazzucato, *Mission Economy*.

57 J. Bradley, S. Gebrekidan and A. McCann, 'Inside the U.K.'s Pandemic Spending: Waste, Negligence and Cronyism', *New York Times*, 17 December 2020, https://www.nytimes.com/interactive/2020/12/17/world/europe/britain-covid-contracts.html

58 'Timeline: Covid Contracts and Accusations of "Chumocracy"', *BBC News*, 20 April 2021. UK: https://www.bbc.com/news/uk-56319927

59 G. Iacobucci, 'Covid-19: One in Five Government Contracts Had Signs of Possible Corruption, Report Finds', *BMJ* 373 (23 April 2021), n1072, https://doi.org/10.1136/bmj.n1072

60 'UK Government's "VIP Lane" for PPE Suppliers Was Unlawful, High Court Rules', *Financial Times*, 12 January 2022.

61 R. Neate et al., 'Healthcare Firm Advised by Owen Paterson Won £133m Coronavirus Testing Contract Unopposed', *Guardian*, 11 May 2020. World news: https://www.theguardian.com/world/2020/may/11/healthcare-firm-advised-by-owen-paterson-won-133m-coronavirus-testing-contract-unopposed

62 A. McGuinness, 'Owen Paterson: Tories Accused of Bringing "shame on Democracy" as Former Minister Avoids Suspension in Commons Vote', *Sky News*, 3 November 2019, https://news.sky.com/story/owen-paterson-former-minister-saved-from-suspension-as-tory-mps-back-standards-process-overhaul-12458870

63 'Boris Johnson Follows Labour Call to Ban MP Paid Adviser Jobs', *BBC News*, 16 November 2021. UK politics: https://www.bbc.com/news/uk-politics-59311003

64 F. Lawrence, 'Hancock's Former Neighbour Won Covid Test Kit Work after WhatsApp Message', *Guardian*, 26 November 2020. World news: https://www.theguardian.com/world/2020/nov/26/matt-hancock-former-neighbour-won-covid-test-kit-contract-after-whatsapp-message; 'Coronavirus: Medical Regulator Investigates £30m Covid Contract Firm', *BBC News*, 21 February

2021. UK politics: https://www.theguardian.com/world/2020/nov/26/matt-hancock-former-neighbour-won-covid-test-kit-contract-after-whatsapp-message

65 H. Siddique, 'Businessman Was Paid £21m of Taxpayer Cash for Securing NHS PPE', *Guardian*, 17 November 2020. World news: https://www.theguardian.com/world/2020/nov/17/businessman-gabriel-gonzalez-andersson-paid-taxpayer-cash-for-securing-nhs-ppe

66 'Procurement Case', *Good Law Project* (blog), accessed 2 July 2021, https://goodlawproject.org/case/procurement-case/

67 L. Weiss and E. Thurbon, 'Explaining Divergent National Responses to Covid-19: An Enhanced State Capacity Framework', *New Political Economy* 0, no. 0 (30 October 2021), pp. 1–16, https://doi.org/10.1080/13563467.2021.1994545

68 W. Lazonick, 'Is the Most Unproductive Firm the Foundation of the Most Efficiency Economy? How Penrosian Learning Confronts the Neo-classical Fallacy', *International Review of Applied Economics* (15 March 2022), https://www.tandfonline.com/doi/abs/10.1080/02692171.2021.2022296

69 D. Lei and M. A. Hitt, 'Strategic Restructuring and Outsourcing: The Effect of Mergers and Acquisitions and LBOs on Building Firm Skills and Capabilities', *Journal of Management* 21, no. 5 (1 October 1995), pp. 835–59, https://doi.org/10.1177/014920639502100502

70 S. Heusinkveld and J. Benders, 'Consultants and Organization Concepts', in *The Oxford Handbook of Management Consulting*.

71 Micklethwait and Wooldridge, *The Witch Doctors*, p. 59.

72 C. J. Lammers, 'Transience and Persistence of Ideal Types in Organizational Theory', in M. Lousbury, S. B. Bacharach and N. Ditomaso (eds), *Research in the Sociology of Organizations* (Greenwich, CT: JAI Press, 1988), pp. 203–24.

73 S. Heusinkveld, *The Management Idea Factory: Innovation and Commodification in Management Consulting* (New York: Routledge, 2013); Heusinkveld and Benders, 'Consultants and Organization Concepts'; N. Brunsson and J. Olsen, *The Reforming Organization* (Bergen: Fagbokforlaget, 1997).

74 M. C. Nippa and K. Petzold, 'Economic Functions of Management Consulting Firms – an Integrative Theoretical Framework', *Academy of Management Proceedings* 2002, no. 1 (1 August 2002), B1–6, https://doi.org/10.5465/apbpp.2002.7516887

75 J.-S. Shin and H.-J. Chang, *Restructuring Korea Inc* (London: RoutledgeCurzon, 2003), p. 56.

76 Wright and Kwon, 'Business Crisis and Management Fashion'.

77 Ibid.; C. Rowley and J. Bae, 'Globalisation and Transformation of Human Resource Management in South Korea', *International Journal of Human Resource Management* 13 (1 May 2002), pp. 522–49, https://doi.org/10.1080/0958519011011512

78 S. Reynolds Fisher and M. A. White, 'Downsizing in a Learning Organization: Are There Hidden Costs?', *The Academy of Management Review* 25, no. 1 (2000), p. 249, https://doi.org/10.2307/259273

79 C. R. Littler and P. Innes, 'Downsizing and Deknowledging the Firm', *Work, Employment and Society* 17, no. 1 (1 March 2003), pp. 73–100, https://doi.org/10.1177/0950017003017001263

80 J. T. Brookman, S. Chang and C. G. Rennie, 'CEO Cash and Stock-Based Compensation Changes, Layoff Decisions, and Shareholder Value', *Financial Review* 42, no. 1 (2007), pp. 99–119, https://doi.org/10.1111/j.1540-6288.2007.00163.x

81 Lazonick and O'Sullivan, 'Maximizing Shareholder Value'.

82 W. Lazonick and J.-S. Shin, *Predatory Value Extraction: How the Looting of the Business Enterprise Became the US Norm and How Sustainable Prosperity Can Be Restored* (Oxford: Oxford University Press, 2020); M. Mazzucato, *The Value of Everything: Making and Taking in the Global Economy* (London: Penguin, 2019 [2017]).

83 W. Lazonick and E. Sakinç, 'Do Financial Markets Support Innovation or Inequity in the Biotech Drug Development Process?', Workshop on Innovation and Inequality: Pharma and Beyond, Scuola Superiore Sant'Anna, Pisa, Italy, 2010; Ö. Tulum, 'Innovation and Financialization in the U.S. Biopharmaceutical Industry', University of Ljubljana, 2018; Ö. Tulum and W. Lazonick, 'Financialized Corporations in a National Innovation System: The U.S. Pharmaceutical Industry', *International Journal of Political Economy* 47, no. 3–4 (2 October 2018), pp. 281–316, https://doi.org/10.1080/08911916.2018.1549842; W. Lazonick et al., 'Financialization of the U.S. Pharmaceutical Industry', Institute for New Economic Thinking, 2019, https://www.ineteconomics.org/perspectives/blog/financialization-us-pharma-industry

84 Citron Research, 'Valeant: Could This Be the Pharmaceutical Enron?' (Citron Research, 31 October 2015), https://citronresearch.com/wp-content/uploads/2015/10/Valeant-Philador-and-RandO-final-a.pdf

85 John Gapper, 'McKinsey's Fingerprints Are All over Valeant', *Financial Times*, 23 March 2016, https://www.ft.com/content/0bb37fd2-ef63-11e5-aff5-19b4e253664a

86 B. McLean, 'The Valeant Meltdown and Wall Street's Major Drug Problem', *Vanity Fair*, 5 June 2016, https://www.vanityfair.com/news/2016/06/the-valeant-meltdown-and-wall-streets-major-drug-problem

87 Congressional Budget Office, 'Research and Development in the Pharmaceutical Industry' (Washington, DC: Congressional Budget Office, April 2021), https://www.cbo.gov/publication/57126

88 The Economist, 'Shop 'til You Drop; Valeant', *The Economist* 407, no. 8838 (1 June 2013), p. 67(US)–67(US).

89 J. Surowiecki, 'Inside the Valeant Scandal', *New Yorker*, 28 March 2016. http://www.newyorker.com/magazine/2016/04/04/inside-the-valeant-scandal

90 McLean, 'The Valeant Meltdown and Wall Street's Major Drug Problem'.

91 Valeant Pharmaceuticals International, Inc., 'Valeant's Perspectives on R&D', https://www.sec.gov/Archives/edgar/data/850693/000119312514232351/d740992d425.htm

92 D. Lutz, '"The Process by Which Drugs Are Discovered and Developed Will Be Fundamentally Different in the Future"', *The Source*, 25 September 2014, https://source.wustl.edu/2014/09/the-process-by-which-drugs-are-discovered-and-developed-will-be-fundamentally-different-in-the-future/

93 Surowiecki, 'Inside the Valeant Scandal'.

94 McLean, 'The Valeant Meltdown and Wall Street's Major Drug Problem'.

95 M. Forsythe, W. Bogdanich and B. Hickey, 'As McKinsey Sells Advice, Its Hedge Fund May Have a Stake in the Outcome', *New York Times*, 19 February 2019. Business: https://www.nytimes.com/2019/02/19/business/mckinsey-hedge-fund.html

96 Gapper, 'McKinsey's Fingerprints Are All over Valeant'.

97 V. Hunt, N. Manson and P. Morgan, 'A Wake-up Call for Big Pharma' (McKinsey, 1 December 2011), https://www.mckinsey.com/industries/pharmaceuticals-and-medical-products/our-insights/a-wake-up-call-for-big-pharma

98 McLean, 'The Valeant Meltdown and Wall Street's Major Drug Problem'.

99 Ibid.

100 A. Pollack, 'Once a Neglected Treatment, Now an Expensive Specialty Drug: [Business/Financial Desk]', *New York Times, Late Edition (East Coast)*, 21 September 2015. B.

101 House Committee on Oversight and Reform, 'Cummings and Sanders Ramp Up Investigation of Staggering Drug Price Increases', House Committee on Oversight and Reform, 14 August 2015, https://oversight.house.gov/news/

press-releases/cummings-and-sanders-ramp-up-investigation-of-staggering-drug-price-increases

102 McLean, 'The Valeant Meltdown and Wall Street's Major Drug Problem'.

103 K. Pistor, *The Code of Capital: How the Law Creates Wealth and Inequality* (Princeton, New Jersey: Princeton University Press, 2019).

8. Colliding Interests: Consultancies and Democracy

1 A. Holpuch, 'Hurricane Maria: Puerto Rico Raises Official Death Toll from 64 to 2,975', *Guardian*, 28 August 2018. World news: http://www.theguardian.com/world/2018/aug/28/hurricane-maria-new-death-toll-estimate-is-close-to-3000

2 J. D. Sutter, ' "The Maria Generation": Puerto Rican Kids Face Harsh Realities', *CNN*, 17 September 2018, https://www.cnn.com/2018/09/17/health/sutter-maria-generation-children-puerto-rico/index.html

3 M. Taylor, 'Climate Change in the Caribbean – Learning Lessons from Irma and Maria', *Guardian*, 6 October 2017. Environment: http://www.theguardian.com/environment/2017/oct/06/climate-change-in-the-caribbean-learning-lessons-from-irma-and-maria

4 A. Holpuch, 'Hurricane Maria Pushes Puerto Rico's Struggling Hospitals to Crisis Point', *Guardian*, 27 September 2017. World news: http://www.theguardian.com/world/2017/sep/27/puerto-rico-faces-a-health-crisis-made-worse-as-majority-of-hospitals-are-inadequate

5 K. Aronoff and A. Brown, 'Sanders and Ocasio-Cortez Call for Reversal of Puerto Rico Austerity Measures', *The Intercept* (blog), 24 September 2019, https://theintercept.com/2019/09/24/puerto-rico-austerity-congress/

6 A. Rice and L. Valentin Ortiz, 'The McKinsey Way to Save an Island: Why Is Bankrupt Puerto Rico Spending More than a Billion Dollars on Expert Advice?', *Intelligencer*, 17 April 2019, https://nymag.com/intelligencer/2019/04/mckinsey-in-puerto-rico.html

7 Ibid.

8 Ibid.

9 Ibid.

10 Steiner, Kaiser and Reichmuth, 'Consulting for the Public Sector in Europe'.

11 M. Williams Walsh, 'House Seeks Clarity on Puerto Rico's Bankruptcy', *New York Times, Late Edition (East Coast)*, 20 December 2018.

12 M. Williams Walsh, 'Debt Adviser To Puerto Rico Stands to Profit', *New York Times, Late Edition (East Coast)*, 28 September 2018.

13 M. Celarier, 'The Story McKinsey Didn't Want Written', *Institutional Investor*, 8 July 2019, https://www.institutionalinvestor.com/article/b1g5zjdcr97k2y/The-Story-McKinsey-Didn-t-Want-Written

14 A. Edgecliffe-Johnson, 'McKinsey Investment Fund Fined $18m by SEC for Compliance Lapses', *Financial Times*, 19 November 2021.

15 Ibid.

16 Securities and Exchange Commission, 'Investment Advisers Act of 1940, Release No. 5912, Administrative Proceeding File No. 3-20656, In the Matter of MIO Partners, Inc.' (2021), https://www.sec.gov/litigation/admin/2021/ia-5912.pdf

17 Edgecliffe-Johnson, 'McKinsey Investment Fund Fined $18m by SEC for Compliance Lapses'.

18 Rice and Valentin Ortiz, 'The McKinsey Way to Save an Island: Why Is Bankrupt Puerto Rico Spending More than a Billion Dollars on Expert Advice?'

19 European Commission, 'Recovery and Resilience Facility', Text, European Commission – European Commission, 2021, https://ec.europa.eu/info/business-economy-euro/recovery-coronavirus/recovery-and-resilience-facility_en

20 Johnson, 'Italy's Destiny Hangs on €248bn Recovery Plan, Says Draghi'; G. Barbacetto and C. Di Foggia, 'Draghi Chiama McKinsey e Soci per Il Recovery Plan', *Il Fatto Quotidiano*, 6 March 2021, https://www.ilfattoquotidiano.it/in-edicola/articoli/2021/03/06/draghi-chiama-mckinsey-e-soci-per-il-recovery-plan/6124061/

21 Barbacetto and Di Foggia, 'Draghi Chiama McKinsey e Soci per Il Recovery Plan'.

22 'Draghi's Hiring of McKinsey Is "an Affront to the Italian People"', *DiEM25* (blog), 24 March 2021, https://diem25.org/draghis-hiring-mckinsey-an-affront-the-italian-people/

23 M. Buissonniere, 'D3: Management Consulting Firms in Global Health', in *Global Health Watch: An Alternative World Health Report* (London: Zed Books, 2019), https://phmovement.org/wp-content/uploads/2018/07/D3.pdf

24 M. Dufour and Ö. Orhangazi, 'Growth and Distribution after the 2007–2008 US Financial Crisis: Who Shouldered the Burden of the Crisis?', *Review of Keynesian Economics* 4, no. 2 (1 April 2016), pp. 151–74, https://doi.org/10.4337/roke.2016.02.02

25 Johnson, 'Italy's Destiny Hangs on €248bn Recovery Plan, Says Draghi'.

26 Buissonniere, 'D3: Management Consulting Firms in Global Health'.

27 Ibid., p. 284.

28 Tax Justice Network, 'What Is Transfer Pricing?', Tax Justice Network, 2021, https://taxjustice.net/faq/what-is-transfer-pricing/

29 R. Syal, S. Bowers and P. Wintour, ' "Big Four" Accountants "Use Knowledge of Treasury to Help Rich Avoid Tax" ', *Guardian*, 26 April 2013. Business: http://www.theguardian.com/business/2013/apr/26/accountancy-firms-knowledge-treasury-avoid-tax

30 Ibid.

31 B. Geys and K. Mause, 'Moonlighting Politicians: A Survey and Research Agenda', *The Journal of Legislative Studies* 19, no. 1 (1 March 2013), pp. 76–97, https://doi.org/10.1080/13572334.2013.737158

32 Hodge and Bowman, '6. The "Consultocracy": The Business of Reforming Government', p. 119.

33 S. Weschle, 'Politicians' Private Sector Jobs and Parliamentary Behaviour', *American Journal of Political Science*, advanced online version (4 September 2022), https://doi-org/10.1111/

34 Geys and Mause, 'Moonlighting Politicians', p. 85.

35 T. Clark, *Critical Consulting: New Perspectives on the Management Advice Industry* (Malden, MA: John Wiley & Sons, 2001); Sahlin-Andersson and Engwall, *The Expansion of Management Knowledge*.

36 Gapper, 'McKinsey's Fingerprints Are All over Valeant'.

37 M. Alvesson and S. Sveningsson, 'Identity Work in Consultancy Projects: Ambiguity and Distribution of Credit and Blame', in C. N. Candlin and J. Crichton (eds), *Discourses of Deficit*, Palgrave Studies in Professional and Organizational Discourse (London: Palgrave Macmillan UK, 2011), pp. 159–74, https://doi.org/10.1057/9780230299023_9; Alvesson, 'Managing Consultants: Control and Identity'.

38 Alvesson and Sveningsson, 'Identity Work in Consultancy Projects'.

39 B. Momani, 'Management Consultants and the United States' Public Sector', *Business and Politics* 15, no. 3 (October 2013), pp. 381–99, https://doi.org/10.1515/bap-2013-0001

40 Alvesson and Sveningsson, 'Identity Work in Consultancy Projects'.

41 J. Costas and P. Fleming, 'Beyond Dis-Identification: Towards a Theory of Self-Alienation in Contemporary Organizations', *Human Relations* 62, no. 3 (2009), pp. 353–78.

42 S. Meriläinen et al., 'Management Consultant Talk: A Cross-Cultural Comparison of Normalizing Discourse and Resistance', *Organization* 11, no.4 (2004), pp. 539–64.

43 Syal, Bowers and Wintour, ' "Big Four" Accountants "Use Knowledge of Treasury to Help Rich Avoid Tax" '.

44 K. Polanyi, *The Great Transformation: The Political and Economic Origins of Our Time* (Boston: Beacon Press, 2001 [1944]).

45 Deloitte, 'Tax Havens and Legitimate Planning', Deloitte South Africa, 2021, https://www2.deloitte.com/za/en/pages/tax/articles/tax-havens-and-legitimate-planning.html

46 Tax Justice Network, 'How Much Money Is in Tax Havens?', Tax Justice Network, 2021, https://taxjustice.net/faq/how-much-money-is-in-tax-havens/

47 S. N. Stausholm, 'Maximum Capital, Minimum Tax: Enablers and Facilitators of Corporate Tax Minimization' (doctoral thesis, Copenhagen Business School, Denmark, 2022).

48 R. Murphy and S. Stausholm, 'The Big Four: A Study of Opacity' (Brussels: GUE/NGL – European United Left/Nordic Green Left, 2017), https://openaccess.city.ac.uk/id/eprint/20066/

49 Ndikumana and Boyce (eds), *On the Trail of Capital Flight from Africa*.

50 Shaxson, 'Angola: Oil and Capital Flight'.

51 Ndikumana and Boyce (eds), *On the Trail of Capital Flight from Africa*.

52 Shaxson, 'Angola: Oil and Capital Flight'.

53 M. Forsythe et al., 'How U.S. Firms Helped Africa's Richest Woman Exploit Her Country's Wealth', *New York Times*, 19 January 2020. World: https://www.nytimes.com/2020/01/19/world/africa/isabel-dos-santos-angola.html

54 R. Soares de Oliveira, *Magnificent and Beggar Land: Angola Since the Civil War* (London: C Hurst & Co Publishers Ltd, 2015), p. 76.

55 International Labour Office, 'The Effective Abolition of Child Labour' (Geneva: ILO, 2022), https://www.ilo.org/public/english/standards/relm/gb/docs/gb280/pdf/gb-3-2-abol.pdf

56 N. Paulsen et al., 'Job Uncertainty and Personal Control during Downsizing: A Comparison of Survivors and Victims', *Human Relations* 58, no. 4 (1 April 2005), pp. 463–96, https://doi.org/10.1177/0018726705055033

57 M. R. Frone and A.-R. Blais, 'Organizational Downsizing, Work Conditions, and Employee Outcomes: Identifying Targets for Workplace Intervention among

Survivors', *International Journal of Environmental Research and Public Health* 17, no. 3 (January 2020), p. 719, https://doi.org/10.3390/ijerph17030719

58 Date of interviews: 23.06.21 and 16.09.21

59 McKinsey & Company, 'USPS Future Business Model' (McKinsey & Company, 2 March 2010), https://about.usps.com/future-postal-service/mckinsey-usps-future-bus-model2.pdf

60 T. Golshan, 'Pete Buttigieg Was Part of McKinsey Team That Pushed Postal Service Privatization', *HuffPost*, 13 December 2019. Politics: https://www.huffpost.com/entry/pete-buttigieg-mckinsey-postal-service_n_5df3dca0e4b0ae01a1e00863

61 American Postal Workers Union, 'NLRB Judge Orders Staples to Stop Handling U.S. Mail', *American Postal Workers Union* (blog), 28 May 2019, https://www.apwu.org/news/nlrb-judge-orders-staples-stop-handling-us-mail

62 Date of interview: 03.08.2022

63 Investopedia, '401(k) vs. Pension Plan: What's the Difference?', Investopedia, 4 July 2022, https://www.investopedia.com/ask/answers/100314/whats-difference-between-401k-and-pension-plan.asp

64 E. Dannin and G. Singh, 'Collective Bargaining: Theory, Data and a Plan for Future Research', SSRN Scholarly Paper (Rochester, NY: Social Science Research Network, 15 September 2005), p. 14, https://doi.org/10.2139/ssrn.805144

65 P. Alon-Shenker, 'Management Consultants and the Employees of Their Client Organizations: Towards a Model of Employee Protection', *Canadian Labour & Employment Law Journal* 21, no. 1 (4 September 2018), p. 160.

66 Ibid.

67 Rice and Valentin Ortiz, 'The McKinsey Way to Save an Island: Why Is Bankrupt Puerto Rico Spending More than a Billion Dollars on Expert Advice?'

68 British Medical Association, 'The Role of Private Outsourcing in the COVID-19 Response' (London: British Medical Association, July 2020), https://www.bma.org.uk/media/2885/the-role-of-private-outsourcing-in-the-covid-19-response.pdf; We Own It, 'How Deloitte Is Failing the NHS', *We Own It* (blog), 2020, https://weownit.org.uk/company/deloitte

69 Gallup, 'Big Business' (Washington, DC: Gallup, Inc, 2021), https://news.gallup.com/poll/5248/Big-Business.aspx

70 P. Pierson, *Dismantling the Welfare State?: Reagan, Thatcher and the Politics of Retrenchment*, 1994, p. 21, https://doi.org/10.1017/CBO9780511805288

71 Ibid.; Collington, 'Disrupting the Welfare State?'

9. Climate Consulting: An Existential Threat?

1 J. T. Houghton, G. J. Jenkins and J. J. Ephraums (eds), *Climate Change: The IPCC Scientific Assessment* (Cambridge: Cambridge University Press, 1990), p. xi.

2 Intergovernmental Panel on Climate Change, 'About – IPCC', 2021, https://www.ipcc.ch/about/

3 'World Chronicle 487: G.O.P. Obasi, WMO', United Nations UN Audiovisual Library, accessed 15 September 2021, https://www.unmultimedia.org/avlibrary/asset/2116/2116949

4 G. O. P. Obasi, 'Climate and Global Change in Relation to Sustainable Development: The Challenge to Science', *Proceedings of the Indian Academy of Sciences (Earth and Planetary Sciences)* 102, no. 1 (March 1993), pp. 27–34.

5 S. Gallagher and E. de Jong, ' "One Day We'll Disappear": Tuvalu's Sinking Islands', *Guardian*, 16 May 2019. Global development: https://www.theguardian.com/global-development/2019/may/16/one-day-disappear-tuvalu-sinking-islands-rising-seas-climate-change

6 J. Hickel, 'Quantifying National Responsibility for Climate Breakdown: An Equality-Based Attribution Approach for Carbon Dioxide Emissions in Excess of the Planetary Boundary', *The Lancet Planetary Health* 4, no. 9 (1 September 2020), e399–404, https://doi.org/10.1016/S2542-5196(20)30196-0

7 IPCC, 'Global Warming of 1.5°C. An IPCC Special Report on the Impacts of Global Warming of 1.5°C above Pre-Industrial Levels and Related Global Greenhouse Gas Emission Pathways, in the Context of Strengthening the Global Response to the Threat of Climate Change, Sustainable Development, and Efforts to Eradicate Poverty' (Intergovernmental Panel on Climate Change, 2018), https://www.ipcc.ch/site/assets/uploads/sites/2/2019/06/SR15_Full_Report_High_Res.pdf

8 J. Watts, 'We Have 12 Years to Limit Climate Change Catastrophe, Warns UN', *Guardian*, 8 October 2018. Environment: https://www.theguardian.com/environment/2018/oct/08/global-warming-must-not-exceed-15c-warns-landmark-un-report

9 IPCC, 'Climate Change Widespread, Rapid, and Intensifying', 9 August 2021, https://www.ipcc.ch/2021/08/09/ar6-wg1-20210809-pr/; IPCC, 'AR6 Climate Change 2022: Impacts, Adaptation and Vulnerability' (Geneva: IPCC, 4 April 2022), https://www.ipcc.ch/report/sixth-assessment-report-working-group-ii/

10 A. Tyson and B. Kennedy, 'Two-Thirds of Americans Think Government Should Do More on Climate', *Pew Research Center Science & Society* (blog), 23 June 2020, https://www.pewresearch.org/science/2020/06/23/two-thirds-of-americans-think-government-should-do-more-on-climate/

11 C. McGreal, 'Revealed: 60% of Americans Say Oil Firms Are to Blame for the Climate Crisis', *Guardian*, 26 October 2021. Environment: https://www.theguardian.com/environment/2021/oct/26/climate-change-poll-oil-gas-companies-environment

12 UNDP, 'World's Largest Survey of Public Opinion on Climate Change: A Majority of People Call for Wide-Ranging Action' (UNDP, 27 January 2021), https://www.undp.org/press-releases/worlds-largest-survey-public-opinion-climate-change-majority-people-call-wide

13 Mazzucato, *Mission Economy*.

14 Coherent Market Insights, 'Global Climate Change Consulting Market Is Estimated to Account for US$ 8,653.7 Mn by End of 2028, Says Coherent Market Insights (CMI)', GlobeNewswire News Room, 4 December 2021, https://www.globenewswire.com/news-release/2021/04/12/2208423/0/en/Global-Climate-Change-Consulting-Market-is-estimated-to-account-for-US-8-653-7-Mn-by-end-of-2028-Says-Coherent-Market-Insights-CMI.html

15 S. Keele, 'Taming Uncertainty: Climate Policymaking and the Spatial Politics of Privatized Advice', in C. Hurl and A. Vogelpohl (eds), *Professional Service Firms and Politics in a Global Era: Public Policy, Private Expertise* (Cham: Springer International Publishing, 2021), pp. 53–75, https://doi.org/10.1007/978-3-030-72128-2_3

16 S. Apparicio, 'One Tenth of UK Climate Aid Spent through Western Consultants', *Climate Home News*, 1 August 2018, https://www.climatechangenews.com/2018/08/01/one-tenth-uk-climate-aid-spent-western-consultants/

17 Boston Consulting Group, 'Boston Consulting Group Announces Expansion of Global Climate and Sustainability Center and COP26 Partnership', *PR Newswire*, 25 March 2021, https://www.prnewswire.com/news-releases/boston-consulting-group-announces-expansion-of-global-climate-and-sustainability-center-and-cop26-partnership-301255504.html

18 McKinsey & Company, 'Launching McKinsey Sustainability: Our New Platform for Helping Clients Innovate to Net Zero', 2021, https://www.mckinsey.com/about-us/new-at-mckinsey-blog/announcing-the-launch-of-mckinsey-sustainability

19 Consultancy.uk, 'McKinsey Acquires Sustainability Consultancy Vivid Economics', *Consultancy.uk*, 8 March 2021, https://www.consultancy.uk/news/27193/mckinsey-acquires-sustainability-consultancy-vivid-economics

20 A. Edgecliffe-Johnson and M. O'Dwyer, 'PwC to Boost Headcount by 100,000 over Five Years', *Financial Times*, 15 June 2021, https://www.ft.com/content/b79e4cd4-e288-4083-a976-47f3e89a0209

21 Consultancy.uk, 'Capgemini Launches Sustainable IT Offering for Clients', Consultancy.uk, 24 June 2021, https://www.consultancy.uk/news/28278/capgemini-launches-sustainable-it-offering-for-clients

22 Consulting.ca, 'EY Canada Appoints Kent Kaufield as First Chief Sustainability Officer', Consulting.ca, 4 June 2021, https://www.consulting.ca/news/2308/ey-canada-appoints-kent-kaufield-as-first-chief-sustainability-officer

23 Keele, 'Taming Uncertainty'.

24 S. Keele, 'Outsourcing Adaptation: Examining the Role and Influence of Consultants in Governing Climate Change Adaptation', University of Melbourne, 2017, http://minerva-access.unimelb.edu.au/handle/11343/194276

25 H. Chenet, J. Ryan-Collins and F. van Lerven, 'Finance, Climate-Change and Radical Uncertainty: Towards a Precautionary Approach to Financial Policy', *Ecological Economics* 183 (1 May 2021), p. 106957, https://doi.org/10.1016/j.ecolecon.2021.106957

26 BCG, 'The Time for Climate Action Is Now' (Boston Consulting Group, April 2021), https://media-publications.bcg.com/BCG-Executive-Perspectives-Time-for-Climate-Action.pdf

27 KPMG, 'Sustainable Finance: It's Decision Time' (Luxembourg: KPMG Luxembourg, 2020), https://assets.kpmg/content/dam/kpmg/lu/pdf/sustainable-finance-it-is-decision-time.pdf

28 PricewaterhouseCoopers, 'Moving to a Low-Carbon and Climate Resilient Future', PwC, 2021, https://www.pwc.co.uk/services/sustainability-climate-change/climate-change.html

29 Boston Consulting Group and World Economic Forum, 'The Net-Zero Challenge: Fast-Forward to Decisive Climate Action', January 2020, https://www.weforum.org/reports/the-net-zero-challenge-fast-forward-to-decisive-climate-action

30 Boston Consulting Group, 'The Biodiversity Crisis Is a Business Crisis', United Kingdom – EN, 23 February 2021, https://www.bcg.com/en-gb/publications/2021/biodiversity-loss-business-implications-responses

31 Boston Consulting Group, 'Making ESG Your DNA: How Wealth Managers Can Grow Through Sustainability' (BCG, September 2020), https://web-assets.bcg.com/10/57/8e4b93cd4be79cb3f200f53c0344/making-esg-your-dna-september2020.pdf

32 Bain & Company, 'Sustainability Is the Next Digital', Bain & Company, 8 September 2020, https://www.bain.com/insights/sustainability-is-the-next-digital/

33 Deloitte, 'Climate Change & Sustainability Consulting Services', Deloitte United Kingdom, 2021, https://www2.deloitte.com/uk/en/pages/risk/solutions/sustainability-services.html

34 Bain & Company, 'Sustainability Is the Next Digital'.

35 Consultancy.com.au, 'PwC Beefs up Sustainability Services with New ESG Advisory Group', *Consultancy.com.au* (blog), 1 September 2021, https://www.consultancy.com.au/news/3884/pwc-beefs-up-sustainability-services-with-new-esg-advisory-group

36 Deloitte, 'Climate Change & Sustainability Consulting Services'.

37 Deloitte, 'Climate-Forward Government: Seven Lessons for Effective Climate Action', Deloitte Insights, 2021, https://www2.deloitte.com/us/en/insights/industry/public-sector/government-policy-climate-change-innovation.html

38 K. Richter, ' "Sustainable Development" Has Been Slow to Take Off ', *Wall Street Journal*, 14 December 1999. Front section: https://www.wsj.com/articles/SB945121700533496759

39 T. Skodvin and S. Andresen, 'An Agenda for Change in U.S. Climate Policies? Presidential Ambitions and Congressional Powers', *International Environmental Agreements* 9 (1 August 2009), pp. 263–80, https://doi.org/10.1007/s10784-009-9097-7; J. McGee, 'The Influence of US Neoliberalism on International Climate Change Policy,' in N. E. Harrison and J. Mikler (eds), *Climate Innovation: Liberal Capitalism and Climate Change*, Energy, Climate and the Environment Series (London: Palgrave Macmillan UK, 2014), pp. 193–214, https://doi.org/10.1057/9781137319890_8

40 McGee, 'The Influence of US Neoliberalism on International Climate Change Policy'.

41 United Nations, 'United Nations Framework Convention on Climate Change', Geneva: United Nations, 1992, https://unfccc.int/files/essential_background/background_publications_htmlpdf/application/pdf/conveng.pdf

42 D. Bodansky, 'The History of the Global Climate Change Regime', *International Relations and Global Climate Change*, 1 January 2001; McGee, 'The Influence of US Neoliberalism on International Climate Change Policy'.

43 McGee, 'The Influence of US Neoliberalism on International Climate Change Policy'.

44 'Global Carbon Markets Value Surged to Record $277 Billion Last Year – Refinitiv,' *Reuters*, 27 January 2021. Environment: https://www.reuters.com/article/us-europe-carbon-idUSKBN29W1HR

45 G. W. Bush, 'Text of a Letter From The President to Senators Hagel, Helms, Craig, and Roberts', 13 March 2001, https://georgewbush-whitehouse.archives.gov/news/releases/2001/03/20010314.html; McGee, 'The Influence of US Neoliberalism on International Climate Change Policy'.

46 McGee, 'The Influence of US Neoliberalism on International Climate Change Policy'; D. van Vuuren et al., 'An Evaluation of the Level of Ambition and Implications of the Bush Climate Change Initiative', *Climate Policy* 2, no. 4 (1 December 2002), pp. 293–301, https://doi.org/10.1016/S1469-3062(02)00067-0

47 McGee, 'The Influence of US Neoliberalism on International Climate Change Policy'.

48 M. Mazzucato and C. C. R. Penna, 'Beyond Market Failures: The Market Creating and Shaping Roles of State Investment Banks', *Journal of Economic Policy Reform* 19, no. 4 (1 October 2016), pp. 305–26, https://doi.org/10.1080/17487870.2016.1216416; A. Voldsgaard and M. Rüdiger, 'Innovative Enterprise, Industrial Ecosystems and Sustainable Transition: The Case of Transforming DONG Energy to Ørsted', in M. Lackner, B. Sajjadi and W.-Y. Chin (eds), *Handbook of Climate Change Mitigation and Adaptation* (New York: Springer, 2020), pp. 1–52, https://doi.org/10.1007/978-1-4614-6431-0_160-1; Mazzucato, *The Entrepreneurial State*.

49 Grantham Research Institute on Climate Change and the Environment, 'What Is Climate Change Risk Disclosure?', *Grantham Research Institute on Climate Change and the Environment* (blog), 26 February 2018, https://www.lse.ac.uk/granthaminstitute/explainers/climate-change-risk-disclosure/

50 J. Andrew and C. Cortese, 'Free Market Environmentalism and the Neoliberal Project: The Case of the Climate Disclosure Standards Board', *Critical Perspectives on Accounting*, Thematic issue: Accounting for the Environment, 24, no. 6 (1 September 2013), pp. 397–409, https://doi.org/10.1016/j.cpa.2013.05.010

51 'About the Climate Disclosure Standards Board | Climate Disclosure Standards Board', accessed 22 September 2021, https://www.cdsb.net/our-story

52 IETA, 'Governance,' 2021, https://www.ieta.org/Governance

53 Andrew and Cortese, 'Free Market Environmentalism and the Neoliberal Project'.

54 Ibid.

55 Ibid.

56 A. Morton, 'Australia Shown to Have Highest Greenhouse Gas Emissions from Coal in World on per Capita Basis', *Guardian*, 11 November 2021. Environment: https://www.theguardian.com/environment/2021/nov/12/australia-shown-to-have-highest-greenhouse-gas-emissions-from-coal-in-world-on-per-capita-basis

57 G. Readfearn, 'Australia Ranked Last of 60 Countries for Policy Response to Climate Crisis', *Guardian*, 9 November 2021. Australia news: https://www.theguardian.com/environment/2021/nov/09/australia-ranked-last-of-60-countries-for-policy-response-to-climate-crisis

58 G. Readfearn, ' "Pure Spin": Experts Pan Coalition Net-Zero Modelling That Allows Gas Sector to Grow', *Guardian*, 12 November 2021. Australia news: https://www.theguardian.com/australia-news/2021/nov/12/pure-spin-experts-pan-coalition-net-zero-modelling-that-allows-gas-sector-to-grow

59 Ibid.

60 Australian Government, 'Australia's Long-Term Emissions Reduction Plan: Modelling and Analysis' (Canberra: Australian Government, November 2021), https://www.industry.gov.au/sites/default/files/November%202021/document/australias-long-term-emissions-reduction-plan-modelling.pdf

61 Ibid., p. 79.

62 Joshi, 'Scott Morrison's Net Zero Modelling Reveals a Slow, Lazy and Shockingly Irresponsible Approach to "Climate Action" '.

63 McKinsey Sustainability, 'The Net-Zero Transition: What It Would Cost, What It Could Bring' (McKinsey Sustainability, January 2022), https://www.mckinsey.com/business-functions/sustainability/our-insights/the-net-zero-transition-what-it-would-cost-what-it-could-bring

64 K. Burkart, 'No McKinsey, It Will Not Cost $9 Trillion per Year to Solve Climate Change', *Climate and Capital Media* (blog), 17 February 2022, https://www.climateandcapitalmedia.com/no-mckinsey-it-will-not-cost-9-trillion-per-year-to-solve-climate-change/

65 Joshi, 'Scott Morrison's Net Zero Modelling Reveals a Slow, Lazy and Shockingly Irresponsible Approach to "Climate Action"'.

66 Readfearn, '"Pure Spin"'.

67 Joshi, 'Scott Morrison's Net Zero Modelling Reveals a Slow, Lazy and Shockingly Irresponsible Approach to "Climate Action"'.

68 M. Forsythe and W. Bogdanich, 'At McKinsey, Widespread Furor Over Work With Planet's Biggest Polluters', *New York Times*, 27 October 2021. Business: https://www.nytimes.com/2021/10/27/business/mckinsey-climate-change.html

69 UN-REDD Programme Collaborative Workspace, 'What Is REDD+? – UN-REDD Programme Collaborative Online Workspace,' UN-REDD Programme Collaborative Workspace, 12 April 2021, https://www.unredd.net/about/what-is-redd-plus.html

70 F. Kesicki, 'Marginal Abatement Cost Curves for Policy Making – Expert-Based vs. Model-Derived Curves', in *33rd IAEE International Conference, 6–9 June 2010* (Rio de Janeiro: UCL Energy Institute, 2011), https://www.homepages.ucl.ac.uk/~ucft347/Kesicki_MACC.pdf

71 Morgan, Sturdy and Frenkel, 'The Role of Large Management Consultancy Firms in Global Public Policy'.

72 A. Buller, '"Doing Well by Doing Good"? Examining the Rise of ESG Investing', *Common Wealth*, 20 December 2020, https://www.common-wealth.co.uk/reports/doing-well-by-doing-good-examining-the-rise-of-environmental-social-governance-esg-investing

73 B. Cornell and A. Damodaran, 'Valuing ESG: Doing Good or Sounding Good?', *NYU Stern School of Business*, 20 March 2020, https://doi.org/10.2139/ssrn.3557432

74 M. O'Dwyer and A. Edgecliffe-Johnson, 'Big Four Accounting Firms Rush to Join the ESG Bandwagon', *Financial Times*, 30 August 2021, https://www.ft.com/content/4a47fb4a-4a10-4c05-8c5d-02d83052bee7

75 N. Kossovsky, 'Fulfilling the Promise of The Business Roundtable's Statement on Corporate Purpose', 25 August 2021, https://www.irmagazine.com/esg/fulfilling-promise-business-roundtables-statement-corporate-purpose

76 Updated Statement Moves Away from Shareholder Business Roundtable, 'Business Roundtable Redefines the Purpose of a Corporation to Promote "An Economy That Serves All Americans"', *Business Roundtable* (blog), 19 August 2019, https://www.businessroundtable.org/business-roundtable-redefines-the-purpose-of-a-corporation-to-promote-an-economy-that-serves-all-americans

77 Bloomberg Intelligence, 'ESG Assets May Hit $53 Trillion by 2025, a Third of Global AUM', *Bloomberg Professional Services*, 23 February 2021. Research and Analysis, https://www.bloomberg.com/professional/blog/esg-assets-may-hit-53-trillion-by-2025-a-third-of-global-aum/

78 Principles for Responsible Investment, 'What Are the Principles for Responsible Investment?', PRI, 2021, https://www.unpri.org/pri/what-are-the-principles-for-responsible-investment

79 M. O'Leary and W. Valdmanis, 'An ESG Reckoning Is Coming', *Harvard Business Review*, 4 March 2021, https://hbr.org/2021/03/an-esg-reckoning-is-coming

80 O'Dwyer and Edgecliffe-Johnson, 'Big Four Accounting Firms Rush to Join the ESG Bandwagon'.

81 A. J. M. Fish, D. H. Kim and S. Venkatraman, 'The ESG Sacrifice', *Cornell University, Working Paper*, 17 November 2019, https://doi.org/10.2139/ssrn.3488475

82 Cornell and Damodaran, 'Valuing ESG'.

83 Reuters, 'G7 Backs Making Climate Risk Disclosure Mandatory', *Reuters*, 5 June 2021. Environment: https://www.reuters.com/business/environment/g7-backs-making-climate-risk-disclosure-mandatory-2021-06-05/

84 TCFD, 'Members', *Task Force on Climate-Related Financial Disclosures* (blog), 2021, https://www.fsb-tcfd.org/members/

85 World Economic Forum, 'Measuring Stakeholder Capitalism: Towards Common Metrics and Consistent Reporting of Sustainable Value Creation', September 2020, https://www.weforum.org/reports/measuring-stakeholder-capitalism-towards-common-metrics-and-consistent-reporting-of-sustainable-value-creation/

86 World Economic Forum, 'Over 50 Global Companies Adopt New ESG Reporting Metrics', September 2021, https://www.weforum.org/our-impact/stakeholder-capitalism-50-companies-adopt-esg-reporting-metrics/

87 World Economic Forum, 'Stakeholder Capitalism: over 70 companies implement the ESG reporting metrics', May 2022, https://www.weforum.org/impact/stakeholder-capitalism-esg-reporting-metrics/

88 Chenet, Ryan-Collins and van Lerven, 'Finance, Climate-Change and Radical Uncertainty'.

89 P. Temple-West and K. Talman, 'The Whistleblower Who Calls ESG a Deadly Distraction', *Financial Times*, 13 August 2021, https://www.ft.com/content/4fdc6cdf-7bd6-41bc-b376-213752103017

90 Cornell and Damodaran, 'Valuing ESG'.

91 Forsythe and Bogdanich, 'At McKinsey, Widespread Furor Over Work With Planet's Biggest Polluters'.

92 Ibid.

10. Conclusion: A Government That Rows So It Can Steer

1 G. Rivett, '1948–1957: Establishing the National Health Service', *The Nuffield Trust*, 13 November 2019, https://www.nuffieldtrust.org.uk/chapter/1948-1957-establishing-the-national-health-service

2 Dunhill and Syal, 'Whitehall "infantilised" by Reliance on Consultants, Minister Claims'.

3 Collington, 'Disrupting the Welfare State?'

4 Mazzucato, *The Entrepreneurial State*.

5 Mazzucato, *Mission Economy*.

6 Mazzucato et al., 'COVID-19 and the Need for Dynamic State Capabilities: An International Comparison'.

7 Ibid.

8 Mazzucato, *Mission Economy*.

9 Ibid.

10 Takala and Kattel, 'Dynamic Capabilities in the Public Sector: The Case of the UK's Government Digital Service'.

11 Mazzucato, *Mission Economy*.

12 UCL Institute for Innovation and Public Purpose, 'Mission-Oriented Innovation Network (MOIN)', UCL Institute for Innovation and Public Purpose, 31 May 2019, https://www.ucl.ac.uk/bartlett/public-purpose/partnerships/mission-oriented-innovation-network-moin

13 UCL Institute for Innovation and Public Purpose, 'Master of Public Administration (MPA) in Innovation, Public Policy and Public Value', UCL Institute for Innovation and Public Purpose, 10 October 2018, https://www.ucl.ac.uk/bartlett/public-purpose/study/master-public-administration-mpa-innovation-public-policy-and-public-value

14 Preston City Council, 'The Definitive Guide to "the Preston Model"', Preston City Council, 2022, https://www.preston.gov.uk/article/1791/The-definitive-guide-to-the-Preston-model

15 'How to Build Community Wealth | CLES', accessed 14 March 2022, https://cles.org.uk/community-wealth-building/how-to-build-community-wealth/

16 M. Mazzucato, R. Conway, E. M. Mazzoli and S. Albala, 'Creating and Measuring Dynamic Public Value at the BBC: A Scoping Report' (London: UCL Institute for Innovation and Public Purpose, 8 December 2020), https://www.ucl.ac.uk/bartlett/public-purpose/publications/2020/dec/creating-and-measuring-dynamic-public-value-bbc

Index

Abadie, Richard, 79
accountancies, 21, 44–5, 47, 79–80,
    101–3, 137, 140–1; auditing as
    loss-leader/low margin activity for
    big firms, 47, 62–3, 65–6; cross-
    selling by auditors, 63, 64–7, 145;
    'opinion shopping' by audit clients,
    65, 231; and regulatory change in
    early 1930s, 39–40; Sarbanes-Oxley
    Act (2002), 66–7, 101 *see also* 'Big
    Four' accountancies
AECOM, 215
Africa, 27–8, 56–7, 58, 159, 161; capital
    flight from, 199–201
'agency theory,' 141–4
Agnew, Lord, 7
AIG, 90
Allende, Salvador, 31–2
AllofUs ('human- centred design'
    agency), 147
Angola, 58, 199–201
Apollo space mission, 167, 238, 242
Appleby (offshore law firm), 97
Aquilent, 70
Arthur Andersen, 44, 66; Accenture
    (formerly Andersen Consulting), 12,
    24, 47, 60, 64–5, 77, 79, 82, 85; and
    Enron scandal (2001), 64–5, 67
Arthur D. Little consultancy, 35, 58,
    140, 217–18

Arup, 215
asset management funds, 141, 58,
    90, 141
asylum seeker/migrant detention
    centres, 94, 95, 96
Atos, 26, 87, 95
Australia, 8–9, 29, 51, 76, 92, 93,
    95–6, 151, 169, 172–3, 223–6

Bain & Company, 1, 30, 114, 136, 147
Barber, Michael, 82
BBC iPlayer, 244
Bear Stearns, 90
Beer, Stafford, 31–2
Bell Report (NASA, 1962), 43
benefits sanctions, 94, 95
Berlusconi, Silvio, 90
'Big Four' accountancies, 1, 3, 17, 21, 23,
    24, 52, 62–3, 98–103, 113–15; as
    Brexit consultants, 133–6, 139; ESG
    clients, 229, 230; and financial crisis
    (2008), 89; and insider knowledge
    of legislation, 191–2, 193, 195, 196;
    'knowledge management' systems,
    121–6; as partnership-based, 140–1;
    and tax havens, 198
'Big Three' strategy firms, 1, 3, 17, 21,
    23, 133–4
biotech companies, 148, 176
BlackRock, 7, 90, 141, 232

Blair, Tony, 18, 76–7, 78–9, 82, 92, 94, 252
Booz Allen Hamilton consultancy, 42, 44, 58, 70, 86
Boston Consulting Group (BCG), 13, 24, 29, 91, 119, 147, 200–1, 214; Australian Senate inquiry into, 29; Brexit as lucrative for, 134, 135, 136; 'Growth Share Matrix,' 38–9, 39; as one of 'Big Three,' 1; as a prime beneficiary of NKS in Sweden, 154, 155
'boutique consultancies,' 18, 22, 145–7
Brackett, Ernest, 167, 238
Brexit, 133–6, 139, 170
British Medical Association, 205
Broadspectrum (previously Transfield Services), 95
Brumer, Justin, 69
Bush, George H.W., 74–5, 218
Bush, George W., 91–2, 219
business schools, 22, 38, 125
business sector: and climate change, 212–22, 223–32, 233; cost accounting methods, 6, 34, 40–1, 54; development of knowledge and resources, 171–4, 175–9; hollowing out of by consultancies, 3, 5, 7–8, 10, 161, 235–6, 252, 253; merger wave of 1980s, 49–50, 60; reform proposals from authors of this book, 239, 247–53; research-intensive firms, 173–9, 197–8; restructuring/downsizing/delayering, 37, 41–2, 106, 171–4, 175–6, 202–3; 'roll-up' companies, 175–9; share buybacks, 1, 174; 'tax strategies,' 196–8; and value creation, 104–8, 111–12, 120–32, 142–3, 144–7, 235–6 see also corporate governance

Cameron, David, 92
Canada, 45, 51, 75, 204, 215
Capgemini, 20, 47, 85, 127, 214–15
Capita, 26, 94, 134
capitalism: and climate change, 212–13, 217–22, 228–32; and government knowledge, 164–70; ills of in modern era, 1, 4, 5, 6, 9–10, 29–30, 235; and risk-reward relationship, 6, 73–4, 136–45, 235, 240–2; subversion of standards in pursuit of profit, 196, 197–8; Taylorism/'scientific management,' 34, 35–7 see also business sector; economies/economics
Carillion, 98–100, 102, 137
Carlos Salinas, 57–8
CGI Group, 17, 71–4
Chicago, 41
Chile, 31–2, 49, 244
China, 25, 59–60
Christmas Island, 96
Citwell (French consulting firm), 12
civil servants, 4, 7–8, 13, 27, 46, 53–4, 70, 75, 157–8, 169–70, 242–5
climate change, 10, 180, 207, 208–11, 235; conflicts of interests over, 9, 226–8, 234, 249; consulting market, 6–7, 8, 9, 213–17, 222–3, 224–8, 229–32, 233–4; COP26 (Glasgow, 2021), 214, 223; deforestation reduction

policies, 226–8; ESG criteria, 6–7, 214, 228–32, 234; fossil fuel companies, 9, 217–18, 219, 221–2, 223–4, 226, 233, 249; green technologies/infrastructure, 215–16, 220, 223, 232, 235, 249; IPCC sets deadline for action (2018), 211–12, 213, 222, 233; Kyoto Protocol (1997), 219; market-driven response to, 7, 217–22, 233; obfuscating and rent-seeking over, 6–7, 217–22, 223–32, 233–4; public opinion on, 212–13; UNFCCC, 214, 218, 219, 223, 226–8

Clinton, Bill, 74, 75–7, 219, 252

Cold War, 41, 42, 58–9, 67

Community Wealth Building principles, 247

Computer Sciences Corporation (CSC), 47

computing/digital technology, 6, 83, 84–7, 162–4, 197–8, 206, 215; 'e-government' IT reforms, 83–6, 87, 162–4, 166, 206, 243–4; Government Digital Service (GDS), UK, 244; HealthCare.gov, 68–74, 96, 138, 241; IT consultancies, 17, 20, 19, 23–4, 45, 46–7, 70–4, 85–6, 140, 144–5, 161, 166–7; key role of public sector in innovation, 45, 84–5, 239; 'masculinization' of in 1960s/70s, 46; need to re-establish public sector expertise, 243–4; outsourcing of, 12, 46, 83–7, 161–4, 166–7, 206, 243–4; Project Cybersyn in Chile, 31–2; Silicon Valley, 84–5, 86–7; and US antitrust laws, 46–7

'confidence tricks,' 3, 108, 109–11

Conservative Party, UK, 32–3, 48–9, 78, 90, 92, 168, 193–4, 238

'consultant engineers,' 34, 35, 108

consulting industry: added value claims/impressions, 3–4, 8, 105–8, 111–12, 114, 120–32, 139, 144–7, 235–6; and aggregated contracts, 78–9, 80–2, 83–8, 97, 138, 241–2; 'alumni networks,' 116–17, 194–5; Brexit as lucrative for, 133–6, 139; and capital flight from Africa, 199–201; conflicts of interests, 3, 5, 9, 52–3, 64–7, 91, 97–103, 184–7, 189–98, 200–1, 226–8, 234, 249–53; 'cost-plus-fixed-fee' model, 73–4; cross-selling by, 63, 64–7, 145; functional theory of, 106–8, 111–12, 144–7; gendered make-up of, 46; history of, 4, 6, 31–45, 46–8, 50–7, 58–67, 104–6, 108; 'knowledge management' systems, 121–6; legitimating function of, 8–9, 41, 42–3, 50, 54, 67, 131–2, 171–2, 180–1, 184, 200–1, 202–3; lowballing, 8, 26, 59, 67, 93, 188, 190, 215, 251–2; and multinational strategy, 50, 60; national/regional divergences in use of, 24–5, 60–1; and NKS in Sweden, 151–2, 154–7; opacity/lack of transparency, 3, 23, 27, 205–7, 250–2, 253; public ignorance of, 5–6, 205–7; public/political scrutiny of, 5, 11–15, 28–30, 91–2, 94–7, 98–102, 204–5; and quasi-academia, 126–30; recruitment and staffing in, 21–2, 46,

consulting industry – *cont'd.*
113–21, 124–8, 192–5; reform
proposals from authors of this book,
238–9, 241–2, 244–5, 247–53; and
rent/value extraction, 3–4, 5, 6–7,
10, 74, 111–12, 132, 139, 145, 173–9,
223–32, 233–4; size/scale of, 2, 22–5,
92–3; structural harms posed by, 5,
9–10, 30, 61–2, 64–7, 73–4, 90–2,
94–103; and tax havens, 197–8,
200–1; taxonomy of, 18–22, *19*;
three critical periods in birth of,
34–41; UK Members of Parliament
working for, 192–4 *see also under*
entries for individual firms
'consultocracy' (Hood and Jackson
term), 54–5
'consultology,' 112–21
Conte, Giuseppe, 188
Coopers & Lybrand, 52, 77
Cornwall, out-of-hours GP
services, 96
corporate governance: and democratic
accountability issues, 196–8; limited
liability, 6, 50, 140–1; partnership
forms of, 139–41; private
corporations, 141; publicly traded
companies, 140, 141, 142;
shareholder value-maximizing
(MSV), 3, 4, 6, 104–6, 131–2,
142–3, 144–5, 173–4, 175, 176–7,
178–9; stock-based executive
compensation, 141–2, 144, 145,
173; and Valeant Pharmaceuticals,
174–7, 178–9, 194–5, 207
Côte d'Ivoire, 199

COVID-19 pandemic, 2, 11–17, 29,
143–4, 158–9, 161, 167–70, 187–8,
205, 239–41, 243, 250–1
credit rating agencies, 182
Cresap, Mark, 42
Cummings, Elijah E., 178
Cuomo, Andrew, 14

DARPA (Defense Advanced Research
Projects Agency), 239, 246
'Delivery Unit' (Blair taskforce), 82
Deloitte, 23–4, 29, 34, 52, 71, 91, 101,
127, 191–2, 197; Brexit as lucrative
for, 134, 135, 136; climate change
consulting market, 216–17, 230;
Covid contracts, 2, 15, 16–17, 205; as
one of 'Big Four,' 1
democracy: in Allende's Chile, 31–2;
consultancies and Brexit, 133–6;
public sector's role in protecting/
maintaining, 158, 164, 169–70, 235–6,
238–53; undermined by consultancies,
9, 10, 33–4, 136, 164–70, 183–7,
189–98, 199–207, 222–34, 249–53
Democratic Party, US, 75–6, 77, 252
Democratic Republic of the Congo, 159
demographic change, 149–51
Denmark, 84, 162–4, 166, 167, 206,
238, 244
developing countries/emerging
markets, 24, 25, 26–8, 55–8, 59, 67,
93, 199–201
development banks, 215–16
Dombrovskis, Valdis, 90
Dorrell, Stephen, 192–3
Draghi, Mario, 187–8, 189–90

Ebola, 159, 161, 240
economies/economics: Asia economic
    crisis (1997), 61, 172; dominance of
    market-driven approach, 7, 25,
    48–60, 74–7, 217–22, 235; dotcom
    recession, 89; eurozone debt crisis, 2,
    90–1, 187; government as a value
    creator, 239–42, 243–7, 252–3; Great
    Depression, 39, 40–1; Great
    Recession, 89–93; international
    governance organizations, 25, 55,
    56–7, 67, 90, 172; Keynesianism,
    48–9; in low-/middle-income
    countries, 27–8; neoliberal
    revolution, 32–3, 47–9, 74–5;
    Nixon ends dollar-gold
    convertibility (1971), 48; post-crisis
    austerity, 6, 90, 93–4, 97; post-war
    spread of American ideas, 44, 67;
    rescues/bail-outs during 2008 crisis,
    89–90, 188–9; Second Industrial
    Revolution, 35; sovereign debt crises
    in Global South, 55–8; 'stagflation,'
    48; Thatcher-Reagan era, 32–3,
    47–9; turmoil of 1970s, 48, 55
Eddie Stobart (logistics firm), 102
Ember (British think tank), 223
Enron scandal (2001), 61–2, 63–5, 67, 89
'entrepreneurial state' concept, 239
Environmental Protection Agency
    (EPA), 52, 55
equality/social justice issues, 31, 76,
    196, 235; capital flight from Africa,
    199–201; Gilded Age in USA, 108–9;
    power elites, 114–15; and responses to
    2008 crisis, 188–9

Ernst & Young, 63, 151–2, 191–2
Eskom, 29
European Union institutions, 18, 90,
    153, 187–8, 190, 192
EY consultancy, 1, 13, 24, 97–8, 101–2,
    136, 215, 229, 230

Factory Act, UK (1833), 201
Fair Labor Standards Act, US (1938),
    201
Fancy, Tariq, 7, 232
Fauci, Dr Anthony, 128
financial crisis (2008), 88–94, 188–9
Financial Reporting Council (FRC),
    UK, 100, 101–2
Flores, Fernando, 31
Fortune 500 companies, 38, 45, 116
France, 11–14, 51
Fukuyama, Francis, 58

G4S, 26, 95
Gaebler, Ted, 75–6, 77, 79, 252
Gates, Bill and Melinda, 190
Germany, 13, 61, 192, 245
Giddens, Anthony, 76
Glassman, Cynthia A., 66
Glennan, Keith, 42–3
Global Reporting Initiative, 230
Godin, Serge, 72
Good Law Project, 168
Gore, Al, 83
governments/governance:
    consultancies and insider knowledge,
    191–2, 195, 196; consultancies'
    systemic conflicts of interest, 9,
    52–3, 64–7, 91, 189–90, 191–5,

governments/governance – *cont'd.*
252–3; critical/core functions given
to consultancies, 2, 3, 11–17, 26–8,
68–74, 81–8, 94–7, 154–7, 162–4,
165–7, 186, 206; history of 'market-
driven climate governance,' 217–22,
233; knowledge of markets/private
sector, 164–70; as not inherently
corrupt, 169, 193; private sector
jobs of UK politicians, 192–4;
reform proposals from authors of
this book, 238–53; short-termism,
1, 4, 67, 93–4, 111–12; state as risk
taker, 240–2; 'Third Way' models/
agenda, 4, 75–82, 83–4, 85, 94,
150–7, 162–3, 252–3 *see also*
democracy; public sector
Grant Thornton, 140
Greece, 91, 187
'Growth Share Matrix,' 38–9, *39*
Guinea-Bissau, 57
Gupta brothers, 29

Hadžialić, Aida, 156
Hancock, Matt, 168
Haskins & Sells, 52
Hawke, Bob, 76
Health Research Authority (UK), 15
healthcare systems, 44, 49, 95, 96,
183–4; global health policy bodies,
190–1; Nya Karolinska Solna (NKS)
in Sweden, 150–7, 241; Obamacare,
68–74, 96, 138, 241; 'value-based
healthcare' approach, 154–6, 183–4
see also National Health Service
(NHS)

Hewitt, Patricia, 77
Hicks, Mar, 46
HIV/AIDS, 159, 190
Hodge, Margaret, 192
Hollande, François, 14
Hollerith machine (IBM), 45*
the Holocaust, 45*
Hong Kong, 58
House of Lies (television show), 117
Howard, John, 92
HP Enterprise Services, 70–1
Hurricane Maria, 2, 180–1

IBM, 17, 45*, 47, 69, 81, 85, 128,
128, 166
In Search of Excellence (Tom Peters
and Robert H. Waterman Jr),
129, 187
India, 24, 27, 158–9, 240, 253
Indonesia, 28
Innisfree, 153
Insolvency Service, UK, 100
intelligence agencies, 86
Intergovernmental Panel on Climate
Change (IPCC), 208–12, 213, 217,
218, 222, 233
International Computers Limited
(ICL), 47
International Monetary Fund (IMF),
25, 56, 57, 172
ISS, 26
Isuprel (drug), 176–7, 178
Italy, 2, 90, 187–8, 189–90

Japan, 24, 84, 104
Johnson, Boris, 168

Joly, Hubert, 117
Joshi, Ketan, 226

Kearney, 140
Keating, Paul, 76
Kenya, 27–8
Killefer, Nancy, 93
KPMG, 26, 29, 45, 52, 77, 93, 102, 120,
    137; audits of Carillion, 100–1;
    climate change consulting market,
    213, 230; and insider knowledge of
    legislation, 191–2, 193, 195, 196; as
    one of 'Big Four,' 1

Laboratorio de Gobierno (Chile), 244
labour: child labour, 201; consulting
    industry's impact on, 98, 100, 143,
    171–2, 184, 202–4, 205; impact of
    2008 crisis, 188–9; laws/agreements,
    9, 98, 172, 184, 201–4; market
    flexibility, 172; and Taylorism, 34,
    35–7; trade unionism, 35–6, 41, 48,
    172, 201–2, 203, 204, 205
Labour Party, UK, 18, 34, 48, 76, 77,
    78–9, 82, 92, 94, 192, 193, 252
Lamar, David, 109
Lansley, Andrew, 34
Latvia, 90
Lazonick, William, 142, 173
learning in organizations: 'absorptive
    capacity' concept, 160; business
    sector development of, 171–4, 175–9;
    and consultants, 7–8, 10, 46, 157,
    159–61, 162–7, 170, 171–3, 174–9,
    206, 238, 245; detrimental
    consequences of outsourcing, 7–9,
    10, 15–17, 46, 97, 156–7, 159–62,
    163–70, 171–4, 206, 238, 241;
    downsizing linked with deskilling,
    172–3; how organizations learn,
    157–9; 'institutional memory,' 157–9,
    160, 161, 163–4, 167–70, 206; need to
    embed in contract evaluations,
    247–9; public sector capabilities/
    knowledge, 7–9, 10, 46, 97, 158–9,
    161, 162–70, 206, 236–8, 239–53;
    transactional mentality of
    consultancies, 157, 247
Leaver, Adam, 99
Lee, Gwanhoo, 69
Lehman Brothers, collapse of, 88
lobbying organizations, 131
Lockheed Martin, 70
LogicaCMG, 85
London Olympic Games (2012), 94–5
Louwagie, Véronique, 11
Lustig, Victor, 109–10
LuxLeaks, 198

Macron, Emmanuel, 13, 14
Madrid, Miguel de la, 57–8
Major, John, 78
Management Consultancies Association
    (MCA), UK, 14–15, 113
'managerialism,' 51, 54
Marsh McLennan, 141
Marshall Field & Company, 40–1
Marshall Plan (1948), 44
Master of Business Administration
    (MBA) courses, 22, 113, 114,
    119, 129
McKenna, Christopher D., 35, 113

McKinsey: acquisitions/consolidation, 147; and Blair's 'Delivery Unit,' 82; Brexit as lucrative for, 134; and capital flight from Africa, 200–1; climate change consulting market, 8, 213, 214, 223, 224–8, 234; consultant resistance over climate change, 234; Covid contracts, 2, 11–13, 14; and Great Recession, 91, 92–3; history of, 34, 40–3, 51–2, 58, 60; impact on labour force of clients, 41, 203, 205; in low-/middle-income countries, 27–8; and macroeconomic restructuring, 180–1, 183–6, 187–8, 189–90, 195, 204–5, 206–7; MIO Partners, 184–6, 189, 206–7; as most well known consultancy, 205; as one of 'Big Three,' 1; and quasi-academia, 116–17, 127, 128–30; recruitment and staffing, 113–14, 116–17, 119; reviews Serco's contracts, 97–8; services/'functions' offered, 20; size of, 24; and Valeant Pharmaceuticals, 174–7, 178–9, 194–5, 207; *Vision* project failures, 27–8; and Zuma presidency in South Africa, 29–30
McKinsey Global Institute (MGI), 128, 130, 172
Mercer, 58
Mexico, 57–8
Micklethwait, John, 112, 129–30
Mills, C. Wright, *The Power Elite* (1956), 114
MindLab (Denmark), 244
'moral hazard,' 139, 144–5

Morrison, Scott, 224
Mulroney, Brian, 75

Nakate, Vanessa, 212
NASA (National Aeronautics and Space Administration), 42–3, 167, 238, 242
National Health Service (NHS), 15–16, 18, 32, 55, 97; Blair's reforms, 80–1, 92, 152, 153; early history of ambition/innovation, 236–8; Health and Social Care Act (UK, 2012), 33–4; PFI contracts, 80, 152, 153
Nazi Germany, 45*
neoliberalism, 4, 32–3, 46, 47–55, 74–5, 76, 169, 218; 'financialization,' 49–50, 179, 235; global exporting of, 55–8; 'Structural Adjustment Programs' (SAPs), 56–7, 67
Netherlands, 84
New York, 14, 44, 81
Nigeria, 56–7, 208
Nitropress (drug), 176–7, 178
Nixon, Richard, 48
non-governmental organizations (NGOs), 27, 118, 128, 194, 221
Nordic Interim AB, 155
Nordic Investment Bank, 153
not-for-profit organizations, 18, 81, 147, 221

Obama, Barack, 68–74, 91–3, 182
Obasi, Godwin Olu Patrick, 208–10, 233
oil crisis (1973), 48, 55

Old-Age Dependency Ratio (OADR), 150

Oliver Wyman consultancy, 61, 91, 134, 141

On the Trail of Capital Flight from Africa (Léonce Ndikumana and James K. Boyce), 199

Osborne, David, 75–6, 77, 79, 252

O'Sullivan, Mary, 173

outsourcing, 6, 11–14, 20–1, 27, 51, 54–5, 136–9, 200; Carillion collapse (2018), 98–100, 102, 137; and civil servants, 4, 7–8, 13, 46, 169–70; costs of re-insourcing, 97, 164; of digital/IT systems, 12, 46, 83–7, 161–4, 166–7, 206, 243–4; and 'downsizing'/budget cuts, 8, 33, 93–4, 97, 111–12, 173–4; and HealthCare.gov, 70–4; impact on capability/knowledge base, 7–9, 10, 15–17, 97, 156–7, 159–62, 163–70, 171–4, 206, 238, 241; of regulatory functions, 165; specialist consultancies, 18, 19–20, *19*, 22, 25, 74, 87–8, 94–103, 113–14, 143–4; Third Way commissioning models, 78–82, 94, 150–7, 252–3; in UK, 14–17, 25–26, 33–4, 46, 78–81, 82, 85, 94–5, 96, 97–103, 137

PA Consulting, 85, 136

Paget, Richard, 42

Panama Papers, 198

Paradise Papers, 96–7

Partnerships UK, 79

Paterson, Owen, 168

Pearson, Michael, 175–7, 178, 194–5

Peters, Tom, 129, 187

pharmaceutical industry, 174–9, 190–1, 194–5, 207

Pinochet, Augusto, 32, 49

Polakov, Walter, 37

'populism,' rise of, 170

Porter, Michael, 105, 154

Preston, 246–7, 253

'prime contracting,' 78, 79, 80, 81, 82, 83, 85, 97, 138, 241–2

prisons, 94, 95, 96

Private Finance Initiative (PFI), 78–80, *80*, 82, 83, 85, 101, 136–7, 138, 150–7, 193

privatization, 3, 6, 47, 51–3, 165, 180–1; in developing countries, 56–7, 58; in former countries of Soviet Union, 59; in Puerto Rico, 180–1, 183–4

Public Accounts Committee (UK), 15, 29, 191–2

public choice theory, 246

public sector: Brexit-related tenders, 135; and capital flight from Africa, 199, 200–1; Clinton's National Performance Review (NPR), 75–6, 83; data as central for, 83–4, 161–2, 243–4; and green technological innovation, 220; HealthCare.gov, 68–74, 96, 138, 241; hollowing out of by consultancies, 3, 5, 7–9, 10, 13–17, 33, 161, 163–4, 165–7, 169–70, 206, 236, 252–3; in-house consulting units, 244–5; impact of budget cuts/austerity, 8, 42, 49, 90, 93–4, 111–12, 236, 246–7; and key innovations in

public sector – *cont'd.*
computing, 45, 84–5, 239; loss of
state's in-house IT capabilities, 46,
83–7, 161, 162–4, 166–7, 206, 243–4;
McKinsey in Puerto Rico, 180–1,
183–6, 189, 195, 204–5, 206–7;
narratives of private sector
superiority, 75, 84–5, 112, 237–8;
need for publishing of contracts,
250–1; need for rebuilding of
capacity/capabilities, 10, 170, 235,
236–8, 239–53; need for reforms to
contracting/evaluation, 241–2, 247–
53; New Public Management (NPM)
credo, 4, 53–4, 84, 129, 157–8, 162–3;
partnerships with research
organizations, 245–6; 'progressive
procurement' process, 246–7; reform
proposals from authors of this
book, 238–53; Reinventing
Government Network, 77, 83; and
risk, 1, 3, 4, 6, 8, 73–4, 79, 136–9,
143–4, 240–2; role of in preventing
corruption, 169–70; Thatcher-
Reagan era, 32–3, 47–9; Third
Way commissioning models,
78–82, 94, 150–7, 252–3 *see also*
outsourcing
'public-private partnerships' (PPPs),
78–82, *80*, 88, 150–7
Puerto Rico, 2, 180–2, 189, 195, 204–5,
206–7; PROMESA Act (2016), 182–6
PwC (PricewaterhouseCoopers), 24,
34, 58, 69, 77, 88, 101, 102, 118, 128,
200–1; Brexit as lucrative for, 134,
135, 136; climate change consulting

market, 213, 214, 216, 230; and insider
knowledge of legislation, 191–2;
Öhrlings (Swedish branch), 151–2;
as one of 'Big Four,' 1; and PFI
contracts, 79, 80, 85

Qvartz, 147

Ramboll, 155–6
Reagan, Ronald, 33, 47–9, 52, 63–4,
74–5, 112
Regenersis, 100
regulatory functions, 24, 39–40, 49–50,
63–4, 137, 165, 203–4, 206–7
Reinventing Government (David Osborne
and Ted Gaebler, 1992), 75–6,
77, 79, 252
Renaissance Florence, 139–40
Republican Party, US, 32–3, 48–9, 69,
74–5, 78
research institutions/organizations,
173–9, 197–8, 239, 245–6
Rio Tinto, 221
risk: and acquisitions/consolidation,
147–8; and 'agency theory,' 141–4;
'Knightian' uncertainty of climate
risks, 231–2; limited liability, 6, 50,
140–1; and outsourcing business
models, 98–101, 137; overlooking of
'moral hazard,' 139, 144–5; and
partnership models, 139–41; and PFIs,
150–7; 'prime contracting,' 78, 79, 80,
81, 82, 83, 85, 97, 138, 241–2; skewed
relationship with reward in consulting
industry, 6, 73–4, 136–9, 143–5, 235,
240–2; state as risk taker, 240–2

Risk Dynamics, 147
Rockefeller Senior, John, 109
Rogers, George, 109
Rolls-Royce, 102
Rosdahl, Torbjörn, 152
Royal Liverpool University Hospital, 99
Rudd, Kevin, 92, 93
Rwanda, 159, 161, 240

Samsom, Melvin, 155
Santos, Isabel dos, 200
Santos, José Eduardo dos, 200
Sarkozy, Nicolas, 13–14
SARS epidemics, 159
Second World War, 41, 42
Securities and Exchange Commission (SEC), 40, 185–6
Serco, 17, 19, 26, 74, 87, 88, 95–8, 143–4
The Shadow Government (Daniel Guttman and Barry Willner, 1976), 206
Shaxson, Nicholas, 199
Shell, 217–18, 221
'shell companies,' 197, 200
Shkreli, Martin, 177–8
Silvers, Damon, 202–3
Skanska, 153
Snowden, Edward, 86
Social Mobility Commission, UK, 115
Sodexo, 17, 26, 74, 87
Somerset County Council, 81
South Africa, 29–30, 199
South Korea, 25, 61, 172
Soviet Union, 37, 58–9
Spain, 91
Stagecoach (transport company), 102

Start Computer Group (China), 60
Sturdy, Andrew, 116
Sustainability Accounting Standards Board, 230
Sutton Trust, 115
Sweden, 91, 149, 150; Nya Karolinska Solna (NKS), 150–7, 241

Tata Consultancy Services, 24, 27
Tax Justice Network, 198
tax law, 191–2, 195, 196–8, 249–50; tax havens, 63–4, 96–7, 191, 197–8, 200–1
Taylor, Frederick, 34, 35–7
Thatcher, Margaret, 32–3, 47–9, 51, 74–5, 78
Thomas Cook (travel firm), 101–2
Thompson, William, 110
Thunberg, Greta, 212
Thurbon, Elizabeth, 168–9
timber companies, 226–8
Toffler, Barbara Ley, 63
Tolba, Mostafa, 208
Toyota, 104
transfer pricing, 191
Transparency International UK, 167
Truman, Harry S., 43–4
Trump, Donald, 170
Turing Pharmaceuticals, 177–8

UCL Institute for Innovation and Public Purpose, 202, 246
United Kingdom: Brexit as lucrative for consultancies, 133–6, 139; climate change consulting market, 214; Coalition government (2010–15), 26,

United Kingdom – *cont'd.*
90, 92, 93–4, 166; 'Compulsory Competitive Tendering,' 53; COVID contracts, 2, 14–17, 29, 167–70, 205, 250–1; liberal market economy, 61; neoliberal governments, 32–3, 46, 47–9, 51–2, 54–5, 74–5; outsourcing in, 14–17, 25, 33–4, 46, 78–81, 82, 85, 94–5, 96, 97–103, 137; privatization of railway system, 51–2; Third Way governments in, 76–9, 82, 85, 94, 151, 152, 153, 252
United States: Affordable Care Act (2013), 68–74, 96; antitrust laws, 46–7; Clinton's National Performance Review (NPR), 75–6, 83; Competition in Contracting Act (1984), 53; consultants in post-war period, 43–4; Covid contracts, 2, 14; Gilded Age, 3, 108–11; and 'market-driven climate governance,' 218, 219, 220–1; military/defence spending, 41–2, 48, 49, 86; neoliberal governments, 32–3, 46, 47–9, 50, 52–3, 55, 74–5; Nixon ends dollar-gold convertibility (1971), 48; Obama pledges consulting cuts, 92–3; Private Securities Reform Act (1995), 50; privatized healthcare model, 154; Reagan's deregulation of energy market, 63–4; regulatory change in early 1930s, 39–40; responses to 2008 crisis, 89–90, 188–9; Sarbanes-Oxley Act (2002), 66–7, 101; Taylorism in, 34, 35–7; 'War on Terror,' 86

United States Postal Service (USPS), 203, 205

Valeant Pharmaceuticals, 174–7, 178–9, 194–5, 207
'value-based competition' theory, 154–6, 183–4
Vanguard, 141
Veblen, Thorstein, 108
Vietnam, 159, 240
Vietnam War, 48
'vulture funds,' 185

Warren, Matt, 69
waste/refuse collection, 94, 95, 161–2
Weiss, Antonio, 46
Weiss, Linda, 168–9
welfare services, 2, 32, 43, 48; and ageing populations, 149–50; negative narratives of, 237–8; in post-2008 crisis period, 93–4, 163; in Puerto Rico, 180–1, 182; retrenching/budget cuts, 180–1; in Sweden, 149, 150–7 *see also* National Health Service (NHS)
Wooldridge, Adrian, 112, 130
World Bank, 25, 56–7, 67
World Economic Forum, 230
World Health Organization, 159
World Meteorological Organization (WMO), 208
WorldCom collapse (2002), 66
Wright, Christopher, 116

Zuma, Jacob, 29